George Herbert

Twayne's English Authors Series

Arthur F. Kinney, Editor

University of Massachusetts, Amherst

TEAS 428

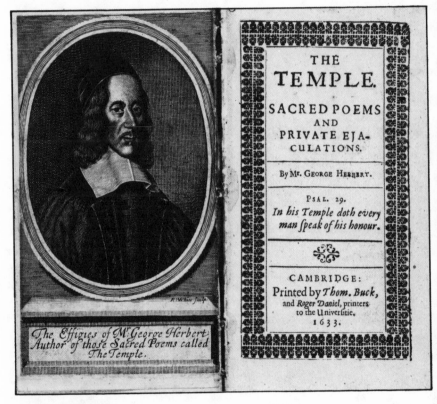

THE
TEMPLE.
SACRED POEMS
AND
PRIVATE EJA-
CULATIONS.

By Mr. GEORGE HERBERT.

PSAL. 29.
In his Temple doth every
man speak of his honour.

CAMBRIDGE:
Printed by Thom. Buck,
and Roger Daniel, printers
to the Universitie.
1633.

The Effigies of Mr George Herbert,
Author of those Sacred Poems called
The Temple.

GEORGE HERBERT
(1593–1633)
Reproduced by permission of The Huntington Library,
San Marino, California

George Herbert

By Stanley Stewart

University of California, Riverside

Twayne Publishers
A Division of G.K. Hall & Co. • Boston

George Herbert

Stanley Stewart

Copyright © 1986 by G.K. Hall & Co.
All Rights Reserved
Published by Twayne Publishers
A Division of G.K. Hall & Co.
70 Lincoln Street
Boston, Massachusetts 02111

Copyediting supervised by Lewis DeSimone
Book production by Marne Sultz
Book design by Barbara Anderson

Typeset in 11 pt. Garamond by
Modern Graphics, Inc., Weymouth, Massachusetts

Printed on permanent/durable acid-free paper
and bound in the United States of America

Library of Congress Cataloging in Publication Data

Stewart, Stanley, 1931–
  George Herbert.

  (Twayne's English authors series; TEAS 428)
  Bibliography, p. 169
  Includes index.
  1. Herbert, George, 1593–1633—Criticism and
interpretation.   2. Herbert, George, 1593–1633—
Influence.   3. Christian poetry, English—History and
criticism.   4. English poetry—Early modern, 1500–1700—
History and criticism.   I. Title. II. Series.
PR3508.S73   1986   821'.3   86–11945
ISBN 0–8057–6921–8

To
Bradford and Duncan

Contents

Editor's Note

This major revisionary study of George Herbert's poetry will be widely welcomed by scholars and critics of Herbert's life and work, as well as by students coming to his probing, meditative, and personal poems for the first time. Taking issue with all the recent views of Herbert, Stanley Stewart argues that Herbert's close friendship with Nicholas Ferrar—to whom he sent his poems for editing and publication—and his interest in the meditative rituals at the religious community of Little Gidding both shaped his religious beliefs and dictated to him the form of *The Temple*. Stewart has uncovered new records and manuscript materials, which he shows, for the first time, to be instrumental in fashioning Herbert's poems. Consequently, Stewart argues, provocatively and compellingly, for the integrity of "The Church-porch" and "The Church Militant" to *The Temple* as, in the tradition of Little Gidding, vital components of the narrative of the odyssey of man's soul. Stewart concludes with an enlightening chapter defining the school of Herbert as analogous to the well-established school of Donne, thereby clarifying Herbert's widespread influence. This study is a thorough, careful, reasoned, and finally convincing interpretation of the lasting significance of George Herbert, the poet and the man. It dispels many of the myths about the Puritan saint, the hymnologist, and the secret recusant that have haunted and shaped erroneous and misleading criticism from the seventeenth century to our own, misguiding among others (Stewart claims) the Wesleys and Coleridge. This is a book that must be reckoned with for the foreseeable future.

Arthur F. Kinney

About the Author

Stanley Stewart, professor of English, has taught at the University of California, Riverside, since completion of his Ph.D. at UCLA in 1961. His main interest in Renaissance studies has led to publication of numerous books and articles on a variety of subjects, including Shakespeare, Spenser, Milton, Marvell, and Herbert. He is probably best known for his thematic study, *The Enclosed Garden: The Tradition and the Image in Seventeenth-Century Poetry* (Madison, 1966), and his work on Traherne, *The Expanded Voice: The Art of Thomas Traherne* (San Marino, 1970). In connection with his teaching, research, and writing duties, Professor Stewart has written and published short and book-length fiction, served as department chairman, served on and chaired statewide academic senate and administrative committees, and coordinated Renaissance conferences and symposia. He has been a recipient of a Senior Fellowship from the John Simon Guggenheim Memorial Foundation. Professor Stewart is currently working on Spenser and Milton.

Preface

Although it is customary to date the beginning of the metaphysical revival from the publication in 1912 of Sir Herbert J. C. Grierson's edition of *The Poems of John Donne,* the rise of critical interest in George Herbert began in earnest in 1941 with the appearance of Canon F. E. Hutchinson's edition of Herbert's *Complete Works,* which was shortly followed by landmark critical studies by Rosemond Tuve, Louis L. Martz and Joseph H. Summers. In the last decade and a half, interest has sharply increased. One need only compare recent issues of the annual *PMLA* Bibliography with those from the thirties or forties—or even with those from the early seventies—to be convinced that the critical focus on Herbert is intensifying. Within the past two years alone, no less than five book-length studies have emerged from university presses dedicated to the single subject of George Herbert. The names of the editorial advisory board and of contributors to the *George Herbert Journal,* which began publication at Sacred Heart University in 1977, read like a who's who of seventeenth-century studies. Moreover, this growing interest in Herbert represents anything but a hegemony of one critical point of view. On the contrary, Herbert's poetry has borne the brunt of an awesome arsenal of old-fashioned and new-fangled methods of historical, ecclesiastical, liturgical, exegetical, iconographic, social, political, metrical, thematic, psychological, textual, intertextual, formalist, structural, and poststructural analysis.

Given such an embarrassment of perspectival riches, one might well ask, why write another book on Herbert? In answer to this question I would begin by admitting that, while I hope this book will be useful to specialists in seventeenth-century studies, I intend it to be accessible to nonspecialists as well. The former will see that it is meant neither as a competitor to, nor substitute for, either Tuve's splendid *A Reading of George Herbert* (London, 1952) or Summers's excellent *George Herbert: His Religion and Art* (London, 1954). They will recognize, also, its debt to both. I trust it will not appear abrupt, even at this early juncture, to observe that one reason for writing this book concerns the shift in recent years away from the wisdom of Tuve and Summers. This shift is discernible in two symptomatic forms. First, critics practicing some of the methods mentioned above have construed Herbert's religious poetry without assuming the burden of Tuve's or Summers's intimate acquaintance with the world of religious controversy, of which Herbert and his poetry were living parts. Their efforts have led to anomalous views of Herbert's texts—to a Herbert expressing feelings and opinions that would have been to him and his audience, in some cases, fantastic, in others, sinful, and in still others, impossible. This body of criticism derives from an excessive faith in individual capacities of mind, unhindered—and unhelped—by anything outside selected Herbert texts. A development of assumptions implicit in the old "New" or formalist criticism, this emphasis on mental virtuosity distorts Herbert with a bias toward modern problems and concerns: we all admire things like *us,* so why not make all things *like* us?

Second, in recent years, another trend in Herbert criticism has produced another species of distortion. Since it proceeds from more historically sophisticated assumptions, it is therefore more difficult to contend with—and more interesting. Historical critics, of which Tuve and Summers must be accounted fine examples, descended into a critical morass of controversy not unlike the one into which the British people themselves stumbled shortly after Herbert died. The historicists split into two camps, one moving in a manner reminiscent of the developing rhetoric of Caroline revolutionaries (from Parker to Harrington to Milton to Lilburne to Overton to Winstanley), progressively interpreting Herbert in ever more Protestant and, finally, even Puritan terms. With equal verve, the other camp placed Herbert as close to the papists as his specifically anti-Roman texts would allow. With the publication in the last few years of such important studies as Barbara Lewalski's *Protestant Poetics and the Seventeenth-Century Religious Lyric* (Cambridge, Mass., 1979), Richard Strier's *Love Known: Theology and Experience in George Herbert's Poetry* (Chicago, 1983), Heather A. R. Asals's *Equivocal Predication: George Herbert's Way to God* (Toronto, 1981), and J. A. W. Bennett's *Poetry of the Passion: Studies in Twelve Centuries of English Verse* (Oxford, 1982), the line separating these schools of thought has only sharpened.

In an attempt to address both species of distortion, this book undertakes a twofold task. First, it will consider the subject of Herbert and his poetry from the viewpoint of his time: well before the Civil War, in the seventeenth century. Accordingly, chapter 1 outlines the facts of Herbert's life and discusses the manner in which their interpretation by early biographers shaped generations of Herbert's admirers. Pursuing this contemporary perspective, chapter 2 inquires into Herbert's views and practices with respect to the Church of England, the offices of which Herbert fulfilled as a priest and the rites and ceremonies of which he vigorously defended in his poetry and in his prose. These two chapters should make the thesis of this study clear: to wit, the emphasis of Herbert's Protestantism and/or Puritanism, having become far too pronounced, requires audience-oriented modulation. Thus, in chapter 3 I attempt to demonstrate that critics have overlooked an important body of evidence relevant to this issue, namely, the "Harmonies" of Little Gidding. These works are valuable aids to our understanding of Herbert's intended audience, which was—I should think incontrovertibly—Nicholas Ferrar and his community of worshipers at Little Gidding. In the nineteenth century the importance of these documents to an understanding of Herbert was taken for granted, but to my knowledge no mention has been made of them in this connection in over a hundred years. Chapter 3 attempts to rectify this omission and, by so doing, to reevaluate the claim of Lewalski and others that such critics as Tuve and Martz have erred in their reliance on medieval, Catholic sources in their interpretations of Herbert's poetry.

Having suggested the manner in which these documents provide us with a strategy for dealing with individual poems, I turn in chapter 4 to a structural analysis of *The Temple* as a sequence, arguing for the inclusion of "The Church-porch" and "The Church Militant" in the Herbert canon—and in *The Temple* as well. Finally, chapter 5 considers the question of Herbert's influence on seventeenth-century poetry. If, with A. Alvarez, we can talk about a school of Donne, we should, *a fortiori,* be able to describe a school of George Herbert, which established its integrity by defining its differences from and objections to many of the poetic features we associate with Donne's poetry. Again, the argument that Donne's school was shaped through the intermediary influence of Herbert would, then, seem to be in need of revision, too.

While working on this book, I enjoyed the constructive help and friendship of many librarians, anonymous readers, and Renaissance scholars, and I would like now to thank all of them. Only James Thorpe will know the full extent of my debt to him; I am deeply grateful for his expressions of encouragement and support. Over the years, Thomas Kranidas has read most of what I have written and has offered helpful criticism. I must also thank C. A. Patrides for his generosity in taking time out from his busy schedule to offer advice on a variety of relevant subjects. I owe a special kind of debt to my good friend Robert F. Gleckner, whose closet preference for Renaissance literature has been a welcome source of informed criticism. Howard D. Weinbrot has remained a loyal friend and critic from whom I have learned much. John Mulryan was especially helpful in encouraging my work on the "Harmonies" of Little Gidding. And I am thankful, also, to Arthur F. Kinney, for suggesting that I do what I had wanted for many years to·do, namely, write a book on George Herbert. In the interim, it was my good fortune to make the acquaintance of a younger generation of Herbert scholars, four of whom, Judy Z. Kronenfeld, Jeanne Clayton Hunter, Chana Bloch, and Michael Schoenfeldt, exchanged ideas and work in progress with me. I have enjoyed their youth and freshness and thank them for their advice. I wish also to extend warm thanks for the encouragement of friends and colleagues at the University of California, Riverside, especially Ralph Hanna, III (who, if he wearied of hearing about the "Harmonies" of Little Gidding, never let on), Ruth apRoberts, Robert N. Essick, John B. Vickery, John M. Steadman, and Marshall Van Deusen. The Research Committee of the University of California, Riverside, made it possible for me to spend the summer of 1983 in London, working at the British Library, and helped with travel and microfilm expenses.

Parts of chapters 3 and 4 of this book have appeared in slightly different forms in *Cithara: Essays in the Judaeo-Christian Tradition* and in *Studies in English Literature* (reprinted in John R. Roberts, *Essential Articles for the Study of George Herbert's Poetry* [Hamden, Conn.: Archon Books, 1979]). I want to thank all of the editors and readers involved for their interest and for their help with numerous revisions. Every idea in this book has received the spirited, if not always friendly, scrutiny of "The Regulars's Caucus" at the Huntington Library: Leland Carlson, Daniel Donno, Elizabeth Story Donno, Christopher Grose, John King, Jonathan Post, James A. Riddell, William Ringler, John T. Shawcross, Hallett Smith, Raymond B. Waddington, Seth Weiner, Joseph A. Wittreich, Jr., and Susanne Woods. Readers familiar with the stringent rules of debate governing discourse at "The Footnote" will expect me to exculpate all of "The Regulars" from any implied legal or moral complicity in the writing of this book. On the other hand, I hope they will consider it no offense if I associate their names with whatever might be found of value in this study.

Renaissance scholars who have enjoyed the privilege of studying at the Henry E. Huntington Library and Art Gallery understand that the many benefits of working in those enviable surroundings are only enhanced by the warm, prompt, friendly, patient, interested—and interesting—assistance of Mary Wright in the Rare Book Room.

Finally, I want to thank my wife, Barbara Stewart, who does not type, but who loves the poetry of George Herbert and agrees with almost everything I say about it in this book.

Stanley Stewart

University of California, Riverside

Chronology

1593   Born 3 April, in Montgomery, Wales, son of Richard and Magdalen Herbert.

1596   Father dies, leaving wife, seven sons, and three daughters.

1597   Mother moves to Oxford to assist eldest son, Edward; makes acquaintance of John Donne.

1601   Mother moves family to London.

1603   Queen Elizabeth I dies. James VI of Scotland crowned James I of England.

1604   At King's request, conference meets at Hampton Court on matters of Church discipline.

1605   Herbert enters Westminster School in London. Gunpowder Plot is foiled.

1608   Magdalen Herbert (40 yrs. old) marries Sir John Danvers (20 yrs. old).

1609   Herbert enters Trinity College, Cambridge.

1612   Henry Stuart, Prince of Wales, dies, and the nation mourns. Herbert contributes poems to Cambridge collection in memory of the popular prince; takes B.A. degree.

1614   Elected minor fellow.

1615   Elected major fellow. Nicholas Ferrar leaves England for tour of Continent.

1616   Takes M.A. degree. Shakespeare dies.

1618   Writes to Sir John Danvers expressing plans to begin divinity studies.

1619   Appointed deputy orator at Cambridge. His brother, Edward, appointed ambassador to court in Paris. Nicholas Ferrar returns from Continent.

1620   Elected public orator for the university; writes to thank King James for copy of *Basilikon Doron;* makes acquaintance of Bacon, who dedicates his translation of the Psalms to Herbert.

1622   Probably writes reply to Andrew Melville.

1623   Delivers oration on occasion of Prince Charles's visit to Cambridge. Virginia Company deprived of patent, and Nicholas Ferrar responds by withdrawing from public life.

1624   Elected member of Parliament for borough of Montgomery, Wales. Ferrar's mother buys manor house and church at Little Gidding.

1625   James I dies. Charles I ascends throne and takes Roman Catholic French princess, Henrietta Maria, as his queen.

1626   Presented to prebend of Leighton Ecclesia, a short distance from Little Gidding, where Nicholas Ferrar has begun to rebuild the church and to establish his society. Herbert offers prebend to Ferrar, who declines. Laud ordains Ferrar deacon. Herbert writes poems commemorating the death of Francis Bacon.

1627   Suffering symptoms of consumption, resigns post as university orator. Mother dies. Writes Latin poems, *Memoriae Matris Sacrum,* which are published with funeral sermon delivered by Donne.

1628   Convalesces at home of brother, Henry, in Essex.

1629   Marries Jane Danvers on 5 March.

1630   Charles I offers Herbert rectory of small church at Bemerton, a short distance from Salisbury. Laud persuades a reluctant Herbert to accept. Installed as rector and ordained a priest.

1633   Dies on 3 March. *The Temple* published, with comments by Nicholas Ferrar.

1634   Edward Lenton describes visit to Little Gidding in letter to Sir Thomas Hetley.

1637   Nicholas Ferrar dies.

1640   Christopher Harvey, *The Synagogue.*

1641   *The Arminian Nunnery.*

1647   Little Gidding sacked by partisans of Parliamentary cause.

1648   Richard Crashaw, *Steps to The Temple.*

1652   *Herbert's Remains* published, with biography by Barnabas Oley.

1654   Thomas Washbourne, *Divine Poems.*

1662   *Musae Responsoriae.*

1670   Walton publishes *Life of Herbert.*

1697   *Select Hymns, Taken out of Mr. Herbert's Temple.*

1739   Wesleys publish *Hymns and Sacred Poems.*

1853   Pickering edition of Herbert's *Works* appears, with comments on Herbert by S. T. Coleridge. Church at Little Gidding restored.

1874   Grosart's 3 vol. edition of Herbert's *Complete Works.*

1905   Palmer's 3 vol. edition of Herbert's *English Works.*

1912   Sir Herbert Grierson publishes edition of Donne's *Poems.* Metaphysical revival begins.

1941   Canon F. E. Hutchinson's edition of *The Works of George Herbert.*

1952   Rosemond Tuve, *A Reading of George Herbert.*

1954   Joseph H. Summers, *George Herbert: His Religion and Art.* Louis L. Martz, *The Poetry of Meditation: A Study in English Religious Literature of the Seventeenth Century.*

1977   Amy M. Charles, *A Life of George Herbert.*

1979   Barbara Lewalski, *Protestant Poetics and the Seventeenth-Century Religious Lyric.*

Chapter One

George Herbert: Life and "Lives"

The Life

The chronicle of Herbert's forty years falls roughly into three epochs, two of almost equal length, and the third much shorter: the early years before his entry into Trinity College (1593–1609); the Cambridge years, including the many years Herbert served as university orator (1609–1624); and the last decade of his vocation and deepening illness. In the first period, Herbert's life was shaped by the predominant influence of his mother, Magdalen Herbert, a beautiful, intelligent, gregarious woman.[1] While Herbert's father, Richard, served in Parliament and was active in county government, his mother, whose family name was Newport, bestowed on her ten children the luster of descent from a Welsh prince. And it was she who provided the greatest influence on her fifth son, George, who was only three years old when his father died.

Shortly after the death of her husband, Magdalen Herbert left Wales, settling for a short time in Oxford, presumably to look after her eldest son, Edward, a student of University College. Two years later she moved the family to London, where she established her large household in a residence near the Strand. It soon became a center of lively social and intellectual activity. Magdalen Herbert entertained often and lavishly, and her guests included some of the most notable names in London. About this time, Herbert began his formal education at Westminster School, known for its teaching of music skills in addition to the usual components of the curriculum: grammar, logic, and rhetoric, studied through imitation and translation of Latin models. Under the tutelage of such learned men as Lancelot Andrewes, Herbert excelled as a student, earning one of three Westminster nominations to Trinity College, Cambridge.

Two nearly simultaneous events mark the end of this period in Herbert's life: his mother's remarriage and his departure for Cambridge. Herbert was sixteen in 1609 when, on the eve of his departure for Trinity College, his mother, then over forty, married Sir John Danvers, an exceptionally good-looking man approximately half her age. Danvers, in turn, became at once a husband and the stepfather of ten children, one of whom (Edward) was about his age. In his first year at Cambridge, Herbert wrote a letter to his mother in which he complained of a severe *"Ague"* and proceeded "to reprove the vanity of those many Love-poems" of the time, and to announce the dedication of his own "poor Abilities in *Poetry* . . . to Gods glory" (*Works,* p. 363). Thus, we know that by New Year's Day of 1610 George Herbert had begun his career as a divine poet.

The epoch of Herbert's attachment to Cambridge University stretches from the fall of 1609 to 1624, when for all practical purposes he severed his connection with the university. During this second period of his life, Herbert was intimately associated with Cambridge as he turned his success as a student into appointments to a sequence of increasingly important academic posts: minor fellow, major fellow, reader in rhetoric, deputy orator, and university orator. This last position provided much honor and visibility; his predecessor in that post, Francis Nethersole, used the appointment as a stepping-stone to knighthood and a career in diplomacy, for the most part in the service of King James's daughter, Elizabeth, the electress of Palatine *(DNB).* Likewise, Herbert's service as university orator included corresponding with King James, thanking him in one instance for a gift to the university of a copy of *Icon Basilike,* and delivering Latin orations on occasions of state at Cambridge.

During this period Herbert wrote his Latin poem on the death of Prince Henry, translated part of Bacon's *The Advancement of Learning,* wrote his rejoinder to Andrew Melville, and composed two other works *(Passio Discerpta* and *Lucus)* in Latin as well. Like *Musae Responsoriae,* which was probably written shortly after Melville's *Apologia, Sive Anti-Tami-Cami-Categoria* (1604) was republished in 1620, *Passio Discerpta* exhibits rather high Anglican attitudes.

On the other hand, Herbert had contact with men aligned with more Protestant elements within the Church as well, men like Bishop Williams, Henry Fairfax, the fourth and fifth earls of Pembroke, and his own stepfather, Sir John Danvers. The question of Herbert's opinions in this matter is not an easy one, and we shall return to it in chapters 2 and 3.

Meanwhile, 1624 was another watershed year for Herbert. Because of " 'many businesses away' " from Cambridge (*Works,* p. xxx), Herbert sought and was granted a leave of absence from his post as orator, and though the leave was only for six months, it appears that he never resumed his official duties. Another indication that Herbert was moving away from the academy may be seen in his successful election to Parliament from the borough of Montgomery.

At his same juncture Herbert was also turning his attention to less public concerns. One of his three sisters, a widow, died, leaving three daughters, whom he helped to care for during his remaining years. As Amy M. Charles has recently shown,[2] Herbert began following the aim spelled out in his letter to Sir John Danvers in March of 1618, namely, of entering "Divinity" studies "to lay the platform of [his] future life" (*Works,* p. 364). With the assistance of John Williams, Lord Keeper and Bishop of Lincoln, Herbert accepted the living of Llandinam and, not long afterward, was named canon of Lincoln Cathedral.

By now, others were assuming his duties as orator at Cambridge, a post he once wanted earnestly enough to argue against suspicions that its duties would militate against his religious goals (*Works,* pp. 369–71). Herbert committed himself to a course destined to end in holy orders. He spent time with family members in Chelsea and Woodford, but the focus of his life was increasingly on divinity. In 1626, he was formally installed as deacon and prebendary of Leighton Ecclesia.

It is hard to date most of Herbert's poetry with certainty, but the Latin poems written in commemoration of his mother were published with Donne's funeral sermon in 1627. Shortly thereafter, Herbert's financial situation took a turn for the better. (As the letters to his stepfather requesting money to buy books make clear, his finances had until this time never been trouble-free.) Some of his newly attained means went into improvements at Leighton. About this time, Herbert wrote a letter to his deputy at Cambridge, Robert Creighton, indicating his virtual abdication of the appointment, and he went to visit Sir John Danvers's brother, the earl of Danby. We assume that during most of the period spent with the earl, Herbert was writing and rewriting many of the poems that would find their way into the revised *Temple.* Another important development during this period was Herbert's marriage to Jane Danvers, a niece of Herbert's stepfather and of his host, the earl. Shortly after

the marriage, Herbert was offered and accepted the living at Bemerton. He was installed as rector of Bemerton on 26 April 1630
and was ordained as priest early in the fall of the same year.

Walton records that Humphrey Henchman, who later became
Bishop of London, was present at Salisbury Cathedral that day: *"He
laid his hand on Mr. Herberts Head, and (alas!) within less than three
Years, lent his Shoulder to carry his dear Friend to his Grave"* (*Works,*
p. xxxv). In those few years Herbert undertook the routine offices
of the Anglican church: saying morning and evening prayer once a
day, offering the Sacraments to his parishioners, and, in general,
providing the many services that he describes in *A Priest to the Temple,*
which he wrote during the same period and which we shall be
discussing in the next chapter. Probably because of the distance
between Wiltshire and Leighton Bromswold, at this time Herbert
urged his friend Nicholas Ferrar to accept the prebendary near Little
Gidding in his stead. Rather than accept the living, Ferrar offered
to assist Herbert in rebuilding the church. Meanwhile, Herbert set
about restoring the church and house at Bemerton, too. Herbert,
his wife, and his nieces settled into the life of a country parson's
household. He wrote *A Priest to the Temple* and finished writing and
revising *The Temple* itself.

Herbert died on Sunday, 1 March 1633 at the age of forty.
Although he is among the greatest lyric poets in the language, none
of the work for which he would be remembered had been published
during his lifetime. Indeed, at the time of Herbert's death, the fate
of his poetry rested with Nicholas Ferrar and his other friends at
Little Gidding, to whom he appears to have sent the finished manuscript of *The Temple.* According to John Aubrey, Thomas Danvers
attended the funeral, at which "the singing men of Sarum," with
whom Herbert had probably himself sung many times, performed
the liturgy for the burial of the dead (*Works,* p. xxxix). Herbert's
will named Arthur Woodnoth, a relative of Ferrar's, as his executor.
It was he who carried from Bemerton most of the remaining un-
published works of George Herbert; according to Walton, Herbert
had already sent the manuscript of *The Temple,* in the hands of
Edmund Duncon, to Nicholas Ferrar at Little Gidding.

Life as Art

The public process of Herbert's canonization began no later than
the publication of *The Temple* (1633), shortly after the poet's death.

Nicholas Ferrar's brief narrative of "the condition and disposition of the Person" of the author depicts a man whose poetic voice had "been inspired by a diviner breath then flows from *Helicon*" (*Works,* p. 3). *The Temple,* he wrote, was dedicated "to the *Divine Majestie* onely," and its author, though "nobly born," set his mind on the way of holiness, "choosing rather to serve at Gods Altar, then to seek the honour of State-employments." Setting aside any knowledge he may have had of Herbert's wishes for preferment at court, Ferrar insists that Herbert's entry into the clergy was "compelled," presumably by God rather than by circumstance. Once on that divinely ordained pathway, Herbert earned his place as "justly a companion to the primitive Saints." He loved God first, his Word second, and after these "the Church and the discipline thereof" (*Works,* p. 4). Ferrar perceived the poet's otherworldly spirit, not only in his faithful discharge of priestly duties, but in the more unusual support that Herbert drew from his wife and nieces, who daily accompanied him to services. Here was an outward sign of "inward Grace." Herbert's "publick celebration," thus accompanied, exhibited how completely the private man's spirit was absorbed in divine functions. Even in his attempt to resign the "Ecclesiasticall dignitie" that went along with these functions Herbert revealed no more than disdain for "worldly matters." When on his deathbed Herbert was comforted by a friend with the reminder that his life was not without its successes, since he had rebuilt the church at Bemerton "that had layen ruinated almost twenty yeares," the poet answered in words reminiscent of the "saints' lives" : *"It is a good work, if it be sprinkled with the bloud of Christ."*

Nineteen years later *Herbert's Remains, Or, Sundry Pieces Of that sweet Singer of the Temple, Mr George Herbert* (1652) appeared, including Herbert's major prose work, *A Priest to the Temple.* Besides this important handbook on the practice of divinity, which will be the subject of the next chapter, the volume included Herbert's address "To the Reader," a second biography, this by Herbert's friend Barnabas Oley (an Anglican divine of strong Royalist sympathies), poems on Francis Bacon and John Donne, and Herbert's "Apothegms" and "Outlandish Proverbs." The subtitle of *A Priest to the Temple, The Countrey Parson,* suggests much about how this handbook shaped the public conception of George Herbert. His aim, as Herbert's preface indicates, was "to set down the Form and Character of a true Pastour."[3] It is evident that Oley thought Herbert had succeeded in presenting a "Speculum Sacerdotale" (sig. alv), challenging every reader's conscience. Oley's "A Prefatory View of the Life and Vertues of the Authour" is actually about three men— or, as Oley thought of it, about *"some confrontments common to"* Thomas Jackson, Ferrar, and Herbert. All three men bore the *"signe of Christ"* (sig. a10) in enduring the most stressful contradictions. Jackson was attacked for taking the side of truth in the libertarian controversy; Ferrar was torn by paradoxical accusations *"that he was a Papist, and that he was a Puritan"* (sig. a11). Herbert embodied extremes of greatness (his family name and his associates) and of humility (his ultimate station in life). And yet all three, despite the stresses of their lives and times, remained true to the tenets of the Church of England. From Oley's point of view, none of them could justly be described as either Puritan or Roman Catholic.

Although Oley's polemical views take up much of this "biography," his felicitous opinion of Herbert's poetry makes a telling contribution to the emerging view of Herbert as a saint: *"he that reads Mr.* Herbert's *Poems attendingly, shall finde not onely the excellencies of Scripture Divinitie, and choice passages of the Fathers bound up in Meetre"* (sig. b1v). It is important to recognize how early and how completely Oley attributes to Herbert's poetry the values of Scripture and of biblical commentary, for Oley's opinion became part of an accepted—if not *the* accepted—way of construing Herbert's poetry. Thus Oley compares Herbert's early verses (*"they be dull or dead in comparison of his* Temple Poems" [sig. b7]) with his mature religious poetry, coming to this similarly influential assertion: *"To write those, he made his ink with water of* Helicon, *but these Inspirations propheticall were distilled from above: In those are weake motions of Nature, In these Raptures of Grace."* (sig. b7). In comparison with Oley's interpretations of Herbert's work, the biography to which he finally turns seems rather gratuitous. And yet this biography erects the scaffolding on which Izaak Walton constructs his more ample *Life.*

Lacking Oley's crankiness, Walton very successfully drew upon and amplified his predecessor's work. By comparison, his style is luminous, and, if opinionated (Walton, like Oley, was a Royalist), it is not as polemical. While Oley's main interest is Thomas Jackson and the theological disputes that bedeviled the times, Walton's *Life of Mr. George Herbert* (1670)[4] did most to shape the image of George Herbert, priest and poet, as a saint. Facing the title page is R. White's engraving of Herbert, whose gaunt, aquiline features and calm, dispassionate expression seem to justify the otherworldly theme of the epigraph from The Wisdom of Solomon: *"He pleased God, and was beloved of him: so that whereas he lived among sinners, he translated him"* (title page). The reference to Enoch and Elisha, whom God translated directly to heaven, is taken up by Samuel Woodforde in a long poem prefixed to Walton's *Life*. Woodforde praises Herbert, not as a loyal servant of the cloth, but as "Heav'ns youngest Son, its *Benjamin*" (*Life*, p. 3), the very Muse of *"Sacred Poesie."* Art and life begin to merge as Herbert takes on mythic identity as God's direct descendant. Accordingly, in his larger-than-life person, Herbert proves that poetry was not inspired by "A Female Muse . . . But" rather by one "full of Vigor Masculine . . . with Angels his Companions." To Woodforde, England was fortunate in having an inheritor of David's "holy rage" (*Life*, p. 4)—one rare throughout the centuries—for no one was more intimately acquainted with David's "mighty *Psaltery*" than Herbert.

To say that such a portrait confuses the man with his work understates the cumulative effects of the imaginative process at work here. Poetry of this magnitude required a poet of like magnitude behind it. Beginning with Ferrar's comments, Herbert's poetry was construed as a natural outgrowth of a supremely pious life. Even while following Oley in tracing Herbert's ancestry and education, Walton expanded the narrative, adding materials and interpretations to demonstrate Herbert's saintly characteristics. So even Herbert's family suffered at the hands of the Philistines during the Civil War:

A Family, that hath been blest with men of remarkable wisdom, and a willingness to serve their Countrey, and indeed, to do good to all Mankind; for which, they were eminent: But alas! this Family did in the late Rebellion suffer extremely in their Estates; and the Heirs of that *Castle,* saw it laid level with that earth that was too good to bury those Wretches that were the cause of it. (*Life*, p. 9).

Just as his family separated itself from the rabble, so does Herbert now distinguish his aims from the common sort. Declaring his independence from the trend of secular love-poetry in a letter to his mother at the age of seventeen, Herbert encloses two "Sonnets," along with his resolution that his *"poor Abilities in* Poetry, *shall be all, and ever consecrated to Gods glory"* (*Life*, p. 19). The two "Sonnets" (*Works*, p. 206) reiterate the theme laid out in the letter:

My God, where is that ancient heat towards thee,
Wherewith whole showls of *Martyrs* once did burn,
        Besides their other flames? Doth Poetry
Wear *Venus* Livery? only serve her turn?

                                                    (ll. 1–4)

The speaker "reproves" the corrosive effects of the poets' preoccupation with romantic love. But he also aligns himself with the zeal
of *"Martyrs"* by making their typical affections his poetic concern.
Implicitly, in Walton's presentation, Herbert assumes the vestments
of martyrdom. As the series of rhetorical questions unfolds, by which
the speaker insinuates his preference for divine over secular poetry,
he propounds a deeper affirmation of the spirit over the flesh: "Why
doth that fire, which by thy power and might / Each breast does
feel, no braver fuel choose / Than that, which one day Worms may
chance refuse?" (ll. 12–14).
    The second of these sonnets continues the same colloquy, as the
poet answers his own questions:

            Sure, Lord, there is enough in thee to dry
            Oceans of *Ink;* for, as the Deluge did
                Cover the Earth, so doth thy Majesty:
            Each Cloud distills thy praise, and doth forbid
            Poets to turn it to another use.

                                                    (ll. 1–5)

This is the rhetoric of the mature Herbert. We sense the intimacy
and conviction of "The Collar": "Sure there was wine / Before my
sighs did drie it" (*Works*, p. 153). But if Herbert is already reaching
for his voice of the soul in colloquy with God, in Walton's presentation he is also separating himself from the mainstream of Western
literature, placing himself under the aegis of the Book of God's
Word ("as the Deluge did") and the Book of God's Creatures ("Each
Cloud distills thy praise"). Writing sonnets in the traditional manner of the unrequited aspirant to adultery is wrong on two counts.
First, such secondhand creation misappropriates Creation itself; it
defies the laws of Nature. Everywhere man looks, he finds evidence
of God's beauty:

            Roses and *Lillies* speak thee; and to make
            A pair of Cheeks of them, is thy abuse.

> Why should I *Womens eyes* for Chrystal take?
> Such poor invention burns in their low mind
> Whose fire is wild, and doth not upward go
> To praise, and on thee, Lord, some *Ink* bestow.
>
> (ll. 6–11)

This sonnet goes beyond Shakespeare's Sonnet 130 in its indictment of the cliché. For this poet, the trite expression is much more than the outward evidence of an uncreative mind. Courtly love is, by its very nature, misprision. It depends entirely on "abusion" of God, who made both *"Womens eyes"* and *"Chrystal."* To confuse the two diminishes both, but—much more—trivializes their Creator. Herbert finds in the perpetually unrequited stance of the courtly lover the very essence of the poetic kind. Whereas the divine poet's praise ascends, like incense from a censer, the anarchic desires of the courtly lover are at once "wild" and immoveable. Like the courtly poet himself, this fire defies the laws of nature and does not ascend in smoke, as do the prayers of the faithful, to God.

And yet this poem is no mere striking of the colors on one side of what Russell Fraser aptly calls the "war against poetry." The speaker does declare himself a partisan in that conflict, but he does so in such a way as to deflect suspicion that his allegiance indicates anything other than a proper awareness of reality: "Open the bones, and you shall nothing find / In the best *face* but *filth,* when, Lord, in thee / The *beauty* lies in the *discovery*" (ll. 12–14). So much for the thousands of lines invested in praise of Beatrice, Laura, Stella, Delia, and the "Dark Lady." "The best *face*," when properly anatomized, has no *"beauty"* at all. Just as the anatomizing of "the best *face*" reveals nothing "but *filth,*" so in the process of *"discovery"*— the seeking of God's face—"lies" intrinsic beauty, for the reasons laid out in the first two quatrains of the poem. Here young Herbert only follows the imagery of the Song of Songs introduced in Sonnet (I) and alluded to again in the second quatrain of Sonnet (II). For who is that *"Dove,"* and why in Scripture do *"Roses* and *Lillies* speak" the Deity? Herbert's mother would have known the answer:

> Behold thou art fair, my love, behold, thou are fair: thou
> hast doves' eyes
> I am the rose of sharon, and the lily of the valleys.
> O my dove, that art in the clefts of the rock, in the

secret places of the stairs, let me see thy countenance, let me hear thy voice; for sweet is thy voice, and thy countenance is comely.

(1:15–2:1, 14)

Walton's introduction of these poems into his *Life of Herbert* does much to suggest that, like Christ, the poet declared himself to be about his Father's work at an early age as the worthiest offspring of a notably virtuous mother.

Walton reprints the two "Sonnets" to show that, at about the age of seventeen, Herbert had "consecrated the first-fruits of his early age to vertue, and a serious study of learning" (*Life*, p. 19). To emphasize further Herbert's spiritual qualities, Walton compares Herbert to the young Christ: "and, as he grew older, so he grew in learning, and more and more in favour both with God and man: insomuch, that in this morning of that short day of his life, he seem'd to be mark'd out for vertue, to become the care of Heaven; for God still kept his soul in so holy a frame, that he may, and ought to be a pattern of vertue to all posterity" (*Life*, p. 21). Herbert was destined for the Church not by fortune or inclination, but by God:

I have now brought him to his Parsonage of Bemerton, *and to the Thirty sixth Year of his Age, and must now stop, and bespeak the Reader to prepare for an almost incredible story, of the great sanctity of the short remainder of his holy life; a life so full of Charity, Humility, and all Christian vertues, that it deserves the eloquence of St.* Chrysostom *to commend and declare it. A life, that if it were related by a Pen like his, there would then be no need for this Age to look back into times past for the examples of primitive piety; for they might be all found in the life of* George Herbert. (*Life*, p. 41)

Walton's self-effacing rhetoric fits the decorum of his hagiographic purpose.

Accordingly, the story that Walton proceeds to recount of Wood-noth's sighting Herbert, prostrate before the altar of his "*Bemerton* Church" (*Life*, p. 42), fits perfectly with the implications of the speech that Herbert supposedly made right after his induction as rector of the Bemerton parish. Just as in the two "Sonnets" the poet rejected the joys of fictional love, so here the priest of God renounces the illusory joys of the world itself:

And I will now use all my endeavours to bring my Relations and Dependants to a love and reliance on him, who never fails those that trust him. But above all,

I will be sure to live well, because the vertuous life of a Clergy-man, is the most powerful eloquence to perswade all that see it, to reverence and love, and at least to desire to live like him. (*Life,* pp. 42–43)

Walton's Herbert follows Christ in life as in art; in both renunciations he seeks the highest authentic model, one that is not much in vogue, but one that is much needed in a world almost bereft of Christian examples.

Just as saints' lives revealed the signs of their peculiar grace, so did their deaths distinguish them from the ordinary faithful. And it was on his deathbed that Walton's Herbert saved the fruit of his knowledge of David's "mighty *Psaltery*," a manuscript of *The Temple,* preserving the record of his very special life. Accordingly, Herbert sent this manuscript to Ferrar, who comments, *"There was the picture of a Divine Soul in every page; and, that the whole Book, was such a harmony of holy passions, as would enrich the World with pleasure and piety"* (*Life,* p. 75). Providence, Walton adds, had already vindicated Ferrar's judgment, in that ten thousand copies of *The Temple* had been sold. Walton recounts a long speech in which Herbert at his death compares himself to Job, happy to be on his way to *"the new Jerusalem"* (*Life,* p. 77). It was Sunday, and Herbert called for his lute. After uttering, "My God, My God," he played and sang a stanza from his poem entitled "Sunday." Walton concludes: "Thus he liv'd, and thus he dy'd like a Saint, unspotted of the World, full of Alms-deeds, full of Humility, and all the examples of vertuous life" (*Life,* p. 79).

Herbert Improved

Walton's view of Herbert as the devout English poet, writing in imitation of Christ, fuses with the cognate image of Herbert as the inheritor of David's "mighty *Psaltery*." George Herbert was the "sweet singer," master of the simple song in praise of God. At its very inception, the "Life of Herbert" involved the concept of religious song, not only for the place Walton accorded it in the "war against poetry," but in the context that Herbert himself sought to establish. Consider, for instance, the two "Sonnets" written to his mother and the "Jordan" poems. It is not surprising in the context of such poetic manifestos that Herbert would come to the attention of those interested in composing hymns. It is more than coincidental that by the turn of the century one of the most important hymnals in England was a slender volume entitled *Select Hymns, Taken out of Mr. Herbert's Temple, And Turn'd into the Common Metre* (1697), *To be Sung* (Herbert's anonymous collaborator declares) *in the Tunes Ordinarily us'd in Churches.*[5]

In his introduction William E. Stephenson points out that this volume was one of the few of its kind published prior to Isaac Watts's *Hymns and Spiritual Songs* (1707). He also reminds us that until the nineteenth century the Church of England unofficially discouraged all singing except that of the approved metrical versions of the Psalms. Just as in the early seventeenth century, contrary to the thinking of the Church of England, Dissenters advanced the cause of spontaneous public prayer, so *Select Hymns* fit the demand of latter-day Dissenters to use less canonically established lyrics in their services. The *Collection of Divine Hymns* (1694) was an anthology of Dissenting hymnody, to which body of songs *Select Hymns* belongs.

When we recall that during the eighteenth century Herbert became a favorite of the Moravian brotherhood and that, in fact, a volume of hymns based largely on *The Temple* was one of the first books they brought to the New World, we can see how completely the myth of Herbert as the saintly inheritor of David had taken hold. It helps explain, too, the development, down to our most recent critical evaluations, of the trend toward Puritanizing the Herbert canon. For it is in the *Select Hymns* and its lineal descendant, the first edition of the Wesleys' *Hymns and Sacred Poems* (1739), that the simple, pietistic, quintessentially Protestant and—yes—Puritan Herbert is established. It is established through a radical process of revision. This is a somewhat controversial point, but since the process of revising Herbert's poems for performance in church no less than that of interpreting "facts" in delineating a "Life of Herbert" laid the basis for the romantic and modern distortions of Herbert's poetics, we must consider these late seventeenth- and eighteenth-century transformations of Herbert as extensions of Ferrar's, Oley's, and Walton's mythmaking.

In the preface to *Select Hymns,* the compiler-collaborator points out Herbert's popularity: *The Temple* had *"undergone Eleven Impressions near Twenty Years ago"* (sig. A2). He complains that, while Herbert is often cited in *"Sermons and other Discourses"* (everybody knows that Richard Baxter admired Herbert), most people were not sufficiently acquainted with the proper tunes to sing Herbert's hymns. In order to make Herbert's lyrics more accessible, the author proposes to rely on *"the New Testament Hymns in Dr.* Woodford's Paraphrase," a portion of which he includes. In a manner reminiscent of Herbert's two "Sonnets" on the state of English poetry, he sees his work as an alternative to secular love-poetry: *"How much more fit is* Herbert's *Temple to be set to the Lute, than* Cowley's Mistress! *It is hard that no one can be taught Musick, but in such wanton Songs as fill the Hearts of many Learners with Lust and Vanity all their Days"* (sig. A2v). By joining Herbert (the speaker insists that he keeps *"strictly to the Sence of the Author"*), this compiler presents himself in the same noble undertaking. The choice for both is between profane and divine love poems. Herbert recognized this, he writes, when he turned *"a light Love-song . . . into a Spiritual Hymn"* (sig. A3).

Clearly, this hymnologist thinks that he merely expresses an intention implicit *in,* though perhaps obscured *by,* Herbert's text. The anonymous composer is referring to Herbert's "A Parodie," the opening lines of which, as F. E. Hutchinson indicates, resemble this popular lyric:

> Soules joy, now I am gone,
>   And you alone,
>   (Which cannot be,
> Since I must leave my selfe with thee,
>   And carry thee with me)
>   Yet when unto our eyes
>   Absence denyes
>   Each others sight,
> And makes to us a constant night,
>   When others change to light.
>   (*Works,* p. 541n)

Compare the opening stanza of Herbert's poem with that of the 1697 version, entitled "Desertion" and sung *"To the Tune* of Psalm 67":

> Souls joy, when thou art gone,
>   And I alone,
>   Which cannot be,
> Because thou dost abide with me,
>   And I depend on thee;
>
>   Yet when thou dost suppresse
>   The cheerfulnesse

Of thy abode,
And in my powers not stirre abroad,
But leave me to my load:

O what a damp and shade
Doth me invade!
No stormie night
Can so afflict or so affright.
As thy eclipsed light.

(*Works,* p. 183)

. . .

Soul's Joy, when thou art gone
(Which yet sure cannot be,
Because thou dost abide in me,
And I depend on Thee.)

Yet when thou dost suppress
The Joy of thy abode,
And in my Power not stir abroad,
But leave me to my Load.

Oh, what a Damp doth seize
My Soul! no stormy Night
Can so afflict or so affright,
As thy eclipsed Light.

(*Select Hymns,* p. 32)

I quote at some length to demonstrate how closely the three texts resemble each other. By altering the context, and so the presumed audience, Herbert alters the tone and substance of the expression. It is not a lover talking about his feelings in the absence of his beloved, but a Christian expressing the vexations endured when God's presence is not felt. But the implication of the minimal changes imposed on "A Parodie" in "Desertion" is that Herbert's text is *already* a hymn. Just sing it *"To the Tune* of Psalm 67." With only the slightest alteration, Herbert's version of David's "mighty *Psaltery"* requires only a selection of familiar psalmic melodies in order to be included in the congregation's public worship. And the same could be said of other poems in the 1697 collection: "Death" (*"To the Tune of* Psalm 100"), "Antiphon" ("To the *Tune of* Psalm 148"), and "Discipline" (*"To the Tune of* Psalm 67").

But the revisions here are not always that simple. Often, poems that involve doctrinal matters indicate a revisionist bias toward Low Church sensibilities. "The Agony" is a case in point. Compare the closing lines of Herbert's poem with those of the hymn sung "*To the Tune of* Psalm 119." This is the stunning close of "The Agonie": "Love is that liquour sweet and most divine, / Which my God feels as bloud; but I, as wine" (*Works,* p. 37). The revised rendition introduces an adverb and a relative construction not present in the original. But the powerful use that Herbert makes of the present tense, according to which God and the speaker feel the same liquid in the here and now is not present in the 1697 text:

> Love is that Liquor passing-sweet,
>   A Drink that is Divine,
> 'Tis what my God did feel as Blood,
>   But what I taste as Wine.
>   (*Select Hymns,* p. 9)

An assertive Dissenter's frame of mind here carries the 1697 speaker away. Lest anyone infer that "Liquor" is not a beverage, the reviser explains ("A Drink that is"). Even more trenchantly, the Dissenter alters the poem in such a way as to save Herbert from the dangers of errant Anglo-Catholic interpretation. The original makes clear early in the stanza that the speaker has tasted "that liquour sweet," for it is on the basis of past experience that the speaker assuredly affirms the proposition that anyone not acquainted with "Love" need only "taste that juice" of the Sacrifice to be convinced that he had never before tasted "the like." The assertion ends in a deflection: "then let him say / If ever he did taste the like." Thus, the final couplet of the poem stands alone, with one subject, one verb (in one tense: the present), and two dependent clauses.

The syntax, important in the original, is radically altered in *Select Hymns.* By making the "I" the subject of "feels" ("Which my God feels as . . . but I [feel] as . . ."), Herbert elicits a powerful sense of immediacy, a sense made stronger by the earlier stress on the liquor's taste:

> Who knows not Love, let him assay
> And taste that juice, which on the crosse a pike
> Did set again abroach; then let him say
>   If ever he did taste the like.

Love is that liquour sweet and most divine,
Which my God feels as bloud; but I, as wine.
(*Works,* p. 37)

Hutchinson states the common wisdom here: "A kind of inversion
of the doctrine of transubstantiation: 'I receive as a refreshing cordial
what was to Christ the blood of sacrifice' " (*Works,* p. 488). But
the primary issue here is neither *"Tran-"* nor *"Con*substantiation."
Herbert sets the sequence up in such a way as to separate protestations concerning the sense of taste from the speaker's categorical
statement in the closing couplet. Even the rhyme accentuates the
speaker's affirmation of the "divinity" of the "wine" and of the act
that so distinguishes God from man, "Sinne" from "Love," and
sinner from communicant. It is precisely this sacramental inclusion
that Herbert's reviser excludes. In so doing, he points the way to
the revisionist Herbert of the 1980s. The Dissenter's Herbert is
more Protestant, more Puritan, more clear, more rational, more
modern, and certainly more relevant to the Dissenter's needs than
is the text of Herbert's poem.

By no means unique, this Dissenter's Herbert, then, is part of
an emerging image of Herbert as the sweet and saintly singer of
simple hymns. In order to make Herbert's songs more attractive to
less liturgically oriented congregations, their doctrine no less than
their meter required adjustment. It is not surprising that Herbert's
poetry began to reflect the tastes and opinions of admirers who
included, besides John and Charles Wesley, framers of the earliest
Moravian hymnals. It has been pointed out to me that because the
Wesleys loved Herbert it must follow that his view of the Sacraments
was palatable to Methodists. If we allow that Herbert's views accord
with those of the Herbert produced by the Wesleys' revisions, then
of course we find the doctrinal harmony that has been propounded.
That is, every Herbert poem revised by the Wesleys points the way
toward a quintessentially "Protestant" George Herbert. We shall
return to consider this question from a different point of view in
chapters 2 through 4, but for now we must concern ourselves with
the way in which the revisions of Dissenters and Methodists shape
part of the emerging picture of George Herbert himself. It is not
enough to say that Herbert was admired by everybody. Indeed this
cliché of Herbert criticism ignores how completely Herbert's texts
were changed by some of his admirers and how completely these

changes reflect, not Herbert's poetic idiom or aims, but social, religious, and poetic ends quite foreign to them. To make this point clear we need only look at the first edition of the Wesleys' *Hymns and Sacred Poems* (1739). I know of no work that more clearly exhibits the importance of George Herbert in the eighteenth century. No work of the period indicates more admiration of Herbert, and no work more clearly shows how completely George Herbert's poetry had become incorporated into the life of the Church.

Forty-two of the songs in this slim collection are based directly on poems in *The Temple*.[6] Several texts bear altered titles, and most of the poems exhibit significant changes in sense. The revision of "Jordan" (II), a poem to which we return more than once as an example of Herbert's poetic views and practices, indicates such a departure. We can see even in the Wesleys' title, "True Praise," a departure from Herbert's primary thematic interest in the source of true poetic inspiration—the Jordan River in contrast to the streams of Helicon. Whereas Herbert's speaker characterizes lines that seem to take on a life of their own ("My thoughts began to burnish, sprout, and swell" [*Works,* p. 102, 1. 4]), the Wesleys depict the singer summoning "Fancy" to the "Aid" of his "feeble Verse" (p. 119). While retaining the figure of "Thousands of notions" running in the singer's brain, they shift the emphasis to the space in the brain these ideas occupy. Indeed, in this new context the life and death of words ("This was not quick enough, and that was dead") are no longer in apposition. Rather, they are replaced by an admixture of biological and geometrical figures accompanied by an unfortunate and probably unconscious rhyme: "This was too flat, that dead."

A look at the Wesleys' revision of the third stanza of "Jordan" (II) shows even better how effectively the text has been turned away from Herbert's thematic interest in the process of writing poetry:

> Mean while I whisp'ring heard a Friend,
>   "Why all this vain Pretence?
> "Love has a Sweetness ready penn'd,
>   "Take that, and save Expence.
>   (*Hymns* [1739], p. 120)

Gone is the agony of creation ("As flames do work and winde, when they ascend"); gone are the poet's doubts about his inordinate love

of self ("So did I weave my self into the sense"). Both are conveniently
reduced into the briefest recognition ("Mean while") of a lapse in
time. The ordeal of composition implodes into a segment of un-
differentiated moments. Then too, "Love" has changed into a being
known only by his possession, as distinct from his attribute, of
"sweetnesse." Finally, since the poem is no longer about "invention,"
but "True Praise," the speaker need not concern himself with the
powerful injunction on which the original ends: *"Copie out onely
that. . . ."* Since "Love" owns a certain quality, it is fitting that
the singer "Take" it.

Clearly, the revision of "Jordan" (II) goes beyond mere metrical
arrangement for singing in church; rather, it results in a shift in
thematic focus away from Herbert's primary interest in poetic composition. A similar uneasiness about the sensuous aspects of Herbert's
art is also evident, for example, in the revision of Herbert's much
admired "Vertue." Compare the Wesleys' version of the third stanza
with the original.

> Sweet spring, full of sweet dayes and roses,
> A box where sweets compacted lie;
> My musick shows ye have your closes,
>   And all must die.
>   (*Works,* p. 88)
>
>   . . .
>
> Sweet spring, so beauteous and so gay,
>   Storehouse, where Sweets unnumber'd lie:
> Not long thy fading Glories stay,
>   But Thou with all thy Sweets must die.
>   (*Hymns* [1739], p. 9)

One could argue that the changes imposed on the first two stanzas
resemble those of "Desertion," which the Wesleys model, title and
all, upon their 1697 predecessor. The apparent aim is to present
the text for congregational singing. And yet throughout, the sensuous effects are systematically altered. The "hue" of Herbert's rose,
so "angrie and brave" as to inflict a tactile response in the viewer
("Bids the rash gazer wipe his eye" [*Works,* p. 87]), only dazzles
the Wesleys' "rash Beholder's Eye." In Herbert's poem, the rose is
"sweet," but we do not know, as we do in the 1739 version, that
it is so because of its fragrance. Still, it is in the third stanza that
the Wesleys' revision most radically diverges. Herbert emphasizes

the compactness of spring's virtues. It is sweet because it is full of "sweet dayes and roses." And yet, though full, it is also "compacted." The Wesleys, in turn, stress the more expansive figure of a storehouse, which encloses "Sweets unnumber'd." The auditory figure of music—Patrides points out how Herbert fuses the olfactory and auditory possibilities of his "box [of] sweets"[7]—and the intensely personal tone of the speaker's affirmation ("My musick shows ye have your closes") are swept away and replaced by abstract clichés from centuries-old traditions of the *ars moriendi.*

Further, it is this expansive sense that governs the close of the 1739 version. Compare:

> Onely a sweet and vertuous soul,
> Like season'd timber, never gives;
> But though the whole world turn to coal,
> Then chiefly lives.
> *(Works,* p. 88)

. . .

> Only a Sweet and Virtuous Mind,
> When Nature all in Ruins lies,
> When Earth and Heav'n a Period find,
> Begins a Life that never dies.
> *(Hymns* [1739], p. 10)

Here, the Wesleys' flight to abstraction leads to an ending that is both trite and corny and results in the excision of one of Herbert's most striking figures. In "Vertue," "season'd timber," endowed with the capacity of resilience, is contrasted to "the whole world," the substance of which can be altered. The eschatological development of this figural comparison follows nicely from the established sense of the way in which one kind of timber "never gives." With the Wesleys we have no timber, no coal, and no figural comparison, but only abstract affirmation of the survival of the "Virtuous Mind" beyond Doomsday. The Wesleys' revision of "Jordan" (II) expunged Herbert's emphasis on the *process* of poetic composition; the changes imposed on "Vertue" eliminate the *effects* of that process. We sense here a simpler, homelier, easier instruction, perhaps more readily grasped by a congregation's singing; we also sense, however, a notably un-Herbertian fondness for abstraction and an un-Herbertian naïveté regarding the true art of imitating Christ while imitating David.

Coleridge and "Constitutional Predisposition"

Evidence that George Herbert's apotheosis had occurred appeared in 1853, with the publication of William Pickering's edition in two volumes of *The Works of George Herbert in Prose and Verse*, originally published in 1841. The editor's reiteration of Oley's belief that "the Divine Herbert" wrote poetry embodying "the excellencies of Scripture Divinitie, and choice passages of the Fathers bound up in meetre"[8] expresses no more than the common wisdom, borrowed from such unassailable sources as Oley and Richard Baxter. Baxter had praised Herbert above all poets, with the exception of George Sandys. Pickering's "Advertisement" notes that along with Herbert's works and Christopher Harvey's *The Synagogue*, he will include Coleridge's "Notes on the Temple and Synagogue":

The Notes by the late S. T. Coleridge, printed at the end of this volume, occur in a copy of The Temple which formerly belonged to him, and with whom it was a great favorite. He appears to have contemplated editing a selection, with a few slight alterations of the verse.
(*Works*, Pickering ed., 2:ix-x)

Coleridge extends the implications of Richard Baxter, who considered Herbert as "a man that is past jest,"[9] and so not to be compared with even such superior poets as Abraham Cowley, who "far excel [him] in Wit" (sig. A7). Baxter claims that, like George Sandys, "*Herbert* speaks *to God* like one that *really believeth a God*, and whose business in the world is most *with God*" (sig. A7v). In other words, Baxter admired Herbert for reasons much like Oley's, because his poetry approximated the values and practices of metrical verse paraphrase. Indeed, this is what Baxter liked about Sandys.

In marked contrast to Baxter's implicit bias for biblical verse paraphrase, Coleridge does not think of Herbert as a member of a school of poets. On the contrary, Herbert "is a true poet, but a poet *sui generis*" (*Works*, Pickering ed., 2:379). Because this is so, it is not enough to read Herbert with "a cultivated judgment." Taste, "classical" or otherwise, will also not do, nor will unaided "poetic sensibility." The argument goes like this: Herbert is, sui generis, a saintly poet, one who is first and foremost a saint. To appreciate such a poet one must "be" like him. If Ferrar and Oley and Walton attribute divine aims to Herbert, Coleridge insists that

Herbert's readers must have them too. Coleridge's view, similar to ethnic formulas popular in the criticism of the 1960s and 1970s, insists that in order to understand George Herbert one must be not only a Christian, but a particular kind of Christian: "To appreciate this volume [*The Temple*], it is not enough that the reader possesses a cultivated judgment, classical taste, or even poetic sensibility, unless he be likewise a *Christian,* and both a zealous and an orthodox, both a devout and a *devotional,* Christian" (2:379). The demands that Coleridge lays upon Herbert's reader reveal more than his religious predilections. We learn how completely his romantic response involved an ecclesiastical conception of Herbert's life: "He must be an affectionate and dutiful child of the Church, and from habit, conviction, and a constitutional predisposition to ceremoniousness, in piety as in manners, find her forms and ordinances aids of religion, not sources of formality; for religion is the element in which he lives, and the region in which he moves" (2:379). "He," the appreciative reader, must be so because Herbert is so. Knowledge of the liturgy is not enough. Nor will it suffice to recognize the pietistic intent behind the forms of Anglican worship. Coleridge lays out biological as well as social determinants of an appropriate readership. Alone or in company, such a critic affirms the rites and ceremonies of the Church effortlessly, for he is, quite literally, born with "a constitutional predisposition to ceremoniousness." The echo from Saint Paul's exhortation to the Athenians would not have been lost upon Coleridge's readers either. So completely does this type of Christian see the "forms and ordinances" of the Church as integral parts of religious experience, rather than decorative devices, that, for him, to be part of one is to be part of the other.

It would be wrong to think that Coleridge wishes only to exculpate Herbert and other seventeenth-century divines from the charge of "yearning after the Romish fopperies and even the Papistic usurpations." He does suggest that Herbert and other seventeenth-century admirers of "forms and ordinances" of the Church could better be described as *"Patristic"* than "Papistic." In this aside Coleridge only follows through on what he has already said about Herbert, his readers, and himself. In Coleridge's view, misunderstanding of Herbert's poetry is inevitable. Herbert was, as many of his readers were not, part of religion's "forms and ordinances" in the same way that he was a part of the Body of Christ. He was "a devout and a *devotional,* Christian," living, moving and having his being in what seemed, to Coleridge's contemporaries, suspiciously "Papistic," but was better described as *"Patristic"* (2:379). On the contrary, Herbert's poetry perfectly reflected a natural propensity "to ceremoniousness." *The Temple,* therefore, reflects a life ("from habit, conviction, and a constitutional predisposition") that remains closed to most readers, who fail to appreciate Herbert's life simply because they cannot understand it. They see in the natural reflection of a devout life signs and symbols of "fopperies," rather than a submerging of the poet's self in the Body of Christ *by* a submerging of his poetic self in the life of the Church. Coleridge explicitly formulates ideas and attitudes implicit in preceding biographies, hymnals, and critical commentary. So totally was Herbert and his work absorbed in the life and forms of the Church that only the handful of readers similarly absorbed will be able to understand and appreciate his poetry. Herbert's saintly life and *The Temple* have become so completely intertwined that this demand is made explicit: to understand the latter one must live the former. Knowledge alone won't help; refined taste will not do. This is not a version of the biographical fallacy, but rather an assertion of a coercively intentional poetics. Coleridge's remarks rest on the powerful assumption that poetry like Herbert's is accessible only to an audience sharing his personal predilections. With respect to Herbert scholarship, it surely represents, in its fullest development, the fusion of life with art.

In 1853, when Coleridge's "Notes" reappeared in London, an edition of *The Poetical Works of George Herbert* was published in Edinburgh, edited by Reverend George Gilfillan, with a twenty-six-page critical biography, "On the Life and Poetical Works of George Herbert." This document has not received much notice from Herbert scholars, yet it represents, especially in contrast to Coleridge's "Notes," something of a departure from the rhetoric of genuflection that had become for all practical purposes the established view of Herbert. There are similarities and continuities, of course. But Gilfillan's approach is more comparative than hagiographic: his assumptions and procedures seem to look forward to those of Alexander Grosart and George Herbert Palmer rather than backward to those of Walton and Oley. Gilfillan takes as his point of departure an extended comparison between Herbert and Milton. He is interested primarily in the differences between two great poets: "His [Herbert's] piety was of a more evangelical cast than Milton's—his purity was tenderer and lovelier—he had more of the Christian, and less of the Jew."[10] Gilfillan assumes that Herbert's readers could appreciate *The Temple* if only they would take the trouble to read the Prayer Book, the Psalter, and other relevant, if too often ignored, texts. For him, the difficulties of Herbert criticism were not determined by one's birth or upbringing. They were not, finally, internal to either the author or his audience. Gilfillan sees the critical problem in terms that we might now think of as concerning the history of ideas: "[Herbert] is often obscure, and his allegorising vein is opened too often, and explored too far; so much so, that had we added a commentary or extended notes on 'The Temple,' it would have necessarily filled another volume nearly as large as the present" (*Works,* Gilfillan ed., p. xviii). Herbert may be quaint, but he is quaint because of certain describable, poetic practices, which can be analyzed and understood accordingly. His allegorical interest, which Gilfillan believes Herbert shared with Donne, Quarles, Giles Fletcher, and Bunyan, is as accessible as Milton's, but it requires patient consideration of the peculiar difficulties of Herbert's language, not of his piety.

Clearly, Gilfillan's outlook differs from that of Coleridge and his antecedent admirers of Herbert's saintliness. Gilfillan does not imply with Coleridge that Herbert critics must incline to one or another kind of Christian worship. Nor does he impute to the liturgical qualities he perceives in Herbert's poetry anything more mysterious than the cadences of the Psalter and the Book of Common Prayer. Herbert's "piety," being "of a more evangelical cast than Milton's," differs from Milton's not in kind but in quantity. If Herbert has "more of the Christian, and less of the Jew," then Milton has less of the Christian and more of the Jew. The comparison is between demonstrably different poetic interests and practices rather than between demonstrably different lives or states of mind.

Toward the end of the nineteenth century, interest in the study of Herbert's art as distinct from his piety took hold. Indeed, Gilfillan's comparison between Herbert and Milton is a convenient point of demarcation in our present study. Now, as we turn to Herbert's writing, it may be well to keep in mind Amy M. Charles's warning that, just as it is wrong to acquiesce to Walton's "portrayal of Herbert as a forerunner of the type of 'gentle Jesus, meek and mild,' " so should we remember too that "the man Herbert is more than the record."[11] He lived in an exciting time, in which much of the social unrest that was to lead to war centered on the institution that he chose to serve and to write about: the Church of England.

Chapter Two

George Herbert
and the Church

As we observed in chapter 1, the tendency to think of George Herbert in pietistic rather than literary terms began with the publication of *The Temple* and continued well into the nineteenth century. Twentieth-century criticism developed its own way of reinterpreting Herbert, but was itself shaped by the image of the sweet and simple singer of *The Temple*. It could be argued that in this meticulously developed image lie the historical bases for the quintessentially "Protestant" and "Puritan" Herbert promulgated by such recent critics as Barbara Lewalski and Richard Strier. Although the present study argues for a more Catholic reading of Herbert, the recent emphasis on doctrinal matters attests to the fact that Herbert's religious views have always been considered of paramount importance to an understanding of him. In this connection, all Herbert scholars are indebted to Joseph Summers's seminal work entitled *George Herbert: His Religion and Art* (1954). But while critics agree on the importance of religious thought in Herbert, their inevitable drift is toward a bifurcated view of the canon, some stressing Herbert's Catholic, others his Protestant, sympathies and tastes.

So it is best to begin our discussion cautiously. Upon what points, if any, do critics agree? Probably those concerning Herbert's ecclesiastical affiliation would be least controversial. After all, while writing a good part of *The Temple* and *A Priest to the Temple*, George Herbert was an active priest of the Church of England. This fact makes him in one important respect like John Donne, whom he admired, and in another important respect unlike Richard Crashaw, who admired him. Donne separated himself from the Roman Catholicism of his family and youth, a fact that John Carey considers crucial in the development of his poetic sensibility. [1] Crashaw moved in the opposite direction, toward a Catholicism that seems more at home in Saint Peter's Basilica than in Saint Paul's Cathedral. In

contrast to both, Herbert underwent nothing like a serious change
in his religious convictions or practices. And yet his spiritual pathway intersected Crashaw's at Little Gidding, where both men found
themselves among kindred souls.

Since George Herbert was an Anglican priest, it seems supererer-
ogatory to say that he could not have been a Roman Catholic. But
as the fate of Archbishop William Laud suggests, such simple statements, when made about the seventeenth century, can be misleading. Then as now, facts may be important, but they are never as
important as their interpretation. Contemporary reactions to activities at Little Gidding are a case in point. It has already been said
that Richard Crashaw's Roman Catholic sensibility did not feel out
of place there, and Archbishop Laud approved of the settlement's
monastic regimen. Charles's biography has only increased our understanding of Herbert's relationship with Nicholas Ferrar and Little
Gidding.[2] In the next chapter we will be discussing the literary
aspects of that relationship. But even now it may be well to recall
that many of Herbert's Protestant brethren hated Little Gidding
and everything that Ferrar was trying to accomplish. We need only
examine that notorious little pamphlet, *The Arminian Nunnery* (1641),
with its engraved title page depicting a nun wearing a rosary and
its contemptuous descriptions of the devotional practices there, to
get a clear, contemporary impression of how that religious society
appeared to sensibilities to the left of Herbert's and Ferrar's. While
this inflammatory pamphlet has been called a Puritan exaggeration
based on the prejudices of an unsympathetic visitor,[3] we must bear
in mind that the boundary between interpretation and exaggeration
is not always easy to discern. And since the pendulum in Herbert
criticism has swung far toward viewing Herbert as a Protestant and
Puritan poet, almost as if the terms were identical, we should
recognize that he was associated with a religious society regarded
by many of his fellow Englishmen as papist.

This association does not make him a Roman Catholic, but neither
does it lend credence to the Protestant or Puritan hypotheses in
Herbert studies. Other evidence must be taken into account. In this
chapter, we will be looking at Herbert's writings on the controversial
religious issues of his day. Although we do not often think of Herbert
as a polemicist (surely Herbert's early biographers did little to encourage that characterization), Herbert in fact wrote extensively on

subjects of religious controversy, and in some works and passages his tone was decidedly, even stridently, polemical.

Herbert and Puritanism

Although Herbert died before the most divisive years of religious controversy overwhelmed England, he was aware of the issues that would soon precipitate civil war: church government, the liturgy, ordination, selection of clergy, "set" prayers, priestly vestments, and so on. We know his views on these important subjects because he wrote on many of them in his poetry and prose. We know that he loved and admired the Church of England, seeing in her via media an aesthetically and politically pleasing form of worship. In "The British Church" (*Works,* pp. 109–10), for instance, the speaker lauds the "perfect lineaments and hue" of his "deare Mother," praising her taste and restraint in makeup and dress:

> A fine aspect in fit aray,
> Neither too mean, nor yet too gay,
>   Shows who is best.
> Outlandish looks may not compare:
> For all they either painted are,
>   Or else undrest.
>   (ll. 7–12)

As in Donne's "Satyre III," so in "The British Church" Rome and Geneva are depicted in figures of feminine extremes:

> She on the hills, which wantonly
> Allureth all in hope to be
>   By her preferr'd,
> Hath kiss'd so long her painted shrines,
> That ev'n her face by kissing shines,
>   For her reward.
>
> She in the valley is so shie
> Of dressing, that her hair doth lie
>   About her eares:
> While she avoids her neighbours pride,
> She wholly goes on th' other side,

And nothing wears.
(ll. 13–24)

Overdressing may be a sign of pride, but it does not follow that one who dresses beneath the occasion is humble. Both women (Geneva, Rome) err in their *overemphasis* on dress, one by an excess of finery, the other by an excess of avoiding finery. Paradoxically, the ends of both excesses are indistinguishable. In their mutual immoderation, these women prove themselves alike: indecorous and ugly.

In his commentary on this poem, F. E. Hutchinson points out the inclusiveness of Herbert's sense of decorum. Not only does he write of "The British" rather than of "The English Church," thereby applauding the reintroduction under the reign of James I of the episcopacy in Scotland, but he includes in his admiration of "the *via media* of the Anglican Church, between Rome and Geneva," her decorum "both in doctrine and in worship" (*Works,* p. 515n). This son admires his "dearest Mother" because she is neither naked nor overdressed in public:

> But, dearest Mother, what those misse,
> The mean, thy praise and glorie is,
>   And long may be.
> Blessed be God, whose love it was
> To double-moat thee with his grace,
>   And none but thee.
>   (ll. 25–30)

Much has been said of Herbert's ostensible gentleness and tolerance in matters of doctrine. But if certain texts can be cited to support those claims, the closing stanza of "The British Church" is not one of them. Even the repetition of the conjunction *And* at the beginning of the paired and rhyming short lines emphasizes the exclusive characteristic of the "grace" accorded "The British Church." Surrounded by water and protected by an enlightened sovereign, the Church of England exhibits the outward sign of the exclusive "grace" claimed by Geneva and Rome.

The figure of dress is not a trivial one in Herbert's time, since the vestiarian controversy was one focus of disagreements among various religious parties in England. In *Musae Responsoriae,* Latin verses written in response to Andrew Melville's *Anti-Tami-Cami-*

Categoria (1604), Herbert excoriates the extremes of both Protestant and Roman Catholic worship. If anything, he is harder on the Puritan's endemic tendency to undress. Indeed, it is not easy to sympathize with the recent trend toward Puritanizing George Herbert in view of the attitudes expressed here and elsewhere on such issues as priestly vestments. Herbert writes, for instance:

> Long ago, when Caesar
> First set foot from his ships
> Upon our isle,
> Noting all the natives of the place
> Living without clothes, he cried,
> "O victory is mine!"[4]

And so it is, he continues, that "the Puritans" want to bring that prophecy to fulfillment by returning in religion to "their fathers' barbaric state"—naked and ignorant.

We should consider Herbert's *Musae Responsoriae* a serious statement of Herbert's views on the prevailing issues of religious controversy. Melville, to whose polemical work Herbert responded, was a controversial figure in his time, which was (Herbert registers sensitivity to this fact) actually more Elizabethan than Jacobean. His rhetorical roots are in the soil of the Martin Marprelate tract wars. Then, Melville struggled mightily against what he designates in *Anti-Tami-Cami-Categoria* as offenses to "sacred worship, as simple and pure."[5] Walton found him a formidable opponent for Herbert: "This Mr. *Melvin* was a man of learning, and was the Master of a great wit, a wit full of *knots* and *clenches:* a wit sharp and satyrical; exceeded, I think, by none of that Nation, but their *Bucanen.* At Mr. *Melvins* return hither [from the Continent], he writ and scattered in Latin many pieces of his wit against our *Altars,* our *Prayers,* and our *Publick Worship* of God; in which Mr. *Herbert* took himself to be so much concern'd, that as fast as *Melvin* writ and scatter'd them, Mr. *Herbert* writ and scatter'd answers."[6] With expressions like this in mind, we can think of Melville as an almost perfect example of the proper use (as Patrick Collinson deems it) of the term *Puritan:*[7] he sought to rid the Church of all vestiges of rites and ceremonies not specifically authorized by Scripture. Thus, Melville answers all of his adversaries at once:

That I by so much as one word should dare
To brand Prelates' pride, and Rites lay bare—
Impious and foolish and absurd,
Such as are found not in The Word;
That I should seek such Rites to expel
As blots on God's chosen; and rebel,

Yea, groan, that an oath exacted should be
Against all law; and that I should see
A sorrowful trap or net spread along,
To catch wretched souls by right or by wrong!
(Grosart ed., pp. 98–99)

The list of rites and ceremonies that Melville excoriates reads like
a litany of complaints enjoined by all Dissenters and leftists dissat-
isfied with church government: bishops, "set prayers," signing,
infant baptism, laying on of hands, wedding rings, the surplice,
the biretta:

Shall he, the Minister of Christ,
Don cap four-squar'd? or o'er him twist
Egyptian robes or pomp externe,
Such as in papal glory worn?
Shall he, Christ's simpleness denying,
Be found old Antichrist out-vying?
(Grosart ed. pp. 99–100)

The tone is reminiscent of the frenzies of the likes of Robert Browne,
Henry Barrow, and John Greenwood, so we are not surprised to
find that Melville praises such heroes of the Puritan cause as William
Whitaker and John Rainolds. On the other hand, Melville does call
upon King James in a manner foreign to the style of these others,
who never look to the crown for comfort. But as a Scotsman ap-
pealing to James's patriotism in the first year of Jacobean rule,
Melville petitions for an end to organ music in the church and for
the extirpation of the entire panoply of papist paganism evident in
the Church of England.

In rejoinder, Herbert also calls on King James, but with a challenge to "beat down the Puritans." Herbert lends a militant hand
himself by declaring war on Andrew Melville, who was, at the time
of Herbert's writing at Cambridge, in his eighties:

> It's not my age that lets me
> Make war on you, a veteran,
> And not my age that lets me
> Beat you down: the case
> Will force me to it. . . .
>
> > (*LP*, p. 7)

Whether fairly or not, Herbert sees the ancient Melville as symptomatic of the Puritan cause. The issues over which Herbert joins Melville in rhetorical combat are virtually every one on which Melville had voiced an opinion in the offending poem: church government ("On the pride of the bishops"), infant baptism ("On the sacred rite of baptism"), signing ("On the sign of the cross"), and priestly vestments ("On the surplice"; "On the biretta"). In each case Herbert heaps scorn on the accusation that Anglican rites and ceremonies are vestiges of Rome. Indeed, in one epigram Herbert reverses the attack, claiming that a blood link exists between zealous Puritans and papists:

> O gracious age! On every side
> The brothers stand around.
> Puritan and Papists have
> Each their own. So now there are
> Good brothers everywhere, though nothing
> Can be rarer than a brother's love.
>
> > (*LP*, p. 31)

Again, in "To His Serene Majesty," Herbert makes the same connection, praising James I's forbearance with extremists of both left and right:

> Endowed with this ability, you endure
> With greater confidence as Puritans
> And Roman Catholics arouse the waves
> Between which you, the Shepherd, drive your sheep,
> Safest in a *via media.*
>
> > (*LP*, p. 59)

Given the way in which Herbert linked Puritans with Roman Catholics as extremes on a continuum, with the Church of England in the middle, he cannot legitimately be thought sympathetic to

those whom he considered sources of iniquity and violence. Herbert
was no Crashaw, but neither was he a Milton or Prynne. Indeed,
Herbert saved his best polemical shots for the Puritans. Of course,
he did write several poems expressly hostile to popes and papism.
We need look at only one of them, *Papae titulus, Nec Deus Nec Homo,*
to make an informed inference about his opinion: "Let us not continue asking / Who is the Antichrist. The Pope is not / God or
man: Christ was both" (*LF,* p. 89). But here it is the brevity that
strikes us. With Melville, Herbert is seldom so. This brevity bears
with it just a hint of cavalier dismissal. For as we have already seen,
Herbert equates Puritans and Roman Catholics, and yet the target
of his rhetoric is Melville. Herbert faults Roman Catholics insofar
as they resemble Puritans. Both groups "arouse the waves" and
threaten the sheep that "the Shepherd" must drive safely. Herbert
alludes to Christ, the good Shepherd, who walked on water, and
to the Old Testament story of God's people crossing the Red Sea.

The fact is, though Herbert wrote several poems against the
papacy, he invariably condemned the arrogance of papal claims but
seldom, if ever, mentioned the differences between the Roman and
the Anglican rites or ceremonies. The target of his attack is Andrew
Melville, not Urban VIII. From a political point of view though,
his elegy "On the death of Henry, the Prince of Wales" refers to
the Gunpowder Plot (*LP,* p. 159). Here Herbert is most impatient
with Puritan assaults on rites and ceremonies of the Church of
England. I think this explains the sense we get of his restiveness
with Melville's perpetual laceration of the papists. The curtness of
the epigram just discussed is typical of the way Herbert brushes
aside the common wisdom as just that—common, and therefore
unworthy of serious poetic labor. *Musae Responsoriae* XXX is an even
more telling example of this tone, as Herbert heaps indignation on
Melville for his facile reference to "the Roman she-wolf" and her
notorious appetites (*LP,* p. 100). Herbert responds:

> Is there no shame
> Or end of slander?
> Will you never cast aside
> Your vain fears of the Vatican
> She-wolf?
>
>   (*LP,* p. 45)

The political point of this epigram is clear: the English are as wary of "the British fox" as of "the Roman she-wolf." Hence the poem, with its tone of exasperation, precedes one of many epigrams in defense of rites and ceremonies observed in common by Roman and Anglican Communions. What difference would the two ceremonies make to Melville? This is the crux of the matter for Herbert: "all rites irritate him" (*LP,* p. 47).

This jibe fits perfectly with the hard fact that Herbert avoids all references to Roman Catholic rites, even those that were repudiated by Anglicans during the preceding century. Not only does he ignore these differences—the use of "holy water" and the rite of "Asperges," for example—but at times he appears to use them in their older, forbidden ways. His use in "The Church-porch" of the figure *"Perirrhanterium"* is a case in point, one that we shall consider in detail in chapter 4. Just where, then, did Herbert stand on points of difference separating factions in the England of his own day? As C. A. Patrides wisely observes, the position of the Anglican Church was often intentionally "flexible if vague."[8] Lines of demarcation were, nevertheless, not hard to find.

The Proper Form of Public Prayer

If we imagine a continuum from left to right, with radical reformers on the left and those who wished to return to the old Roman ways on the right, we might have a means of conceptualizing the complex structure of religious controversy in Herbert's time. Herbert himself used such spatial figures ("arouse the waves / *Between* which you" [*LP,* p. 59, italics mine]). This is not to deny that such a two-dimensional analogy implies neatness where in fact overlapping and confusion abound. Yet differences did simplify themselves into violent actions: the Gunpowder Plot, the Civil War. Religious differences were not the only ones that motivated partisans, but social, political, and economic conflicts focused in those days on the Church, which was the means by which the crown governed the universities, urged obedience of subjects to the established order, obtained money for hospitals and aid for widows and orphans, and governed major events in the daily lives of people in the local parishes (birth, marriage, death). It is well to remember that it was no more feasible in the seventeenth century to separate religious from political questions than it would be today to separate economic from political questions. So when Herbert wrote on the rites and ceremonies of the Church of England, he took a stand on the most important political issues of his day.

By now we can agree that Herbert's views were neither to the extreme right nor left. And yet we know that such a continuum is easiest to imagine when it is of least use—as when discussing Herbert's poems on Pope Urban VIII or Andrew Melville. Common sense tells us that an imaginary continuum has only an imaginary center. It should be clear from even the few examples we have discussed that Herbert valued the via media, and so we must infer that he thought himself safely in it. And yet, notwithstanding his energetic defense of the Church of England, the tendency in recent criticism has been to shift Herbert too far to the left on the religio-political continuum. Let us take one of the more divisive issues as a test case: the proper "form of prayer." I doubt that any question of the time was more highly charged. Even the vocabulary tended toward polarization: "prescript forms of prayer" and "conceived prayers," by consent of all participants, designated mutually exclusive sets. Further, the distinction carried with it a burden of invective remarkable even for that immoderately contentious age. Pamphlets issued from all segments of the continuum—Puritans, Brownists, Anabaptists, Shakers, priests and bishops—all of them tending toward a polarized rhetoric. One view even held that God himself was the author of set forms: "No doubt from God it hath proceeded." Consequently, for Richard Hooker, "voluntarie dictates proceeding from any mans extemporall wit" could bear no institutional weight.[9]

On the other side, Dissenters like Robert Browne, Henry Ainsworth, Henry Barrow and John Greenwood—Puritans all—found "prescript" prayers not merely boring and unedifying, but pernicious utterances purveyed by Antichrist. The very terms Dissenters used for such prayers—*read, set, stinted, prescript*—suggested absurdity. For instance, in *An Aunswer to George Giffords Pretended Defence of Read Prayers* (1590), John Greenwood ridicules the Church of England for adhering to a practice in which "whole congregations do make no other prayer to God then reading over certeine numbers of wordes upon a booke from yeare to yeare . . . the same matter and words as they were stinted, even out of that *Portuis,* englished out of Antichrists masse-booke; besides private reading of mens writings instead of praying."[10] We can easily proliferate examples here from divines along the spectrum (Greenwood, Barrow, Francis

Johnson, Joseph Hall, Richard Bernard, Gifford, Hooker), but in none of them will we find proponents who designate "conceived prayers" as a "form of prayer." It is as if, by tacit agreement, partisans of every opinion encourage the greatest possible contra-distinction as a necessary benefit to the truth.

In prayer, as in the vestiarian controversy, our continuum roughly corresponds to the range of possible public utterances. At one end of the spectrum, we have the same prayer uttered many times over, with the repetitions themselves taking on meaning (the Rosary). At the other, we have a denial of all *"Form of Words,"* with the affir-mation in its place of the *"Apostle's Doctrine* and *Practice* of *Praying* by the *Spirit,* as it gave words and utterance?"[11] With the Anabap-tists, the *"Spirit"* was known to move congregations to loud singing or "deep sighs, Groans and Tears and Roaring,"[12] which expressions, popular in the so-called "Prophesying" groups of the time (leftist counterparts of the more genteel religious societies associated with Traherne and Herbert), dismayed such Anglican spokesmen as George Gifford and Richard Hooker.

The focus of all this controversy was, of course, the Lord's Prayer. If the Roman Catholics repeated the Paternoster one hundred fifty times, in imitation of the Psalter, certain Puritans refused to utter it even once, holding that it was not a prayer, but as John Greenwood argued, "a doctrine to direct al prayers."[13] He held to this opinion to the bitter end; an eyewitness at Tyburn records that he could not be induced to recite the Lord's Prayer, even to save his life. It is easy to understand why King James would speak out on the issue of the Lord's Prayer. The subject was intrinsically political. James linked Puritan opposition to "set prayers" to rebellion against "the government of Bishops."[14] James was correct in recognizing their preoccupation with the immediate mind of the individual, for in rejecting the Our Father in "dayly Common prayer,"[15] Puritans effectively repudiated "all set prayers."[16] Obviously, this left only spontaneity in their place, which for James had no place in public prayer: "But this monstrous conceit of conceived prayers, without any premeditation, spoileth both *Puritans* and *Brownists.* I justly call it monstrous, since they will have a thing both conceived and borne at once, contrary to nature."[17]

So, for James, to whom Herbert dedicated his response to Mel-ville, tradition and restraint went hand in hand. When upstarts rejected the Paternoster they spurned "the onely Prayer that our

Saviour dictated out of his owne mouth,"[18] replacing it with their own "private spirit," which answered to no public standards of intelligibility or taste. By shifting the locus of taste in prayer, these modern "Donatists" destroyed prayer by transforming it into something else, to wit, preaching. Puritans slid from *the* Word to *their* words, "turning the commandement of the Apostle from *Pray continually*, to *Preach continually*."[19] The end of "privat spirit," namely *"Chaos,"*[20] could be seen in the Low Countries, in "those little start-up sects in *Amsterdam,* where two or three make a Church."[21] Even more tellingly, Joseph Hall defined the political objective of spontaneous prayer as asserting a Congregation's right to select its own pastor ("chosen the mouth of many")[22] and so "Democracie, or popular state (if not Anarchie)."[23]

We can see, then, that Herbert's views on this subject were in line with the customary Anglican distinction between extemporaneous prayer, appropriate only in private and so not answerable to external, public norms of decorum, and prayers said in church, which had to meet the severest tests of social, artistic, and spiritual decorum. With Herbert, the distinction was as "easie" and "quick" as mental prayer itself. Indeed, the tone of "Prayer" (II)—and one of its main themes—is *"Ease."* The speaker has no doubt of the potential immediacy of communication with God: "If I but lift mine eyes, my suit is made" (*Works,* p. 103). Herbert's pronounced emphasis on the present moment encourages comparison with the persistent Puritan demand that "present wantes" of the Congregation could not be read from a book in "divers formes of wordes, as though they [the authors] had knowen the heart of man."[24] Here, the intense personal quality of the expression dramatically represents one soul in colloquy with God:

> Since then these three wait on thy throne,
> *Ease, Power,* and *Love;* I value prayer so,
> That were I to leave all but one,
> Wealth, fame, endowments, vertues, all should go;
> I and deare prayer would together dwell,
> And quickly gain, for each inch lost, an ell.
>
> (ll. 19–24)

Indeed, the voice in this poem—and in "Prayer" (I), for that matter— is familiar throughout "The Church" portion of *The Temple.* This is the voice of a Christian pilgrim, making his way within the corporate Body of Christ, knowing the universal impact of the Sacrifice ("for our sakes in person sinne reprove" [l. 16]), but experiencing gratitude, anxieties, and doubts, alone.

But, again, the norms of public and private prayer differ. In *A Priest to the Temple* (1652), Herbert includes a chapter on *"The Parson praying,"* which balances the liturgical aspects of the priest's performance against the dramatic requirements of the congregation: "The Countrey Parson, when he is to read divine services, composeth himselfe to all possible reverence; lifting up his heart and hands, and eyes, and using all other gestures which may expresse a hearty, and unfeyned devotion." (*Works*, p. 231). By his emphasis on expressiveness and spontaneity, Herbert certainly shares an interest with his brethren to the left of center on our continuum, but he parts company with them in the sacramental role that he envisages the priest fulfilling: "yet not as himself alone, but as presenting with himself the whole Congregation, whose sins he then beares, and brings with his own to the heavenly altar to be bathed, and washed in the sacred Laver of Christs blood." For Herbert, public prayer is an intrinsic part of the Eucharist. In his emphasis on expressiveness, Herbert incorporates interests of importance to those urging continued church reform; but as he sees in that expressiveness a preparation for, and enactment of, the Eucharist, he exhibits values important to those content with Anglican rites and ceremonies.

My point is that Herbert is both explicit and firm in his statement about the priest's role in public prayer. Fervency is not just permissible, it is essential. His opinion in this matter requires that the priest actually *feel* intense emotions in order that he "may affect also his people." Because prayer is more moving than a sermon, it must be uttered with just the proper balance "between fear and zeal," and in just the right tempo. But, again, not only his prayers but the peoples' responses to them must meet the specific demands of the liturgy and of decorum. The people must kneel correctly, pay strict attention to the proceedings, and make all proper responses loudly and they must think "while they answer . . . meditate as they speak" (*Works*, p. 231). As if in answer to the Puritan's accusation that "read prayers" were a contradiction in terms, Herbert turns to Scripture, and expands on this important point:

This is that which the Apostle cals a reasonable service, *Rom.* 12. when we speak not as Parrats, without reason, or offer up such sacrifices as they did of old, which was of beasts devoyd of reason; but when we use our reason, and apply our powers to the service of him, that gives them. (*Works,* p. 232)

Herbert not only rejects that specific accusation, but he argues against the principle that just because a prayer is read from a book, it must be devoid of sense or feeling. His epigram, "On the Lord's Prayer," is an epitome of extensive arguments advanced in defense of including this most notable and controversial of "set prayers" in the daily life of the Church. As would be expected, Melville's diatribe included the obligatory attack on "stinted prayers": "How dare I roll out set words of prayer / In magic rotation through the air?" (2. 99). And Herbert's "On the Lord's Prayer" may be the sternest of his rebukes to Melville, for he ends the poem with the awful suggestion that, for his troubles in attacking the Word of God itself, Melville may have earned reprobation: "But you, whoever you may be, take care, / Lest, evil one, while you deny / The words of God, God's Word / Abandon you" (*LP,* p. 43).

Here, Herbert does more than merely remind his opponent that as one of his last acts before departing to paradise Christ himself delivered this prayer to his disciples. Anglican apologists customarily argued simply that the Lord's Prayer was not proscribed, but prescribed, by Scripture, as amply shown by texts from the Old and New Testaments. Thus, at God's direction, Moses told the people to pray in a certain way (Num. 6.22–26); Richard Bernard takes this "forme of blessing" as not merely permissible, but "prescribed by the Priests."[25] As for "saying the same words," Matthew records that Christ left his disciples for the third time, going apart to pray, "saying the same words"; and in the Gospel according to Luke, likewise, when Christ's disciples asked him for instruction in how to pray, he answered, "When you pray, say thus." "I said," writes cantankerous George Gifford, "Christ saith not when ye meditate, but when ye pray say thus, *Our Father which art etc.* Do I not say truly that Christ saith not when ye meditate, but when yee pray, say thus, *Our Father which art.*"[26] Even his own repetition *("When you pray, say thus")* is designed to hurl defiance in the face of those who criticize prayers only because they have appeared in print: Christ's only prayer, in the context of his instruction, was printed in Holy Scripture.

Herbert follows tradition by dividing the Lord's Prayer into seven parts. Like Gifford, he points to the fact that Christ's instructions on prayer were virtually the last he uttered on earth. And yet, by personalizing Melville's attack as if it were made against Christ rather than against a particular liturgy, Herbert is, if anything, more severe than Gifford:

> Who will receive
> A friend the way the Puritans, who dare
> Touch up anew the symbol
> Of holy love, do their God?
>
> (*LP*, p. 43)

And then he ends the poem by reminding his Puritan adversary of the dangers inherent in tampering with God's Word. It would have been hard in Herbert's day to read these words without remembering those toward the close of the Apocalypse: "And if any man shall take away from the words of the book of this prophecy, God shall take away his part out of the book of life, and out of the holy city, and from the things which are written in this book" (Rev. 22.19).

The Parson Preaching

In this idea of the pastor as one "chosen the mouth of many" the domains of Church discipline and political order converge. If prayer must be freed from past constraints, means must be found to effect that liberation. "Chosen," yes, but by whom? Since election was the only means of guaranteeing that a pastor would be responsive to all and only his congregation's wants and needs, "form" and "order" involved government. So the standards of extemporaneous prayer required nothing less than renovation of the method of selecting clergy: "everie one here hath freedome and power (not disturbing the peaceable order of the Church) to utter his complaintes and griefes. . . . Here is no intrusion or climing up an other way into the sheepfolde, then by the holy and free election of the Lordes holie and free people."[27] Guided by the Word in selecting "what kinde of men the Lorde will have" (sig. A3), writes Henry Barrow, the congregation obtains the voice of a pastor in whom civil and spiritual virtues coexist; he is "temperate" and "holie." In the church and in his family, this saintly man of God leads a "life unreproveable."

Herbert's defense of "signing," the surplice, infant baptism, the biretta, and the like may seem at times obligatory and uninspired, but his rejoinder to Melville's version of the demand that clergymen

lead a "life unreproveable" may be his most severe rebuttal of the
Puritan cause:

> You reproach us for
> Imperfections, stains.
> Why? Is it so
> Strange? We are
> Travelers. What
> Is Christ's blood for, save
> To wash stains off,
> Which the body's clay, too intimate,
> Sprinkles on the spirit?
>
> (*LP*, p. 31)

Here, the sharp contrast between Anglican sacramentalism and the
Puritan focus on the "inner light" and "sanctification" is plain. Not
that Melville would eradicate all outward signs of reverence in public
worship, nor that Herbert would reject the claims of the Word and
conscience—but they impart a different emphasis to the relative
value of both. For Herbert, "life unreproveable" is an ideal to guide
action, but one met only by Christ. Melville's insistence on the
clergy's "spotlessness" distorts Scripture. Herbert's perspective is
close to Donne's in *Devotions upon Emergent Occasions* (XIII). Here,
the "spots" on the speaker's skin, symptoms of his disease, are
transformed in the speaker's mind by the process of meditation into
a vehicle for his recognition of human frailty ("Lord, if thou look
for a spotlessness, whom wilt thou look upon?")[28] and for his acceptance of God's mercy as well:

I know, O Lord, the ordinary discomfort that accompanies that phrase,
that the house is visited, and that, that thy marks and thy tokens are upon
the patient; but what a wretched and disconsolate hermitage is that house
which is not visited by thee, and what a waif and stray is that man that
hath not thy marks upon him? These heats, O Lord, which thou hast
brought upon this body, are but thy chafing of the wax, that thou mightst
seal me to thee: these spots are but the letters in which thou hast written
thine own name. (pp. 87–88)

If Herbert believed in an achievable "life unreproveable," *The Temple*
would exhibit few rather than "many Spiritual conflicts betwixt God
and [the] Soul." For Herbert, even the earnest Christian experiences

anxiety as certainly as assurance, and on occasion he may seem to hurtle precipitously between the two. Both Donne's and Herbert's conceptions of the "Visible Church" differ from Melville's and from Barrow's. For Donne and Herbert, the church is a "sanctuary of the troubled soul," a place for sinners to seek respite from the "body's clay," which clings to all souls—"too intimate"—regardless of their sincerity, regardless even of their calling as shepherds of Christ's flock.

This point can hardly be overemphasized. George Herbert wrote one of the few handbooks for priests published during the seventeenth century, and if it is not a book much given to doctrinal dispute, it is nevertheless one that points away from any notion of a "life unreproveable." Herbert took the role of the parish priest as a model of behavior seriously, but we must take him at his word, too. He did not imagine that one became a model priest merely by laying out prose directives for such a model. Thus, in an address *"to the Reader,"* Herbert states very explicitly that he wrote *A Priest to the Temple* (1652) to please God, and because the "way to please him" was "to feed [his] Flocke diligently and faithfully" (p. 224). Now, for Herbert, the model of the priesthood is Christ, and so his directions are practical versions of an exhortation to imitate Christ:

since our Saviour hath made that the argument of a Pastour's love, I have resolved to set down the Form and Character of a true Pastour, that I may have a Mark to aim at: which also I will set as high as I can, since hee shoots higher that threatens the Moon, then hee that aims at a Tree. (*Works,* p. 224)

As he writes in *"Of a Pastor,"* "a Priest is to do that which Christ did, and after his manner, both for Doctrine and Life" (p. 225). But to understand Herbert, we must avoid literalism. Unlike Melville, he lays on no demand for a priestly "life unreproveable." The good priest is not one who attains every goal laid out by Scripture or conscience. Implicitly, Herbert acknowledges the likelihood of his own failure in attaining them. But such a failure does not mean that the priest "presently sinns, and displeases God," but only that man is *not* God.

In the chapter entitled *"The Parsons Life,"* Herbert emphasizes, not the priest's "life unreproveable," but the practical means he must take *"to reprove"* his flock. The nondoctrinal nature of this book is especially evident in this chapter, for the directives to any "Country Parson" are offered in the specific context of the actualities of rustic living. Since the people in the countryside "live hardly" (*Works,* p. 227), the priest, regardless of his own means, must avoid material displays. The needs of the congregation determine the emphasis of the priest's moral concerns. Thus "because it is the most popular vice," the priest avoids drinking, and taverns where drinking occurs: "For sins make all equall, whom they finde together; and then they are worst, who ought to be best." To be able *"to reprove"* errant members of his congregation, the priest takes avoidance of reproach as "a Mark to aim at." Hoping to give an *impression* of spotlessness, he does the best he can, using the physical means at hand: "and his apparrell plaine, but reverend, and clean, without spots, or dust, or smell; the purity of his mind breaking out, and dilating it selfe even to his body, cloaths, and habitation" (p. 228). Discipline in dress may not be the same as a "life unreproveable," but it is achievable.

As we observed in chapter 1, Herbert's conception of a priestly life is not a simple one. Rather, like much of his poetry, it reflects his belief that Scripture is deeply intertwined with every aspect of Christian life. That belief applied a fortiori to one called to priestly duties. In an ingenious analysis of Herbert's "Collos. 3.3," Chauncey Wood shows how completely Herbert presupposes an audience awareness, not only of the Pauline text, but of a number of interrelated biblical and figurative associations.[29] As the poet's meaning is wittily dispersed in the poem's acrostic form, so is the speaker's life hidden in Christ. It is hidden not only in its daily movements, but in their liturgical counterparts: the death and resurrection of baptism. As we read often in *The Temple,* the "Christians destinie" (*Works,* p. 58) has already been told in Scripture; likewise, the liturgy exhibits shared features of the Christian life. Just as prayer is "the soul in paraphrase" (p. 51), so is the priestly life a transliteration of the actual into something purer. We see this not only in the tension in such poems as "The Priesthood" and "The Collar," but also in the Herbertian sense of the priestly performance as just that—a "set" form, like prayer, in which the limited life of an unworthy servant is translated into the canonical imitation of the life of Christ. In his priestly guise, the parson leads a life "hidden" in a life beyond life, much as the story in a stained glass window comes into being only through the penetration of light. Both are transformed by "Grace" and the decencies of Anglican rites and ceremonies into a different story, with a more hopeful end.

We find quite similar thematic material in Herbert's ideas on preaching. For Herbert, preaching to a simple, unworldly congregation is an effort to induce recognition of the truth in Jeremiah's words, *"Oh Lord, I know that the way of man is not in himself"* (p. 234). As the difficult task before him is nothing less than to separate the listening souls from all wordly distractions, including overly intellectual doctrinal concerns, the priest resorts to "all possible art" (p. 232). Thus, in *"The Parson preaching"* we learn that he avoids witty, verbal "crumbling" of the "text into small parts" (p. 235) in order to reach these "Countrey people; which are thick, and heavy, and hard to raise to a poynt of Zeal, and fervency" (p. 233). Just as in "The Church-porch" "a verse may finde him, who a sermon flies" (p. 6), so here neither doctrine nor eloquence counts, but rather the priest's and the congregation's "attention" to the end of preaching, namely, "Holiness."

In addition to Herbert's chapter *"The Parson preaching,"* several poems are relevant here. Most obviously, "The Priesthood" (*Works*, pp. 160–61) plaintively voices the distinction between, on the one hand, "earth and clay," and on the other, "pure things" and "the sky." This preaching "I" feels "much unfit / To deal in holy Writ"— indeed, so unfit as to invite comparison between his preaching and Uzzah's blasphemy in touching the Ark of the Covenant. And yet his appropriate humility is one of several motions the speaker makes toward the discharge of priestly duties. A sense of unworthiness precedes assertion of the speaker's will to submit completely to "high uses meet," which are insulated from the natural effects of "earth and clay."

> There [at Christ's feet] will I lie, untill my Maker seek
> For some mean stuffe whereon to show his skill:
> Then is my time. The distance of the meek
> Doth flatter power. Lest good come short of ill
> In praising might, the poore do by submission
>   What pride by opposition.
>
>   (ll. 37–42)

In this context, humility is only one gesture in a dramatic sequence aimed at the end of service. It is just so in one of Herbert's most powerful poems, "The Crosse" (pp. 164–65), in which the speaker endures a similar sense of his unworthiness to serve. Thematically similar, too, is the apposition in "The Crosse" between the speaker's and God's "designes." The conflict here subsides only when the speaker comes to recognize the truth—close to that of "Collos. 3.3"—of the relevant biblical text:

> Ah my deare Father, ease my smart!
> These contrarieties crush me: these crosse actions
> Doe winde a rope about, and cut my heart:
>   And yet since these thy contradictions
>   Are properly a crosse felt by thy Sonne,
> With but foure words, my words, *Thy will be done.*
>   (ll. 31–36)

As in Donne's "The Crosse" and Herbert's "On the sign of the cross," so in this poem: wherever the speaker looks, even if at his own objections and sufferings ("designe," "aim," "bent . . . bow," "crosse actions," "contradictions"), the same design appears. And as we read in "On the sign of the cross," "who has arms / And does not stay afloat / In the clearest cruciform?" (*LP*, p. 19)

In "The Windows" (pp. 67–68), one of several of Herbert's poems on common architectural features of a Church, he exhibits the same conflict and the same apposition between God and man:

> Lord, how can man preach thy eternall word?
>   He is a brittle crazie glasse:
> Yet in thy temple thou dost him afford
>   This glorious and transcendent place,
>   To be a window, through thy grace.
>   (ll. 1–5)

By using the third person, Herbert manages to look at the conflict in a different way from that evident in "The Priesthood" and "The Crosse." Here, the speaker asks how, given the actualities of his nature, it is possible for any man (not *this* man, or *a* man, but "man") to preach. In a provocative essay, Judy Z. Kronenfeld discusses Herbert's use of a variety of meanings and associations of the major figure in the poem ("glasse") to draw out the pathos of the situation and to express an ideology of union between forms of worship and the inner convictions that they represent.[30] Accord-

ingly, the glass is both a mirror of humankind—"brittle crazie"—
and a stained glass window in which the individual pieces, "an-
nealed" of different colors, tell the story of Christ's life.

In *"The Parson preaching"* Herbert suggests that the end of pulpit
oratory is to elicit a picture of "Holiness." Likewise, in "The Windows," the pure light of the Word shines through the stained glass
windows, bringing the various colors to life:

> But when thou dost anneal in glasse thy storie,
>   Making thy life to shine within
> The holy Preachers; then the light and glorie
>   More rev'rend grows, and more doth win:
> Which else shows watrish, bleak, and thin.
> (ll. 6–10)

"The Windows" is a verse analogue not only of *"The Parson preaching"*
but of the theme of *A Priest to the Temple* itself. Throughout this
handbook, Herbert stresses the aesthetic union between the priest's
daily life and the decencies imposed on public worship. Because of
his unique status, the priest is always under scrutiny for his behavior,
and so his life can never be completely private.

As we have seen, then, public standards of decorum apply to the
conduct of prayer and preaching in the church, and they apply also
to the parson's life in the community. With respect to the decencies
of public worship, they are the outward signs of the inner Grace
that marked, for Herbert, "the middle way between superstition,
and slovenlinesse" (p. 246). If pains are taken with the parson's
dress and demeanor outside of church in the highways and byways
of the parish, even greater efforts are exerted to make the Church
appear "decent, and befitting his Name by which it is called." This
entails preparation of the sanctuary to meet all the demands of the
five senses. The church is clean, and when appropriate "stuck with
boughs, and perfumed with incense." Texts from Scripture are "every
where painted," all of the appointed books properly bound are in
their places, and all of the altar dressings, including the chalice and
the "Communion Cloth," are expensively and finely turned out.
Furthermore, these efforts reflect serious religious concerns:

And all this he doth, not as out of necessity, or as putting a holiness in
the things, but as desiring to keep the middle way between superstition,

and slovenlinesse, and as following the Apostles two great and admirable Rules in things of this nature: The first whereof is, *Let all things be done decently, and in order:* The second, *Let all things be done to edification,* 1 *Cor.* 14. (*Works,* p. 246)

Holiness is not in the liturgical signs themselves any more than the priest's life, insofar as it is acceptable to God, is his own. The mottoes from Scripture, painted decorously "every where," are constant, "grave, and reverend" reminders of this Grace behind and beyond all outward signs. In his penetrating analysis of "Collos. 3.3," Chauncey Wood reminds us of Walton's assertion that "Herbert himself caused" the Pauline text ("For ye are dead, and your life is hid with Christ in God") "to be painted at his wife's seat at Bemerton Church" (p. 16).

Herbert and the Eucharist

We have been discussing Herbert's ideas on prayer and preaching in the context of religious controversy in his time. It seems clear that he had aesthetic no less than doctrinal differences with those Protestants to the left on our continuum. To him, apparel mattered. Whether inside or outside of church, whether of a priest delivering a sermon or of one moving about the parish, outward appearances were never *merely* outward appearances. By the same token, one's "inner light" could not be taken as the only criterion of "Holiness." With King James, Herbert imputes to the Puritan disdain for Anglican rites and ceremonies a "slovenlinesse" of mind. It has been pointed out often that Herbert balances preaching with prayer, including in *A Priest to the Temple* a chapter of about equal length on each. And we have noted, too, that Herbert defends liturgical prayers, insisting that they need not be divorced from spontaneous and fervent feelings appropriate to worship.

Much of what has been said about prayers and preaching (and the political contexts involving arguments on their proper forms) could be applied to most ecclesiastical matters on which Herbert wrote. This is so partly because his defense of the received wisdom on rites and ceremonies rather unexceptionally follows the Anglican line, which aimed to balance competing claims of public and private man. For Herbert, no less than for other Anglican apologists, this balancing act was hardest to sustain when it came to the holy sacraments. Arguments over the Eucharist went beyond aesthetic and social concerns to the very substance and meaning of the ceremony itself. Even so, as C. A. Patrides rightly observes, "the Eucharist is the marrow of Herbert's sensibility" (p. 17). In his chapter *"The Parson in Sacraments,"* Herbert readily concedes the difficulty of the situation: "The Countrey Parson being to administer the Sacraments, is at a stand with himself, how or what behaviour to assume for so holy things. Especially at Communion times he is in a great confusion, as being not only to receive God, but to break, and administer him" (*Works,* p. 257). Writing about the surplice, the "Communion Cloth," the flagon, the chalice, the wedding ring, the sign of the cross, and the like, Herbert is at pains to insist that "holiness" is not "in the things." Vestments, accoutrements and gestures are merely signs of reverence. But in the Eucharist the priest dealt with "things" *intrinsically* "holy." Nor does Herbert turn this chapter into a doctrinal thesis on such ideas as transubstantiation and consubstantiation. Rather, with the unworthy supplicant in "The Priesthood," he avoids the issue by prostrating himself:

Neither findes he any issue in this, but to throw himself down at the throne of grace, saying, Lord, thou knowest what thou didst, when thou appointedst it to be done thus; therefore doe thou fulfill what thou didst appoint; for thou art not only the feast, but the way to it. (pp. 257–58)

Moreover, Herbert deals with the question of "the manner of receiving" (p. 259) in much the same way: "The Feast indeed requires sitting, because it is a Feast; but man's unpreparednesse asks kneeling." As with other aspects of worship, this rite answers to demands of propriety. (Puritans preferred that communicants sit.) Although Herbert seems initially inclined to imply that the form does not really matter, he proceeds to separate himself from attitudes which he feels are conveyed by the communicant who remains seated at this particular banquet:

Hee that comes to the Sacrament, hath the confidence of a Guest, and hee that kneels, confesseth himself an unworthy one, and therefore differs from other Feasters: but hee that sits, or lies, puts up to an Apostle: Contentiousnesse in a feast of Charity is more scandall then any posture. (*Works,* p. 259)

So it is not the Puritan observance, but what it implies—"Conten-tiousnesse"—that gives offense. Nothing could express a more in-appropriate response to the Sacrifice than truculence. So, again, the decencies of external form are not vain vestiges of Rome, but gestures with inner significance. Because this feast is unlike all others, it generates its own decorum; it is "holy," which is why the "Countrey Parson . . . is at a stand with himself" how to deliver it (p. 257).

In this matter of the Eucharist Herbert does equivocate a bit. Having argued that holiness is not in the "things" themselves, Herbert now reverses himself, proclaiming that the "things" them-selves are "holy." I do not mean to imply that this equivocation is a fault in the work, which, after all, does not purport to be a systematic doctrinal treatise. But as Patrides points out, even if it were such a treatise, the position of the Anglican Church on the Eucharist was not marked by systematic thought, but was, instead, typically "flexible if vague" (p. 17). Fashioned during Elizabeth's reign, it bore the impress of her determination to establish a middle ground between the extremes of Zwingli and Luther, on the one hand, and Rome on the other. The most radical theorist of the Sacrament, Zwingli, held that Christ was present in the bread and wine only in the communicant's memory: "Take this in *remembrance* of me." Roman Catholic doctrine held that Christ's Body and Blood were physically present in the bread and wine, which were trans-formed at the moment of "Consecration" through a process called transubstantiation. In an important essay, Jeanne Clayton Hunter suggests that lines from Herbert's Passion poem, "The Sacrifice," "could be read as evidence of Roman transubstantiation or Lutheran consubstantiation."[31] In the manner of the *Improperia* of Passion Week, Christ scornfully poses the awful irony of his suffering in light of his infinite love for man: "Then with a scarlet robe they me aray; / Which shews my bloud to be the onely way / And cordiall left to repair mans decay" (*Works,* p. 31). Rosemond Tuve's land-mark *Reading of George Herbert* (1952) examines this and other poems— "The Agonie," "The Bunch of Grapes," and the "Jordan" poems, to mention only a few—against a rich background of liturgical, exegetical, and iconographic expression.[32] Hunter correctly indicates that "a reevaluation" of Herbert's Catholic and medieval character-istics, emphasized by Tuve, has taken place. Even so, it is hard to read Herbert ("Love is that liquour sweet and most divine, / Which my God feels as bloud; but I, as wine" [p. 37]) without lending credence to Tuve's thesis. (In the next chapter, I will argue that the time has come to reevaluate the "reevaluation" of Tuve.)

"The Sacrifice," "The Agonie," "Love unknown," "The Bunch of Grapes"—many of Herbert's finest poems are either about the Eucharist or richly infused with imagery allusive to it. Nevertheless, we probably learn more about Herbert's views of the Sacrament from his two poems entitled "The H. Communion" than we do from isolated image clusters and traditional phraseologies, important though they may be. It should be pointed out that Hunter regards only one of these poems as indicative of Herbert's settled views on the subject. She buttresses her opinion with the fact that Herbert included only one of the poems in *The Temple* sequence, inferring that the Williams Manuscript poem represents an early formulation—later discarded—of the poet's opinion.

Hunter's closely argued views deserve serious attention. Yet it seems to me she relies too heavily on inferences about Herbert's reasons for removing the Williams Manuscript Communion poem from "The Church." Other reasons for that excision are equally plausible. The poem is, after all, a touch tendentious, and so does not fit the theme, mode, and tone of "The Church" as well as the included selection on the Sacrament does. *The Temple* is not a devotional miscellany, but a patterned sequence. Artistic criteria apply. Why didn't Herbert include the Williams Manuscript "Love" in *The Temple?* Though a good poem, its material and diction somewhat overlap that in "The Reprisall." What about "Perseverance"? Had this poem *been* included in *The Temple,* would we have reason to argue that it does not belong there? (Where? In which of the interstices would the poem be notably out of place, and why?)

Hunter's thesis on Herbert's settled Calvinist predilections regarding "the holy Eucharist," as Richard Hooker refers to it (5. 173), is burdened by other inconveniences, not least of which is her dissent from Patrides's commentary on "Love" (III). Hunter sees the poem as an illustration of the Calvinist belief in the "Real Presence" by "ascension." And yet her argument diminishes the structural function of that poem. I have argued elsewhere, and shall again (in chapter 4), in agreement with Patrides's understanding of the poem.[33] Its position at the end of "The Church," preceding "The Church Militant," is the context in which we must construe the dramatic exchange between guest and host. "Love" (III) surely has eucharistic overtones, but the temporal context is important as

well. Indeed, the stunning close of this great poem ("So I did sit
and eat") does not support a *purely* eucharistic reading of the situation. Hooker and other Anglican centrists held that communicants
receiving the Body and Blood of Christ should kneel rather than
"sit": "Our kneeling at communions is the gesture of pietie. If wee
did there present our selves but to make some show or dumbe
resemblance of a spirituall feast, it may bee that sitting were the
fitter Ceremonie, but comming as receivers of inestimable grace at
the hands of God, what doth better beseeme our bodies at that
hower then to bee sensible witnesses of minds unfainedly humbled?"
(5.183). We will remember that in *"The Parson in Sacraments"* Herbert makes virtually the same argument in strikingly similar words:
"The Feast indeed requires sitting, because it is a Feast; but man's
unpreparednesse asks kneeling."

I have quoted Hooker at some length here because of the signal
importance of his *Lawes of Ecclesiasticall Politie* (1597) as a quasi-
canonical commentary on the official position of the Anglican Church,
spelled out in the Convocation of 1582 and reaffirmed in that of
1604. The first thing we note is that Hooker's statement on Holy
Communion follows, as does Herbert's, discussion of baptism as a
logical development of a biological metaphor. Following birth, the
body requires nourishment, and this requirement lasts as long as
life remains: "But as long as the daies of our warfare last, during
the time that wee are both subject to diminution and capable of
augmentation in grace, the wordes of our Lord and Saviour Christ
will remaine forceable, *Except ye eate the flesh of the Sonne of man and
drinke his bloud ye have no life in you*" (5.173–74). It is "not by
surmised imagination" (or memory, as Zwingli would have it) that
Christ's body is made food, and his blood drink. And yet, though
Hooker mentions Zwingli and Oecolampadius, expressing dismay
at inferences that must be drawn from their work, his aim is to
articulate only the kernel of consensus among all Christian commentators on the Sacrament. Indeed, in this passage we perceive
something like a defense of an idea that was to have great impact
on seventeenth-century intellectuals—the idea that those religious
beliefs commanding reasoned assent were those "common notions"
affirmed by proponents of every religion:

But seeing that by opening the severall opinions which have beene held,
they are growne for ought I can see on all sides at the length to a generall

agreement concerning that which alone is materiall namely the *reall participation* of Christ and of life in his body and bloud *by meanes of this Sacrament,* wherefore should the world continue still distracted and rent with so manifold contentions, when there remaineth now no Controversie saving onely about the subject *where* Christ is? (5.174)

Thus, Hooker argues that it is unnecessary to decide between such versions of the Eucharist as transubstantiation and consubstantiation. It would be better if Christians regarded more in "silence what [they] have by the Sacrament, and lesse to dispute of the manner how."

In the Williams Manuscript Communion poem (*Works,* pp. 200–201), the speaker likewise dismisses the issue of the location of Christ's body in the Sacrament, and he does so simply because there is no certain way of ending controversy on the subject. The Eucharist was and would remain a mystery. This being so, one does a disservice to Christ's Body of the Church by asking imponderable questions. Not only do such questions draw their propounders into polemical quagmires, dividing Christians from each other, but they also direct attention away from the Christian's proper concern, which must still be the nourishment of spiritual life. In this same spirit Herbert writes:

> First I am sure, whether bread stay
> Or whether Bread doe fly away
>   Concerneth bread, not mee.
> But that both thou and all thy traine
> Bee there, to thy truth, and my gaine,
> Concerneth mee and Thee.
>   (ll. 7–12)

As Canon Hutchinson points out (p. 548), Herbert's poem is a veritable epitome of the Anglican flight from strict doctrine on the Eucharist. Herbert's speaker dismisses all disputes, taking refuge in the "Real Presence" of Christ as the only relevant concern. Nor does it matter what steps in what sequence to what group of communicants Christ moves in presenting himself:

> And if in comming to thy foes
> Thou dost come first to them, that showes
>   The hast of thy good will.

> Or if that thou two stations makest
> In Bread and mee, the way thou takest
>   Is more, but for mee still.
>   (ll. 13–18)

As in Hooker, so in Herbert, doctrines that separate communicant from communicant contradict the very nature of the Sacrament. Christ did not die "for Bread," so "Impanation" must be, at best, an irrelevant distraction and, at worst, the extremist's means of causing schism in the Church. Nor do the senses permit one to believe in the strict demands of transubstantiation. As in his earlier polemical poems, and as in "The British Church," here Herbert poses the answer to this doctrinal dilemma as a reasonable choice between polar alternatives. Reason insists that the problem, in intellectual terms, is insurmountable:

> Into my soule this cannot pass;
> Flesh (though exalted) keeps his grass
>   And cannot turn to soule.
> Bodyes and Minds are different Spheres,
> Nor can they change their bounds and meres,
>   But keep a constant Pole.
>   (ll. 37–42)

Since reason and the senses convince the speaker that the penetration of the Host contradicts the laws of nature, it is unreasonable and senseless to formulate divisive rules governing this mystery.

Hunter astutely remarks on the tone of dismissal in the closing stanza of this poem:

> This gift of all gifts is the best,
> Thy flesh the least that I request.
>   Thou took'st that pledg from mee:
> Give me not that I had before,
> Or give mee that, so I have more;
>   My God, give mee all Thee.
>   (ll. 43–48)

Not only this stanza, but the entire poem has something about it of the wit of Donne: obscure syntax, arcane vocabulary, esoteric theories, scholastic technique. But we have already suggested that the poem does not fit the major theme of spiritual progress in "The Church." And yet, behind the superficial insouciance of its typically Anglican pose of doctrinal indifference, the poem is still imbued with an ecumenical spirit. The speaker insists, as Hooker does, that the life-giving gift itself is what matters, not knowledge, or the pretense of knowledge, concerning the imperceivable mystery of its *"way"* of giving life.

The tone of "The H. Communion" in *The Temple* (pp. 52–53) is altogether different, and so is the point of view. There is no hint here of the wunderkind who has boned up on abstruse theories of the Eucharist. As in the Williams Manuscript poem, controversy does intrude, but not so obstreperously. The dramatic situation is, of course, very different. The tone is more intimate and subdued. And the emotional content differs partly because this poem begins where the other ends—with the emphasis on gratitude:

> Not in rich furniture, or fine aray,
>   Nor in a wedge of gold,
>   Thou, who for me wast sold,
> To me dost now thy self convey;
> For so thou should'st without me still have been,
>   Leaving within me sinne:
>
> But by the way of nourishment and strength
>   Thou creep'st into my breast;
>   Making thy way my rest,
> And thy small quantities my length;
> Which spread their forces into every part,
>   Meeting sinnes force and art.
>
> (ll. 1–12)

The contrast here between the seen and the unseen derives a measure of its sharpness from a polemical context shared with the Williams Manuscript poem and with the Latin poems defending Anglican rites and ceremonies. But here the speaker counts the cost of lavish vestments, which are, like the "goodly Babylonish garment" described in Joshua (7.21), costly, but not nearly so dear as the priceless though freely given body of Christ. And yet in this poem the rhetorical battles are not foremost in the speaker's mind. He is more concerned with personal experience, as the bartered Christ is conveyed to the soul. Rather than struggling toward theological insight, the speaker feels "nourishment and strength" creep into his breast, and "spread . . . into every part."

Again, these stanzas employ the same metaphoric conception that we find in Hooker. The soul is nourished by spiritual food, but just how the speaker does not say. The Sacrament creeps into every part of the spiritual body, and though the speaker knows that, he cannot surmise either how that penetration occurs or how his assurance of it came to be: two mysteries in one. Hooker writes: "The reall presence of Christs most blessed body and bloud is not . . . to bee sought for in the Sacrament, but in the worthie receiver of the Sacrament" (5.176). And Herbert's speaker can describe only the feelings of one unworthy receiver. Hooker writes:

Let it therefore be sufficient for me presenting my selfe at the Lords Table to know what there I receive from him, without searching or inquiring of the maner how Christ performeth his promise . . . the very letter of the word of Christ giveth plaine securitie that these misteries doe as nayles fasten us to his verie Crosse, that by them we draw out, as touching efficacie force and vertue, even the bloud of his goared side, in the wounds of our redeemer we there dip our tongues, wee are died red both within and without, our hunger is satisfied and our thirst for ever quenched. (5.181)

And in "The H. Communion" the speaker likewise affirms that no one knows the means or manner of the Sacrament's transcending the walls between flesh and spirit:

> Onely thy grace, which with these elements comes,
>   Knoweth the ready way,
>   And hath the privie key,
>   Op'ning the souls most subtile rooms;
> While those to spirits refin'd, at doore attend
>   Dispatches from their friend.
>
>   (ll. 19–24)

Although the tone here differs from that of the Williams Manuscript poem, the two poems share a skepticism on questions of the "how" and "where" of the Eucharist. Here, as in the earlier poem, the speaker dismisses the efforts of "sharp-witted men" with their theories of how that nourishment transcends "the wall that parts / Our souls and fleshy hearts" (ll. 14–15). Only God knows the "how" of this divine mystery; man only experiences its effects, which are like those of messages from a friend.

"A Lover of Old Customes"

Returning to the question asked at the beginning of this chapter, I think we have begun to shape an answer. Although we have not dealt with every relevant example, such evidence as we have considered seems clearly to support Joseph H. Summers, who suggested in his seminal critical biography that "we cannot identify George Herbert with a specific ecclesiastical party.[34] He was a priest, apparently an obedient and loyal priest, of the Church of England, and did not align himself with any one of the many troublesome factions of his day. Surely it would be a mistake to push him toward either extreme on our imagined continuum. Indeed, when applied to Herbert even the term *Protestant* is somewhat inaccurate. Herbert, himself, never uses the term, and it is hard to imagine the character who typically speaks in his lyric poetry protesting anything but his own unworthiness. With the examples we have discussed in mind, perhaps when describing Herbert we should emulate Ira Clark in using the word *Reformed* rather than *Protestant.*[35] We have seen no credible evidence either that Herbert had any quarrel with the established Church, or that he protested even one of its rather archaic ways. Rather, he seems consistently to have admired his "deare Mother" ("The British Church") for her beauty as well as for her circumspection: *"Let all things be done decently, and in order"* (p. 246).

Even so, we must admit that Summers is right, too, in pointing out that "Herbert died just five months before Laud succeeded to the episcopal throne, and [therefore] we have no information as to how he would have reacted to Laud's attempt at enforced conformity" (ibid.). The fact is Herbert did not live to see the horrors of religious warfare that would wreak havoc in the life of his good friend and religious fellow traveler, Nicholas Ferrar. Both wanted to preserve the best of the old ways, and both wished to follow the Psalmist in worshipping God "in the beauty of holiness." Granted, there is room for argument here, and one need only look at recent bibliographies of work on Herbert to concede that an era of the Protestant Herbert is upon us. But the evidence thus far seems to point in another direction. The Herbert whom we have been reading does not run after novelty in religion. Nor does he protest liturgically

prescribed prayers and rites of the Church. On the contrary, he not
only defends them, one by one, but he defends the ancient ways in
general. One of the most revealing chapters in *A Priest to the Temple*
comes near the end of that work and sums up much of what Herbert
has been saying all along. In *"The Parson's Condescending,"* Herbert
writes that "The Countrey Parson is a Lover of old Customes" (p.
283), insisting that he tries to interpret every one of them (the
"Procession" into the fields during Rogation Days, for instance) in
a manner accordant with Scripture. Where others turn up evidence
of "superstition," Herbert looks for and finds occasions of prayer
and praise. He dismisses the facile charge of "superstition" wherever
older forms and practices occur: "and those that thinke this super-
stitious, neither know superstition, nor themselves" (p. 284). The
true priest of God is not afraid to use any "forme," but rather he
takes the old "forme" and "reformes, and teaches" with it. Like the
hard heart of man in "The Altar," the corporate heart of the congregation stands in need of "Grace."

And yet, despite these disclaimers, I think that Peckard's words,
meant to describe Nicholas Ferrar and his Little Gidding "family,"
also fit the facts of Herbert's record and writing. He was "firm" as
a member of "the Church of England" (p. 238). Although he did
not suffer, as did Ferrar, for his beliefs, he might have had he lived
much longer, for these two friends shared many religious and aesthetic values. For instance, Herbert approved of the motto in Ferrar's
living room, which Bishop Williams—as a friend rather than as a
powerful official—recommended Ferrar remove. Williams proceeded to tell Ferrar that he had recently seen terrible punishments
heaped on others in London for displays far less suspicious of "superstition" than this large brass motto (with its jesuitical inscription). As for Herbert, Peckard writes that he valued as "an inestimable
jewel" the copy of the "Harmonies" sent to him. Shortly thereafter,
another copy of this work was presented by Archbishop Laud to
King Charles I. No single work has greater bearing on the literary
and religious relations between Ferrar and Herbert than the "Harmonies," and yet no work relevant to those relations has been more
steadfastly ignored. It is to analysis of this body of evidence of
Herbert's religious and poetic practices that we now turn.

Chapter Three
Herbert and the "Harmonies" of Little Gidding

Since publication of Rosemond Tuve's *Reading of George Herbert* (1952) and Louis L. Martz's *Poetry of Meditation* (1954), critical commentary has emphasized the importance of specific religious contexts to an understanding of George Herbert's poetry. Diverse studies have recounted the relevance of the *Biblia Pauperum,* missals, primers, Books of Hours, the *Improperia,* the liturgical calendar, devotional handbooks, sermons, stained glass windows, Augustinianism, and the like. The implication seems to be that Herbertians must become historians of ideas: the bibliography of primary sources in Stanley Fish's *Living Temple* (1978), which includes titles of dozens of Renaissance catechisms, runs to more than sixteen pages; the bibliography of exegetical and doctrinal materials in Heather A. R. Asals's *Equivocal Predication* (1981) is no less daunting. And Barbara Lewalski's chapter on Herbert in *Protestant Poetics and the Seventeenth-Century Religious Lyric* (1979) assumes that readers are familiar with an awesome body of biblical lore, especially with traditions surrounding the Psalms and the Canticles. No doubt the reader could add, or has already added, to this list of studies.

And yet it seems that what the history of ideas giveth, the history of ideas taketh away. Lewalski's study alone suggests that the common interest of historicists has not produced consensus on even the most basic matters of Herbert criticism. We have, Asals points out, two diametrically opposed camps on the question of Herbert's view of the Eucharist.[1] Scholars may concede that Herbert criticism owes much to historicists (not even Helen Vendler, whose formalist study preempted Lewalski's strictures by more or less ignoring the implications of *A Reading of George Herbert* and *The Poetry of Meditation,* explicitly denies the relevance of more Catholic traditions), but they nevertheless have failed to sort out contradictory claims of Herbertian historicists themselves. For example, assuming that Herbert must have been impressed by "the poetic implicit in the sermons of Donne," Lewalski argues that in *The Temple* (1633) Herbert develops "fully and harmoniously as the very foundation of his poetry" what she describes as a "new Protestant aesthetics."[2] It follows from this that approaches to Herbert's poetry through "medieval iconography" (Tuve) and "Salesian meditation" (Martz) require "a necessary corrective." Lewalski does name other contexts whose claims also need correction, but I single out her differences with Tuve and Martz because they most pointedly concern her thesis that Herbert's poetic practice is quintessentially Protestant, a thesis that flatly contradicts analyses based on such artifacts as missals, breviaries, primers, pontificals, rosaries, Books of Hours, the *Biblia Pauperum,* responsories from Holy Week, and directives on devotion from the saints, including Saint Ignatius.

Admittedly, we cannot easily distinguish between necessary corrective and gratuitous overcorrection. But the assumption that Herbert criticism has too much emphasized Catholic sources tends toward the view that it has therefore nurtured a false understanding of Herbert's poetry. Herbert either was or he was not expressing himself in the manner of those Good Friday Complaints cited by Tuve; the iconography of medieval Books of Hours either is or is not relevant to interpretation of *The Temple.* Contrariwise, the evidence either does or does not justify the designation of Herbert's poetics as "fully" Protestant, much less, as Richard Strier argues, as radically Puritan.[3] Even so, despite their apparent disarray, Herbertian historicists do share one important assumption: they believe that correction is possible, because a valid criterion of accuracy enables critics to distinguish between descriptions in need of correction and those not in need. With respect to judgment in the present case, the issue stands or falls on evidence of the comparative relevance of Protestant and Catholic analogues. For the historicists agree that as we alter the contexts in which the Herbert canon is construed, so we alter the canon.

Since questions of context concern all the values that we ascribe to Herbert's art, they cannot be dismissed as merely academic. The Protestant poetry of Herbert may be no better or worse than the Catholic, but it is patently different poetry. In addressing these questions we may do well to consider the audience for which Herbert wrote. If members of that audience were notably linked with groups accurately described as Protestant, were they also thought of as Puritan? Did Herbert's manner of expression differ markedly from Catholic ones on similar themes? Were Anglican poets Protestant, and if so, why were certain members of Parliament outraged by men like Nicholas Ferrar? Would it be fair to say that Ferrar was an important (if not the most important) member of Herbert's audience? If so, would it not follow that his tastes and attitudes must figure prominently in any historical account of Herbert's poetry?

Scholars have long recognized the personal and religious affinity between Herbert and Ferrar, to whom the poet probably sent copies of *The Temple* and *A Priest to the Temple*. Of course, Herbert had no way of knowing that Ferrar would become his first editor, but the record is replete with evidence that he could expect a sympathetic reading from him. Furthermore, Herbert had reason to suppose that Ferrar and his "Little Academy" would prepare his manuscript for print—or at least copy it: "They were," writes J. Max Patrick in his spirited "Critical Problems in Editing George Herbert's *The Temple*," "experienced in such work, and the Bodleian Manuscript resembles similar volumes turned out by the Little Gidding community."[4] In fact, copying, gilding, book binding, and other quasi-literary interests were energetically pursued at Little Gidding, where they were looked upon as acts of devotion.

In the following pages, I hope to show that work done at Little Gidding provides valuable evidence about the audience for which Herbert wrote and that this context was not medieval, but rather topical and lively. I shall argue, too, that these typical expressions of biblical tradition there were not uniquely Protestant, surely not Puritan, and might even be described as Catholic. At the same time we must acknowledge, with Joseph Summers, that even in Herbert's day, religious categories, Catholic and Protestant among them, were slippery[5] and often weighted with political controversy. Even so, we may recall that, as part of morning prayer, Herbert intoned the Creed ("I beleeve in the holy Ghost, the holy Catholike Church, the Communion of Saints . . ."); and at Holy Communion he led the congregation: "And I beleeve in one Catholike and Apostolike Church."[6] Then too, many of the opinions separating Herbert from Andrew Melville concerned the role of rites and ornaments in public worship shared by the Anglican and Roman Communions. More often than not, issues of aesthetics implicit in the critical language we are discussing involved notions of prayer and worship. Relevant attitudes and images were everywhere evident, not only in the literary practices at Little Gidding, but also in Herbert's personal life and in *The Temple*.

Although criticism has recognized the deep personal and religious bond between Herbert and Ferrar, it has yet to pay comparable attention to relevant evidence of their literary relations. Fortunately, an important literary context of that relationship, though rarely noticed in the twentieth century, allows us a valuable perspective on *The Temple*. I am talking about a number of volumes, famous[7] in their own time, though ignored even by scholars today: *The Actions and Doctrine and other Passages Touching Our Lord and Saviour Jesus Christ* (1630–37).[8] In the early 1630s, at precisely the time Herbert was writing and rewriting more than half of *The Temple*, much of the time at Little Gidding was spent either composing, reading, or reciting aloud from these artifacts.[9] Often referred to as the "Harmonies" (the subtitle reads: *as they are Related by the Foure Evangelists*), these volumes were second only to the Psalms in the order of worship at Little Gidding. And yet a glance through John R. Roberts's valuable *George Herbert: An Annotated Bibliography of Modern Criticism 1905–1974* will show that such comment as we do have on the writing done at Little Gidding concerns the *Story-Books* and letters.

It should be noted, however, that this anomaly is new. In the nineteenth century, the importance of the connection between Herbert's poetry and the "Harmonies" of Little Gidding was taken for granted. For example, Jane Frances Mary Carter casually linked "The Harmonies, or, as they are always called in the family manuscripts, the Concordances," with the pair of Herbert sonnets entitled "The H. Scriptures," believing that they alike represented "close and thoughtful study of Holy Scripture, an earnest desire to learn and to teach its lessons."[10] The context and tone of Carter's remark reveal two assumptions that bear on my thesis. First, she took for granted that the affinity between the devotional life of Little Gidding and the poetry of George Herbert was most clearly represented in the "Harmonies" and in "The H. Scriptures I" and "II." Second, she inferred that Herbert's poetry and the "Harmonies" of Little Gidding derived from a common practice of "close and thoughtful study of Holy Scripture," this accomplished with "an earnest desire to learn and to teach its lessons" (p. 182).

If, as I believe, this dual assumption is correct, then Herbert critics have in our own day overlooked one of the most important contexts for the understanding of his poetry. Further, if it is correct, historicists do have evidence bearing on the propriety of the claim that the analyses of Tuve and Martz rely too heavily on other than Protestant sources.

The "Harmonies" of Little Gidding

In *The Living Temple* (1978), Stanley Fish demonstrates the importance of the catechism to our understanding of Herbert's thought and art. Its place in the liturgical life of the Church, as Herbert understood it, can hardly be overemphasized. For Herbert, learning and teaching were integral parts of the priestly function; as Judy Kronenfeld has recently reminded us, he did not attempt to restrict that function to activities within the architectural boundaries of the sanctuary.[11] Rather, the light of God's Word was to shine through in every aspect of the priestly life. In the process of learning and teaching, knowledge precedes its application. Thus, in *A Priest to the Temple,* Herbert expands upon a figure also employed in "The H. Scriptures I" ("There he sucks, and lives"):[12] in reading the Bible man discovers precepts for life, doctrines for knowledge, examples for illustration, and promises for comfort. With respect to Herbert's poetic practice, the third of these is immediately relevant:

The third means is a diligent Collation of Scripture with Scripture. For all Truth being consonant to it self, and all being penn'd by one and the self-same Spirit, it cannot be, but that an industrious, and judicious comparing of place with place must be a singular help for the right understanding of the Scriptures. (p. 229)

With the possible exception of the Authorized Version of the Bible, no sustained literary effort in seventeenth-century England better manifests the ethical judgment of these sentences than that lavished by Nicholas Ferrar and his religious society on the "Harmonies." At Little Gidding, the "Harmonies of the Four Evangelists" figured prominently in the daily practice of the "Little Academy"; under his direct supervision, Ferrar's young novitiates spent at least an hour a day on these volumes, and recitation of chapter headings from memory and reading aloud from the chapters themselves were a regular part of the group's worship.

This is not the appropriate place to recount the devotional practices and doctrines that prompted some people to think of Little

Gidding as an "Arminian Nunnery."[13] Some thing, or many things, so outraged the adversaries of Archbishop Laud that, when opportunity presented itself, they wreaked havoc on the settlement. Setting aside the question of Ferrar's political judgment, we may still recall that he did have a serious commitment to the kind of knowledge Carter attributed to him in her 1892 biography. Happily, records of the day-to-day life of the community survived the Puritan invasion. We know that much of the time there was given over to one or another means of instructing the young ladies under Ferrar's protection. These Little Gidding novitiates, in turn, spent many hours with "This Booke of the Concordance of the 4: Evangelists contrivement, [which] was directed to be made in that manner by N. F. appoyntment and direction. N.F. having first spent Some time in the contrivance of the Work."[14] In the task of composition, these dedicated young virgins worked painstakingly by hand on the "Harmonies" "an hour every Day":

They with their Cizers cut out of each Evangelist such and such Verses, and layd them together, to make and perfect such and such a Head, or Chapter, which when they had first roughly done, then with their Knives and Cizers they neatly fitted each Verse So cutt out, to be pasted downe upon sheets of Paper, and So artificially they performed this new-found-out-way, as it were a new kind of Printing. (p. 42)

Anyone who has had the privilege of examining one of these volumes will not be surprised to learn that one copy was a year in the making (p. 43). The young ladies cut, trimmed, copied, pasted, wrote and ciphered; and they learned how to bind the volumes as well as how to construct their pages in what they believed was "a new kind of Printing." Each line—sometimes single words or syllables of a line—was scissored and arranged to give the impression that the text was intended to appear in just that way. Knowing the thought process behind this careful practice, and knowing also that George Herbert had one such volume in his possession,[15] gives vivid meaning to lines from "The H. Scriptures II," which Carter closely associated with the "Harmonies": "This verse marks that, and both do make a motion / Unto a third" (p. 58).

Albeit striking, the literal sense in which verses from various parts of Scripture made "a motion / Unto" others in and of itself would hardly justify Carter's linking of the "Harmonies" with Herbert's poetry. Rather, she referred to the intention behind two

seemingly different types of literary expression. The "Knives and
Cizers" were tools only to put together what belonged that way in
the first place. In the seventeenth century, harmonizing "the foure
Evangelists" was akin to unveiling "the Sanctuary," which, like the
Gospels, was upheld by four pillars. The narrative linking of the
Tabernacle with "the living temple" was embodied in the Gospels,
although as Augustine, an early harmonizer of the Evangelists,
pointed out, understanding that narrative required great effort. Augustine claimed that his work on *The Harmony* ranked among his
"most toilsome and exhaustive."[16] The sense of such effort is no
more concisely stated than in an engraving in the most magnificent
of the Little Gidding "Harmonies," depicting a text from Matthew.
The picture illustrates the forbearance of Moses ("Now the man
Moses was very meek, above all the men which were on the face of
the earth" [Num. 12.3]) when confronted by the carping of Aaron
and Miriam about his "Cushite" bride, Zipporah. Although Moses
failed in his attempt to intercede for Miriam, that action presaged
his plea soon afterward on behalf of the children of Israel. A hand-
written comment explains the connection between the Old and New
Testament texts: "This example of Moses Meekne[s] is heer brought
in as the opposite of that Anger which Christ forbids v. 22" (cols.
119–20). The reference is to the Sermon on the Mount: "But I say
unto you, That whosoever is angry with his brother without a cause
shall be in danger of the judgment" (Matt. 5.22). Beneath this scene
from the life of Moses is an engraving of Christ seated at a table
with two open books. The scene is illuminated, presumably, by the
candle near the Book of the Evangelists, the candle being reminiscent
of Christ's words in the same sermon: "Ye are the light of the
world. . . . Neither do men light a candle and put it under a
bushel, but on a candlestick" (5.14–15). Here, representations of
Moses and Christ are associated by the "meekness" which a proper
understanding perceives in these distant passages from Scripture;
Moses' story "brings in" the life of Christ. This association is apposite
in meaning to the use of parallel columns in Thomas Middleton's
Mariage of the Old and New Testament (1620), of which the following
example is typical:

59   Moses *made a serpent of Brasse, and set it up for a signe, and when
a serpent had bitten a man, then he looked at the serpent of brasse and lived* . . .
. . .

59   *As* Moses *lift up the Serpent in the Wildernes, so must the Sonne of man be lift up, that whosoever beleeveth in him should not perish, but have eternal life.* [17]

The "Method of this booke" (the employment of parallel texts in facing pages) "is for the matter of the one is answerable to, and makes plaine the other" (p. 7). The assumption is that these scenes and figures elucidate—"make a motion / Unto"—each other. So, in the Little Gidding illustration, with his open palms Christ indicates the open volumes: the Books of the Prophets and of the Evangelists. As this and similar comparisons show, the Little Gidding "Harmonies" are a subspecies of the larger body of "Harmonies" of the Old and New Testaments, a body of commentary to which many Elizabethans, Jacobeans, and Carolines contributed, Thomas Middleton, James Bentley, Hugh Broughton, John Huid, Henry Garthwait, John Lightfoot, and William Gould among them.

Thomas Middleton's *Mariage of the Old and New Testament* is indicative of the metaphoric way in which these "harmonies" seek to fuse the two books. Thus, the author, who sees himself as a *"Chronologer,"* sets forth a *"Genealogy"* or *"Pedigree"* of Christ in texts from the two Testaments, whose "mutuall sounds . . . their heavenly musicke sends forth" (p. 8). Here, even the musical metaphor fits the oblique method of Scripture: "To preserve the memory of this expected *Redeemer,* more lively, sundry pictures of him (as it were) were drawne in the persons of others" (p. 3). Architectural figures also implied that the two gates of the spiritual Temple were the Prophets and the Evangelists. Accordingly, John Lightfoot thinks of his *Harmony of the Foure Evanglists* (1644) in English as "something toward the building of the Tabernacle": *"The veile of the Sanctuary was supported by foure Pillars. . . . So is the Story of the veile Christs flesh by the foure Evangelists . . . of like variety."* [18] Such spatial and temporal figures were held *"to cleare and open the sense and meaning of the Text . . . especially where it was of more abstrusenesse and obscurity"* (sig. A4v). As in the "Harmonies of the Four Evangelists" from Augustine's to Middleton's, so in Herbert's "The H. Scriptures," the meaning of the written Word was not immediately accessible but was, rather, mysterious.

This conception is very important to the structure of *The Temple.* We must remember that commentators have always held one level of scriptural interpretation to be literal and historical. [19] Invariably,

God's ways to man were revealed in the history of his people, whose story only appears discontinuous; as the speaker affirms in "The H. Scriptures II," "all the constellations of the storie" present a single unified narrative. Thus, we find prefaced to *The Actions and Doctrine Touching Our Lord* a description of the complex meaning behind the cut-and-paste method of biblical interpretation. Someone, perhaps Ferrar himself, points out that the "Harmonies" are divided into two parts, "COMPARISON and COMPOSITION, . . . which are Joyntly Related by Two or more of the Evangelists" (fol. 4v). Thus he uses as conceptual synonyms *Harmony* and *Concordance*. In addition to this arrangement of the one or more Evangelists, Ferrar presents a single narrative, devoid of conflicts, extrapolated from one, two, three, or four sources:

the whole Evangelical Historie is included in that, which is termed the COLLECTION. which is that in the Great English Letter together with those Additions in the Romane Letter. . . . And in both these together is fully Conteined what ever is related by the Foure Evangelists. So that no one Word is omitted in this COLLECTION or BODY. (fol. 4v)

The "Context" and the "Supplement" permitted "Every of the Evangelists" to be read "as if they were alone." To expedite this presentation of "Agreements and Differences," the exegete indicated the Evangelists by letters of the alphabet in four colors: "Observe, That, A [black], signifies Mathew, B [blue] Mark, C [red] Luke, D [brown] John." The effect of this elaborate system was to permit comparison among the Evangelists, but also to form a single "COMPOSITION" or narrative—the "story." Especially in relation to "The H. Scriptures II," the implicit assumptions about the meaning of Scripture and the bookmaker's art are revealing. The reader has the choice of following "from Section to Section" in the "same Evangelist, whose Gospel is indicated by a colored letter," notwithstanding any "Differences," by looking beyond the "Collection" (or, as Herbert designates the process, "collation") to the "Composition." Accordingly, the "Preface" to Luke becomes the "Preface" to a synthetic narrative, "to all the Evangelical Historie as well as to St Lukes Gospell" (fol. 7v).

With these considerations in mind, we may better understand the manner in which the "Harmonies" fit into the daily routine of Little Gidding. Ferrar and his "Little Academy" kept twenty-four

hour "Vigils, or Night-Watches," recited the Psalms, received honored guests (including royalty), and worked in a place called the
Concordance Room composing their "Harmonies." Rather than an
indication of a Puritanical preoccupation with "arts and crafts" intended to keep young hands busy, the "Harmonies" were an integral
part of worship. Like the Psalms, they were recited daily: every day,
Monday through Saturday, at six in the morning "they all came to
the Great chamber again," where they said the Psalms for the second
time that day, and "then one of them sayd one of the heads of the
Concordance of the four Evangelists without Booke, For the Booke
conteyned 150: heads or Chapters" (p. 42). Whereas the Psalms
were read at every service over the twenty-four hour period (a practice, we will recall, of which Herbert approved), and so were completed daily rather than monthly (as in the typical Anglican parish),
the "Harmonies," read three times daily, were completed in monthly
rounds.

By becoming intensely involved in the most intricate aspects of
the "Harmonies," members of the "Little Academy" were reminded
of the way in which "some Christians destinie" lay in perception of
one story, the life of Christ:

> Such are thy secrets, which my life makes good,
>   And comments on thee: for in ev'ry thing
>   Thy words do finde me out, and parallels bring,
> And in another make me understood.
>   ("The H. Scriptures" [II], p.58)

When these lines are read in the context of the Little Gidding
"Harmonies," they make very different sense from that perceived
by Helen Vendler, who says of the first quatrain of this poem:

In answer to the imagined charge that generalized exegetical systems of
interconnection are only invented by the poet and are unverifiable, Herbert
replies that his insights are "more than fancy" because they are vindicated
by his lived experience. . . . Such searching out of parallels and confir-
mations can issue in fantastic and far-fetched "correspondences," but Herbert, though he usually does not go beyond the first step in this poetic
method, seeing only "how each verse doth shine," in what we might call
the personal reinterpretation of the sacred, does that so well that had he
lived longer, we might have had configurations as well as single shining
verses.[20]

It seems to me that Vendler overlooks both the immediate textual and the relevant historical contexts, which are crucial to the complex rhetorical function of the sonnet in the unfolding sequence of *The Temple*.

First, it is a mistake to overlook the way in which these lines "bring in" others in the collection. As Herbert conceives the interpretation of Scripture, so he presents his own lines as part of a composite expression, which in turn reflects a continuing process of the speaker's struggle to grasp the hidden meaning ("Such are thy secrets") of God's Word and, so, his intentions for one particular "Christian." This process transforms shards of experience that seem unrelated and confused into a new and refreshing recognition or "story." Thus, we cannot separate the first quatrain from the rhetorical demands of the sonnet itself. Nor should we overlook how integrally the sonnet emerges from and develops feelings expressed in the preceding poem—a sonnet bearing the same title.

Both poems are addressed to Scripture, and both concern the way in which God organized his message to mankind. And yet it should be clear that, not only do the two poems relate to each other, amplifying a common theme on the same topic, but they obliquely reflect the way in which *The Temple* is organized as well. Not only are both poems about the method of Scripture's organization, but the first sonnet ends with the same figure ("heav'n lies flat in thee") that is its successor's dominant concern. In "The H. Scriptures II," the speaker expostulates as if he were—the phrase belongs to Nicholas Ferrar—a "Discerner of the Skie." This figure emerges as early in the sequence as "The Agonie." In a similar way, in all three poems astronomers and serious readers scan God's "Books" for evidence of meaning. This is so because the Book of God's Creatures and the Book of God's Word alike conceal *and* reveal the mind of God.

In *The Actions and Doctrines Touching Our Lord,* the figure of an astrologer, with his "Jacob's Staff" for measuring distances among heavenly bodies, stands with a panoramic view of land, sea, and sky. His raised right hand points to the transparent Zodiac above, and we have another representation of the same "Discerner" in the middle panel below.[21] The meaning of these engravings emerges disjunctively. Below the engravings already described, two opposing illustrations depict Jonah being disgorged by the whale onto dry land. What, we may ask, is the connection? What "lights combine" to reveal the "constellation" of meaning represented here? The answer lies in the way the "Harmonies" were put together. In the flesh, those with ears often cannot hear, and those with eyes are blind. These engravings illustrate chapter 49, a "harmony" of texts on Christ's teaching by parables drawn from Matthew, Mark, and Luke. Ferrar draws special attention to the words of Matthew: "A wicked and adulterous generation seeketh after a sign; and there shall no sign be given, but the sign of Jonas." We recall that the Pharisees, exhibiting their lack of understanding, had asked Christ for a sign in the heavens. Christ's parables of the Kingdom should have convinced them of their folly in such questioning. It is foolish to read the "face of the sky but not discern the signs of the times." Ferrar's discerner of the sky, then, "brings in" Christ's claim that only "the sign of Jonas" will be given. The implication is that those with functional senses will know that sign to be Christ himself ("a greater than Jonas is here" [Matt. 12.41]). Jonah remained in the belly of the whale three days, and Christ would be resurrected on the third day, thus razing and raising the Temple in three days. The Pharisees look for signs and wonders in the heavens, but are deaf to the Word heralding the Kingdom at hand. The disjunction here is between two kinds of seeing and hearing, between humble understanding and willful obfuscation.

I am not suggesting that Herbert's poem alludes to Jonah, nor even that we need think of Christ's response to the Pharisees's obtuse provocations. I am suggesting that, like the "Collection" of chapter 49 in *The Actions and Doctrine Touching Our Lord,* "The Agonie" develops its theme by appositions like those in "The H. Scriptures II":

> Philosophers have measur'd mountains,
> Fathom'd the depths of seas, of states, and kings,
> Walk'd with a staffe to heav'n, and traced fountains:
>   But there are two vast, spacious things,
> The which to measure it doth more behove:
> Yet few there are that sound them; Sinne and Love.
>
> (p. 37)

In contrast to the one who understands the Word, "Philosophers" neither see nor hear the witness of one truth: the story of the human race was fully manifest in two tableaux from the life of Christ. As in the "Harmonies," where the scene depicting Moses' "meekness" "brings in" the life of Christ, so in "The Agonie" we find attention focused on the life of Christ. In an engraving already mentioned, Christ points to the two books of the Prophets and the Evangelists. Implicitly, it is not Moses, but Christ—"the meek / And readie Paschale Lamb"—who "Finish'd and fixt," by his perfect "Sacrifice," the work that his predecessor only "pursu'd":

> Who knows not Love, let him assay
> And taste that juice, which on the crosse a pike
> Did set again abroach; then let him say
> If ever he did taste the like.
> Love is that liquour sweet and most divine,
> Which my God feels as bloud; but I, as wine.
>
> (ll. 13–18)

Herbert critics owe much to Rosemond Tuve's discussion of the complex iconographic meanings of this poem.[22] As the evidence of the Little Gidding "Harmonies" indicates, the iconographic and liturgical traditions which informed those intentions were understood and used well into the seventeenth century. It follows that the visual and semantic implications of this fact bear on our understanding of Herbert's method, or at the very least on how that method would be construed by his intended audience. Just as verses from various parts of Scripture interrelate, so figures set out in one Herbert poem are developed in others. "The H. Scriptures II" depends on "The H. Scriptures I," and is "brought in" by the astrological development in "The Agonie," which, in turn, is figuratively and structurally related to "The Bunch of Grapes." Indeed, the latter poem not only amplifies the eucharastic motifs developed earlier in "The Sacrifice" and "The Agonie" and alludes to the passage in Numbers recounting Joshua's return from Canaan with a heavy bunch of grapes, but it also associates a surprising figure from the Old Testament, one not depicted in the contexts cited by Tuve. Admittedly, most of these date from the Middle Ages and carry a distinctly Catholic flavor,[23] but they are prominent in the "Harmonies" of Little Gidding as well.

It is no secret how richly "The Bunch of Grapes" is infused with allusions to the trials and tribulations of Israel during the days of Moses. But Moses is also important in the poem, for at one point the speaker expresses the disappointment of one who, like him, has drawn near the Promised Land, only to be denied entry. Further, Moses brought to mankind "the Laws sowre juice," the same concoction, but as yet unmellowed by the coming age of "*Noahs* vine," that would bring redemption from its bitter condemnation. In chapter 67 of the "Harmonies," two engravings indicate that the sign mistakenly sought in the heavens has already been given. One engraving depicts two men carrying a heavy bunch of grapes suspended from a large staff (cols. 229–30). Another shows Moses holding the tablets of the Law juxtaposed against a scene of "The Transfiguration" (the chapter's title), the subject of which is extrapolated from Matthew, Mark, and Luke. Ferrar explains the connection: "As the Bunche of Grapes was a proofe of the excellency of the Lande of Canaan Soe Christs Transfiguration was an Earnest and foresigne of the Glory of heaven" (col. 229). The surprise here might almost be guessed from the hat one of the carriers is wearing; it has a pronouncedly forked brim. The commentator writes: "And divers Allegorize the story, Making Christ the Cluster of Grapes And the Pole wheron it was carried to signify his Cross—The 2 Bearers—Moses and Elias."

In this context, the disjunction between types of representations fits into a single narrative that explains why in one of the engravings the "Discerner of the skie" has a yoke around his neck. Like the Pharisees, he is burdened by misguided notions of heavenly signs. In this context, we can see how poignantly Herbert has drawn on a theme introduced in "The Agonie." The vastness of the universe, the "contrarieties" of experience—these two seemingly unrelated manifestations of a mystery—when understood, explain "some Christians destinie." The meaning of the speaker's life, which is bound up in reading verses only in the context of other verses, emerges from a spatial and temporal fusion. Scripture changes the attentive reader; just as experience reminds him of relevant verses, the verses in turn jointly infuse different events in the speaker's life with a fashioning virtue. It is not only that his life makes the "secrets . . . good." The "secrets" invest his life with value as well.

The "Harmonies" and the Order of Worship

Since it bears directly on the difference between Protestant and Catholic poetic norms, we return now to reconsider the connection at Little Gidding between the "Harmonies" and the Psalms. Parallel use of the two works implied a similarity between subjects treated by David and by the four Evangelists. It emphasized, too, literary and aesthetic attitudes associated with David ("O worship the Lord in the beauty of holiness" [Ps. 99.9]), involving inferences about structural similarities between the Psalms and the composite Evangelists' narrative. Specifically, Ferrar borrowed from Jensenius an arrangement, reminiscent of the Psalter ("For the Book conteyned 150: heads or Chapters" [p. 42]), suggesting a parallel between the Psalms and the "story" of his divine descendant. In *The Actions and Doctrine Touching Our Lord* the analogy does not depend on a random numerical arrangement but is explicitly asserted in an engraving prefixed to Ferrar's sequence on the Passion. Here, the illustration demands comparison with the *Great Psalter, Or, Our Ladies Psalter.* We see a circular border of spheres, suggesting beads, thirty-three in all, each of which bears the impress of a specific virtue manifested in the life of Christ. In *The Poetry of Meditation* (1954), Louis L. Martz demonstrated how Donne employed the Rosary tradition in *La Corona* and elsewhere.[24] In *The Actions and Doctrine*, the explicitness of that tradition tells us something about the reactions of Ferrar's leftist adversaries. It was not without cause that Charles I admired the work, nor that Archbishop Laud, on examining a copy, supposedly "declared that the Name of Little Gidding should be altered from 'Parva' to 'Magna.' "[25]

It seems to me that Laud's response to the "Harmonies" of Little Gidding requires that we reexamine the conception of Herbert's sensibility as dominantly or characteristically Protestant. We should ask whether his intended audience would have considered it so. The evidence indicates that important contemporaries, Puritans as well as the Archbishop, do not seem to have associated Ferrar and his followers with Protestant views or practices. And yet the trend in criticism is to view both Herbert and his audience as Protestant, even Puritan, in outlook. In perhaps the most influential study of Herbert, even the untendentious Joseph Summers writes: "At least one visitor to Little Gidding described the family as 'orthodox, regular, puritan protestants'; and for the attitude it expresses toward profane literature, Nicholas Ferrar's death-bed statement might have been written by an Anabaptist" (p. 49). I should add that Summers warns against the perils posed by such categories: "To simplify the religion of Nicholas Ferrar or most other seventeenth-century religionists is to falsify; to understand, one must see individual religious experience within the light of the various movements of the time" (p. 50). On the other hand, even while conceding the difficulties of the question, we may with Laud acknowledge that the "Harmonies" represent just such solid evidence of "individual religious experience"—not only Ferrar's but that of community members whose practices reflect his values. Clearly, the "Harmonies" involve considerations broader than Ferrar's attitude toward secular literature (some examples of which offended compilers of the *Index Prohibitorum* no less than Anabaptists). We must see the "Harmonies" as an integral part of the religious observances at Little Gidding, with their devotional reliance on the senses: stained glass windows, pictures, engravings, vestments, incense, liturgical music.[26] And we should recall that not only did Ferrar consult Herbert in such matters, and not only did Herbert approve of Ferrar's tastes and practices, but Herbert himself employed many of the same "helps" in his own home and parish life.[27]

We should remember, too, that in the late sixteenth and earlier seventeenth centuries the most divisive aesthetic issue separating Protestants from Catholics—and from each other—concerned the proper form of public prayer. Dissenters such as Anabaptists defined their positions on repeated prayers in opposition to that of the Roman Catholic Church and to that of the Church of England as well. Such leftists as Robert Browne, Henry Barrow, John Greenwood, and Henry Ainsworth considered "signing," use of the surplice, placing of the altar, and the like as issues subordinate to the larger question of how the congregation conducted itself at prayer. We need not read far in the literature of this controversy to see that polemicists of all points of view affirmed the distinction between "conceived" and "set forms of prayer" and that this distinction carried with it a burden of invective remarkable even for this immoderately contentious age. The established clergy, men like Richard Hooker and George Gifford, held that God himself was the author of set forms, while their leftist antagonists ridiculed "read prayers" as an abomination conceived in the mind of Antichrist. John Greenwood ridiculed Gifford and the Church of England for the idolatrous practice in which "whole congregations do make no other prayer to God then reading over certeine numbers of wordes upon a book from year to yeare . . . the same matter and words as they were stinted, even out of the *Portuis,* englished out of Antichrists masse-booke;

besides private reading of mens writings instead of praying."[28] One could easily offer many such examples of radical Puritan invective against the use of the written word in public, and even in private, worship. On the other hand, Hooker and Gifford praised liturgical form ("No doubt from God it hath proceeded"),[29] disparaging the "voluntarie dictates proceeding from any mans extemporall wit." The most controversial of all "set prayers" was, of course, the Lord's Prayer; an eyewitness at Tyburn wrote that John Greenwood and Henry Barrow could not, even to save their lives, be induced to recite the Our Father. King James associated Puritan objections to its use with rebellion: "Thus yee see, how that letting slippe the holde of the true Church, and, once trusting to the privat spirit of Reformation, according to our *Puritanes* doctrine, it is easie to fall and slide by degrees into the *Chaos,* filthy sinke and *farrago* of all horrible heresies, wherof hell is the just reward."[30]

By now it should be clear where Little Gidding and the "Harmonies" of Little Gidding fit in this rhetorical war over the role of "reading upon a book" in worship. As we have seen, the rote repetition of headings and passages extrapolated from the four Evangelists was an important part of daily worship with Ferrar's "Little Academy." Then as now, people are known by the company they keep, and the same practices that Charles I and Archbishop Laud supported were those their adversaries condemned. Whereas Little Gidding was steeped in repetitious forms of worship anathema to Puritans—the Psalter, the "Harmonies," Vigils—and whereas George Herbert's poetry seems at times best described as "a *meditation* upon the liturgy" (Martz, p. 92), devotional practices of more Protestant sects tended toward spontaneous expression "as neede and occasion urgeth, and the spirit giveth utterance,"[31] leading at times, or so it seemed to many Anglicans, to a confusion of "deep sighs, Groans and Tears and Roaring."[32]

In the context of this religious controversy, the more one looks at the *Story-Books* and "Harmonies" of Little Gidding the more one is likely to register doubt regarding Ferrar's and Herbert's Puritan presentiments. Herbert loved Ferrar, was consulted by him, and as Amy Charles suggests, may have seen more of him than is usually believed during the years of his being prebendary for Leighton.[33] We cannot miss in Herbert's self abnegating efforts to rebuild the church there an imitation of Ferrar's unselfish work in refurbishing the special environment that became home for about thirty people of Little Gidding. Further, Herbert's rigorous monitoring of his nieces and the ritual presence of his entire family at all liturgical offices at Bemerton are likewise reminiscent of the twenty-four hour "Vigils" at what its detractors called "The Arminian Nunnery."

Repetition in prayer was only one divisive issue; the visual aspect of worship was another. Here, Puritan works just do not look like the *Story-Books* or "Harmonies," and while appearances do not mean everything, they do mean something. Every letter generated at Little Gidding and every page of the *Story-Books* bear the sacred symbol of the Society of Jesus: *IHS*. In the "Harmonies," the monogram appears frequently with the more explicit Jesuitical signs of a Crucifix above the *H* and three nails beneath the letters. Like the invocation of the Rosary tradition in the *"Coronae"* section of *The Actions and Doctrines* (cols. 479–80), the repetition of this symbol cannot suggest Protestant, much less Puritan, sentiments. Rather, they go hand in hand with the numerous representations of the Madonna and Child, and of such saints and martyrs as one will not find chronicled in Foxe: Saint Catherine, Saint Peter, Saint Nicholas, and the like.[34] Many of the engravings were executed by or drawn after artists of the Roman or Mannerist tradition (Marten de Vos, Marten van Heemskerck, and Jon van der Straet, to mention only three), and as such they reflect subjects and treatments commonplace to workshops and altarpieces of Renaissance Rome and Florence. Their dominant artistic influences are Michelangelo, Titian, and Veronese. One of the charges laid against Laud was that he possessed books engraved by Boethius Bolswert, whose engravings of the life of Christ George Henderson describes as "the backbone of the King's [i.e., Charles's] great Concordance" (Henderson, p. 191). We know that the sensitivity of such representations was more than once pointed out to Ferrar, and yet at Little Gidding he fostered such insignia and such modes of expression. We need only think of Thomas Rogers's opinions on the visual representations of such saints to recognize the impropriety of describing Ferrar and his religious family at Little Gidding—at least from the standpoint of aesthetic taste—as Protestant or Puritan.[35] Rather, they were thought by many of their contemporaries—and not in my judgment without cause—to be of a high-Church, if not Romish, stamp.

What is true of one's sympathetic audience is often true of the speaker. In the context of the "Harmonies" and other documents from the life of one member of Herbert's audience, we will more likely infer that Ferrar's Royalist and Puritan contemporaries thought of him as of the Laudian persuasion. And if we consider relevant parts of *The Temple* from the point of view of this intended audience, we will perceive feelings and tastes not "characteristically" Protestant, although the author of "The British Church" and *"Papae titulus"* was no Father Garnet in disguise. "The Sacrifice" is not an English translation from Latin liturgical sources, alhough J. A. W. Bennett has reminded us of the way in which those sources inform the dramatic structure of numerous English poems, Herbert's included.[36] As Chana Bloch has eloquently argued, Herbert melds many of the sources noted by Tuve with his own "diligent Collation of Scripture with Scripture."[37] Agreeing with both Bloch and Bennett, I would add that he "brings in"—as does Ferrar in the "Harmonies" of Little Gidding—many of the old images, often with their Catholic and liturgical associations.

In this context of the relationship of the "Harmonies" to pertinent questions regarding forms of worship, the point of view and tone of Herbert's "To all Angels and Saints" (pp. 77–78) take on, as Louis Martz rightly observes, an ambiguity of feeling not evident in a Protestant context (p. 97). Tuve points out that, except for "Trinity Sunday," this is the only feast day "outside the great days of Christ's own mission . . . which Herbert chooses as subject of a poem in *The Temple*" (p. 143). She goes on to say that the speaker's invocation of Mary is reminiscent of Donne's list of saints in "A Litanie," which is, for the most part, "the conventional medieval and Catholic (not Anglican) list" (p. 144n). It should be noted, too, that not even in Donne's "A Litanie," a poem which harks back to the Sarum Missal for its list of saints, do we find a speaker addressing the departed as does Herbert's speaker. And this is only one of the ways in which "To all Angels and Saints" commemorates an ancient, Catholic feast day. As with the two sonnets on Scripture, we cannot appreciate the full complexity of Herbert's poem without considering its place in *The Temple*. "To all Angels and Saints" follows "Anagram", and this setting, a result of Herbert's final revision of the sequence,[38] underlines the Marian emphasis. Preceded by this apostrophe to the Virgin, "To all Angels and Saints" is a prayerful address to the saints and to her (notwithstanding its speaker's protestations to the contrary). On the surface, the speaker disavows the practice of addressing either Mary or the saints. But that disavowal is tentative and defensive:

> Not out of envie or maliciousnesse
> Do I forbear to crave your speciall aid:
>   I would addresse
> My vows to thee most gladly, Blessed Maid,
> And Mother of my God, in my distresse.
>
>   (ll. 6–10)

It seems to me that Protestant attitudes of Herbert's day become less and less controlling here, while those of his Little Gidding audience remain untouched. The point of view is determined not just by the fact that the speaker addresses "glorious spirits," all of them departed and in the presence of God, but by his declaration that he would "Chiefly" unburden his "soul" to the "Mother of . . . God." Although both expressions would fit neatly with the many representations in the "Harmonies" of the Blessed Virgin— often nimbed and in the presence of other saints and often accompanied by Jesuit insignia—they would, I think, have dismayed more Protestant sensibilities. Structurally, the speaker's statements of disavowal are further muted by being squeezed between expressions of extravagant praise of the Blessed Virgin:

> Thou art the holy mine, whence came the gold,
> The great restorative for all decay
>   In young and old;
> Thou art the cabinet where the jewell lay:
> Chiefly to thee would I my soul unfold.
>
>   (ll. 11–15)

So, in the company of all the saints, a company in which, we have been told, "ev'ry one is king, and hath his crown" (1.4), hierarchy is still observed, a hierarchy nonetheless among equals. Here, the "Blessed Maid" seems, by virtue of the speaker's inclination ("Chiefly to thee would I my soul unfold") no less than by that of her own merit, to elicit what the speaker "would" do, namely, precisely what he *does:* address the "Blessed Maid" directly with a mind to unburdening his "soul."

    C. A. Patrides comments on the rhetorical difficulties in the poem: "A tactful censure of Mariolatry, especially the Roman Catholic tendency to regard the Virgin as co-redemptrix with Christ."[39] Patrides emphasizes the speaker's tact while softening the speaker's stress on the doctrinal controversy involved: the Roman Catholic

Church has no firm position on the issue, but only a "tendency to regard the Virgin as co-redemptrix with Christ." Patrides's perception of tact here draws attention to the complexity of the rhetorical situation. Perhaps the doctrinal issue is not the poem's central concern, but if it did not provide a basis of tension, what need would there be for tact? Clearly, an answer to this question is central to our interest, and it involves two notions of audience. It seems doubtful that the composer of the Little Gidding "Harmonies" would have taken offense at the Marian sentiments in the poem, so any tactfulness on Herbert's or the speaker's part must be aimed elsewhere. Ferrar did have trouble getting *The Temple* past the censors at Cambridge University, but the lines that gave offence are not from this poem. Nor does it appear that Ferrar agreed with Herbert's censors in the first place.

Since the poem is addressed to the saints and to the Blessed Virgin, any tactfulness displayed must concern the speaker's fictive audience, and so we can envisage Herbert's intended audience recognizing feelings and ideas of which it might approve, yet from which it might distance itself. If the tactfulness here is in the speaker's address to the departed, it will concern us in one way, if with the wider reading audience, in another. In the latter case, we know that any tactfulness would concern readers other than Ferrar. Here, the imagery and tone of the "Harmonies" enter in. In that context, the requirement of tactfulness in the speaker's censure would concern objections that a Protestant audience, one inclined toward what King James called "the privat spirit of Reformation," might have. But who or what would require censure? And if it is censure, why doesn't the speaker include "prayers" or any other form of address, to the other departed saints? I think the answer to this question must include the lovely stanza that follows the speaker's disavowal, in which he states that he cannot, because he dares not, unburden himself to the Virgin, because their "King . . . Bids no such thing" (ll. 16, 18). He elaborates: where the King's "pleasure no injunction layes" (l. 19), the Virgin herself (" 'Tis your own case") does not "move a wing" (l. 20). The following stanza, a parenthetical reflection on "worship" in general, seems to justify Patrides's comment:

> All worship is prerogative, and a flower
> Of his rich crown, from whom lyes no appeal
> At the last houre:

Therefore we dare not from his garland steal,
To make a posie for inferiour power.

(ll. 21–25)

Now, the speaker attributes to "All worship" a quality of being
laden—in Herbert's time—with overtones of royalty. The Stuarts
were locked in battle with Parliament for decades over such questions
of the royal "prerogative" as "ship money" and the right to appoint
bishops. Here we read that "All worship" is identical with this
abstract concept of sovereignty; that is, it has the highest earthly
claim on the speaker and everyone else—until the speaker adds an
"and." With that addition, what has been given is taken away, and
the regal figures introduced in the first stanza are developed in a
different, even contradictory, manner.

In the first stanza, everyone has a crown, "If not upon his head,
yet in his hands" (l. 5); "ev'ryone is king." Patrides reminds us of
the biblical allusion here: "I saw four and twenty elders . . . and
they had on their heads crowns of gold" (Rev. 4.4). We will remember, too, Saint John's counsel to Smyrna during her tribulations: "be thou faithful unto death, and I will give thee a crown of
life" (Rev. 2.10); and the similar promise in the Epistle of James:
"Blessed is the man that endureth temptation: for when he is tried,
he shall receive the crown of life" (l. 12). This collation of texts
seems to fit the sense in Herbert's poem that the saints are those
who, faithful to the end, survive tribulations. Like them, the speaker
holds to their values, and so, because of his faithful understanding
of the Word, he can see the saints around the throne and, implicitly,
ally himself with them through the medium of direct address. The
rhetorical effect of all this is equivocal and ambiguous:

Although then others court you, if ye know
What's done on earth, we shall not fare the worse,
            Who do not so;
Since we are ever ready to disburse,
If any one our Masters hand can show.

(ll. 26–30)

It is equivocal because, especially in the context of "Anagram,"
which registers exultant praise of the Blessed Virgin ("In whom the
Lord of Hosts did pitch his tent!" [p. 77]), it does not actually re-

pudiate prayerful address to the "Blessed Maid," though *not* for intercession. On the contrary, the poem ends in an address to her and with a steadfast assertion of the speaker's earlier claim that, if he could, he "would . . . unfold" his "soul" to the Virgin Mary. He and worshippers like him are in fact "ever ready to disburse" their praise and love (as in stanza 1, the expression here is courtly), if only one condition could be met: if "any one" were able to show their "Masters hand."

On the surface, the poem does invite a sense of restrained censure, but not necessarily of the saints or the Virgin. They have earned their place in God's presence. It is important to note that the apostrophe to Mary in stanza 3 is never retracted. Nor does the speaker fully disclaim his feelings of allegiance to her. If "All worship is prerogative," it has its own claim to sovereignty, even if that sovereignty is—as we know from stanza 1 it is in heaven—subject to hierarchical order. The speaker never identifies his own wish to unburden himself to Mary as a desire to worship her; hence, we cannot overlook the subtle suggestion that "What's done on earth" is affected in large measure by powers on earth. Thus, "If any one" can prove otherwise to the speaker and the members of the group ("we") to which he belongs, they stand ready to do as he would do—and *does*— namely, talk in his "distresse" to the "Mother of . . . God."

Presumably, Christ's "garland" is not diminished by the crowns awarded to the saints, much less by any given to the "Mother of God." In Herbert's time, "worship" had much to do with "prerogative," in the strict, political sense of the term. While at one level the speaker suggests that kingship exists "On earth as it is in heaven" (we cannot miss the echo in the last stanza of the Lord's Prayer), he also suggests that its heavenly "prerogatives" cannot claim absolute sovereignty. If "any one" can justify address to the Blessed Virgin, the speaker stands ready to do in the future as he has done in the present of the poem. We are left with an undercurrent of political irony here; neither spontaneous nor decreed forms of prayer are permissible. The earthly "King" claims his prerogative, too. Hence, the speaker's longing, which persists undiminished throughout the poem, is not politically feasible. It may be true that "all" do not or should not "joyntly adore and praise" (l. 17) the King of England. But, on the other hand, with respect to "forms of prayer," the crown determines "What's done on earth," and only the most foolish of men—the Henry Barrows and John Greenwoods of the world—"dare" defy its "prerogative."

The Temple at Little Gidding

On the basis of our brief look at the Little Gidding "Harmonies" in relation to several Herbert poems, I think we can consent to Jane Carter's estimate of their mutual relevance. Study of the "Harmonies" seems to indicate that Herbert's audience would have recognized many of the symbols thought by Lewalski to be excessively medieval and Catholic, but held by Tuve to be important to our understanding of Herbert. "To all Angels and Saints" may be a Puritan poem to Richard Strier,[40] but it would not have been so construed by Nicholas Ferrar. Very likely, Ferrar would have perceived the impropriety for certain readers—not those at Little Gidding—of the strictest meaning of the speaker's invocation of the Virgin Mary in "To all Angels and Saints," and yet he himself would have taken no offense. Indeed, the poem would accord with the Mariolatry and martyrolatry evident in many panels of the "Harmonies."

On the basis of this body of evidence, it seems reasonable to infer that the pendulum in recent Herbert criticism has swung too far toward a Protestant reading of the poet's work. And yet, in raising questions about that emphasis, we need not demand reversal in an equal and opposite direction. I suggest instead that, in discussing Herbert's art, we deemphasize ideology, in particular the polarity between Catholic and Protestant poetic norms. In so doing, I offer no more than consent to the wisdom of T. S. Eliot, who found in Herbert, Ferrar, and Little Gidding values associated with "High Churchmanship."[41] From that vantage point Herbert's poetry resists reduction to doctrinal statements, expressing instead equivocal impulses, evasions, and doubts.

Close examination of the "Harmonies" also supports Tuve's observations on the similarity between Donne and Herbert:

Both wrote short poems, and were devotional poets in a way their predecessors were not (except Southwell, a Catholic), both escaped an earlier—and a later—Protestant hesitancy to make striking use of 'Papistical' symbolism, and both had reason to know particularly well traditions which after all had remained most alive in devotional, liturgical, or other religious materials. (pp. 136–37)

The current emphasis on Protestant poetics, represented most notably in Lewalski's impressive study and (more recently) in Strier's *Love Known: Theology and Experience in George Herbert's Poetry* (1983), tends to ignore this period of freedom following the days of the Tudors but preceding the era of the most dangerous discontents of Charles's reign. Tuve's remark emphasizes the liveliness of the older Catholic traditions and the means in religious practice of maintaining them, not as enclaves of Rome (as some Puritans believed), but as acceptable, indigenous expressions of devotion, neither Puritan nor Roman, but Catholic and Reformed. As Carter wrote, "The popular feeling was settling down upon the lines on which the Church, as reformed, was intended to continue, preserving the old Catholic traditons, free from what had been rejected of mediaeval development" (p. viii). Evidence from the "Harmonies" of Little Gidding indicates that the liturgical, meditative, and iconographic traditions cited by Tuve and Martz are neither medieval nor irrelevant, but rather the received contexts of expression at Little Gidding, where the most visible and important member of Herbert's audience resided, prepared to read, copy, edit, and, above all, understand Herbert's work.

Nicholas Ferrar and his group were, as modern critics can aspire to be, prepared readers of Herbert's texts. From the atoms of single syllables, words, and phrases, they put together a seamless wonder of a story, which when read correctly, explained the reader and the Word. Here, as in *The Temple,* one "word is all, if" understood. That story, as Carter suggests and as Carter's Victorian colleagues well knew, was told by Herbert in an idiom that would have been well received at Little Gidding. But times did change. And if critics point to the acceptance of Herbert among later Puritans—Baxter, Taylor, the Wesleys—it must be said that the poet they admired was apt to be a Herbert of their own making. If we want a Herbert who answers to Protestant poetic norms, we might better look for him in the first edition of the Wesleys' *Hymns and Sacred Poems* (1739) than in the poet that Ferrar presented to the reading audience, along with his own statement of critical appreciation, in 1633. In contrast to the Wesleys, Ferrar did not revise Herbert's poems; he saw them through press. Moreover, as time passed, Ferrar's views— namely, those of Herbert's intended audience—became less tenable. As controversy in the seventeenth century deepened, the distinction between Protestant and Catholic sensibilities resumed the political significance it had in earlier Tudor days and in the period immediately surrounding the Gunpowder Plot. But at Little Gidding, as at court when Anne of Denmark and Henrietta Maria openly affected Roman sympathies, the negative associations perceived in certain symbols and attitudes were less important. As time passed they gained in importance, especially to the ascending Puritan majority. We can recognize their differences with Ferrar and those like him, and in so doing agree with Carter, who two centuries later could look to the "Harmonies" of Little Gidding as the key to a historical understanding of Herbert's poetic method.

Chapter Four

The Sanctuary of
the Troubled Soul

In the last chapter, we examined the literary relationship between the "Harmonies" of Little Gidding and Herbert's poetic method. For Herbert, discrete moments of the Christian life were like parts of just such a composite text, cohering in an enlightened understanding of superficially unrelated contexts. Within this composite method, as individuals in their historical context were conjoined with ancestors or descendants in a manner expressing an order of meaning and understanding, visual images often took on particular density: "all the constellations of the storie." Necessarily, our discussion focused on only a few examples of the way in which Herbert linked sometimes distant poems in *The Temple*. But a more comprehensive view reveals that, like Sidney's *Astrophil and Stella*, Spenser's *Amoretti*, Watson's *Passionate Centurie of Love*, and Donne's *La Corona*, *The Temple* tells a story. Accordingly, a proper appreciation of Herbert's art must take account of the larger arrangement of poems into a patterned sequence.

Izaak Walton was the first critic to recognize the narrative aspect of *The Temple*. In his fascinating (if apocryphal) account of Herbert's disposition of the manuscript of *The Temple*, Walton imparts to his narrative perspective the special ethos of authorial intent. He has Herbert speaking to Edmund Duncan: *"Sir, I pray deliver this little Book to my dear brother Farrer, and tell him, he shall find in it a picture of the many spiritual Conflicts that have past betwixt God and my Soul, before I could subject mine to the will of Jesus my Master."*[1] Clearly, uncritical belief in this account would tend to elevate our understanding of *The Temple* from spiritual autobiography, a literary form with honorable antecedents of its own, to biography as known in the "lives of the saints," a related but distinct form with accompanying different claims. Well-documented studies by Amy M. Charles and David Novarr encourage a healthy skepticism toward Walton's historical reliability.[2] As we found in chapter 1, the hor-

tatory aims of early biographical accounts of Herbert's life owe much
to the norms of hagiography. Even so, as literary criticism, Walton's
word remains relevant and helpful. It is through his eyes that we
first see Nicholas Ferrar as the poet's intended audience and we first
see Herbert communicating with that audience. We can reasonably
infer from Walton's description that Ferrar would read *The Temple*
in accordance with the norms of spiritual autobiography. Thus,
Walton links *The Temple* with traditions well known in the period
through the works of Augustine, Thomas á Kempis, Saint Teresa,
and Saint John of the Cross. Behind these, of course, stood the
greatest of confessional poets to sing of man's relationship with God:
the Psalmist.

Perirrhanterium

In *The Poetry of Meditation* (1954), Louis L. Martz demonstrates
the importance of the Psalms and the traditions of spiritual meditation to a proper understanding of *The Temple*. Since publication
of that seminal study, critics have increasingly recognized *The Temple*
as a patterned work of art of some length made up of relatively
short poems, most of which exhibit a structural integrity of their
own. The few poems in the work which do appear weak when
considered apart from the sequence—"The Thanksgiving," for instance—only point up the importance of considering their narrative
function within the larger context.

It is no secret that *The Temple* is divided into three parts: "The
Church-porch," "The Church," and "The Church Militant." But
despite the surge of interest in Herbert's poetry, the first and third
sections of the work have received little attention and less praise.
Critical studies devoted entirely to Herbert's poetry have recently
appeared that effectively ignore both of these long poems. Helen
Vendler's study bears the ambitious title *The Poetry of George Herbert*
(1975), but makes no mention of "The Church Militant" at all and
takes only passing notice of "The Church-porch," a poem which,
Vendler observes, "can be thought of, at least in part, as an ethical
address to the self."[3] This omission is no mere lapse in the thinking
of one well-known critic, for Vendler's study only makes explicit
what is implicit in the annals of Herbert criticism and in the emphasis of anthology selections: in practice, the term *Herbert's poetry*
designates those lyrics found in the second and longest section of

The Temple, "The Church." Such commentary on "The Church-porch" and "The Church Militant" as we do have suggests that the first and third sections are viewed as something on the order of the "Cetology" chapters in *Moby-Dick.* As a favor to a great author, critics either ignore the poems completely, or apologetically dismiss them as embarrassing excrescences on an otherwise admirable literary work.[4]

And yet, as Martz points out, the didactic, proverbial qualities of "The Church-porch" fit the decorum of "preparation for spiritual communion in prayer and meditation," which "The Sacrifice" and its succeeding liturgical pieces represent.[5] Michael Schoenfeldt has eloquently shown how *"The Dedication"* prefixed to *The Temple* depicts the proper relations between God and the poet,[6] and between both and the proper readers, namely, those who would do violence neither to themselves nor to the work prayerfully submitted. "The Dedication" introduces the temporal theme of preparation, which part 1 of *The Temple,* "The Church-porch. / Perirrhanterium," further develops. In the Williams Manuscript, "Perirrhanterium" accompanied "Superliminare" as the title of two verses placed between "The Church-porch" and "The Church":

> Thou, whom the former precepts have
> Sprinkled and taught, how to behave
> Thy self in church; approach, and taste
> The churches mysticall repast.
>
> Avoid, Profaneness; come not here:
> Nothing but holy, pure, and cleare,
> Or that which groneth to be so,
> May at his perill further go.[7]

In revising the work, Herbert transformed the latinized Greek work *Perirrhanterium* into the subtitle of "The Church-porch." The change more closely associates sprinkling with the doorway to "The Church" and accentuates the link between "Superliminare" and "The Church-porch." The significance of this revision, while often noticed, has not received much commentary. And yet that revision draws attention to the paradoxical fact that the the speaker, despite his good efforts in "The Church-porch," appears to be sprinkled at the beginning *and* at the end of his tutelage under the supervision of a more experienced instructor.

As in such poems as "The Agonie" and "To all Angels and Saints," so here the tone and substance of associating sprinkling with the soul's entrance into the narthex of the Church and its entrance, after instruction, into the nave, suggests a sense of nostalgia for rites and ceremonies cast aside with the Reformation. As F. E. Hutchinson and C. A. Patrides note, the term refers to the instrument used "for sprinkling holy water prior to entry into the church proper."[8] George Herbert Palmer thought the use here refers to the "scattering" of topics in the poem.[9] And yet his uncertainty about the place in *The Temple* that the term occupies is indicative of an unease shared by others with a figure suggesting a stoup of holy water set just inside the church door.[10] Ordinarily, the practice of sprinkling holy water on the faithful upon their entrance into the main sanctuary was associated with the ceremony of Asperges, hence, the latinized word designating the "Sprinkler," or *aspergillum*.[11] Never part of the Mass proper, this ceremony was based on texts from Psalm 51: "Purge me with hyssop, and I shall be clean: wash me, and I shall be whiter than snow (51.7). The antiphon, followed by the Miserere from the same Psalm, accompanied the priest's sprinkling of the faithful in a manner reminiscent of baptism.[12] Normally, the Asperges was associated with Ash Wednesday, Easter week, Rogation Days, Ascension Day, visitation of the sick, and extreme unction.[13]

The uneasiness of Palmer and others with Herbert's use of a figure associated with the ceremony of Asperges is not hard to understand. In seventeenth-century England, sprinkling holy water at the church door, or anywhere else, would have been neither common nor legal, because the use of holy water went out with the Reformation. Accordingly, the Convocation Journal of 1536 sought to expunge Romish elements from mass books and portuisses.[14] On this subject, John Foxe remarks: "As concerning holy water, which they used to sprinkle at the church door upon them that entered in, I will not say that it sprung from the idolatrous rise of the Gentiles."[15] He proceeds, instead, to link the practice with the Roman art of conjuring by water. Catalogs of holdings of London churches at the time of the Reformation make clear that many churches had in their possession the stoups and sprinklers that Herbert employs as figures to coincide with, first, "Superliminare" and then, in 1633, "The Church-porch."[16] But by then, as Foxe indicates early on and as Thomas Jackson states in Herbert's time, the use of holy water, being considered of pagan origin,[17] fell from use in England. The

Roman understanding of the practice as legitimately derived from the Old Testament mixing of ashes with water reflected, Jackson argues, a misinterpretation of the sacrifice of the red heifer in Numbers (19.9).

The *OED* records uses of *aspergillum* that accord with this sense of the sprinkling of holy water upon entrance to church, but that may not work for Herbert. Although nostalgia may be reflected here, it is also possible that Herbert had never seen the Asperges ceremony performed. While sprinkling was the common practice in baptism, priests customarily used either a small cup or their hands to sprinkle infants. Be that as it may, the evidence points away from an architectural understanding of the movement from "The Church-porch" to "The Church." Indeed, the sprinkling of the faithful during the Asperges also seems to contradict the temporal sense conveyed of the individual soul's progress. In this vein, John Donne described the "sanctuary of the soule" as "the *Communion Table*,"[18] and the means by which one entered it was clear: "we are put over the Threshold into the Body of Church, by Baptisme." Again, *"Limen Ecclesiæ,* The threshold over which we step into the church" was baptism (8:157). It is well known that Anabaptists inveighed against infant baptism, but Anglicans christened newborns as soon as possible, and then, at what Donne referred to as the "age of discretion," catechizing and confirmation took place, followed by full participation in the Eucharist. This was the traditional sequence. Thus, in the Salisbury pontifical, confirmation immediately follows baptism,[19] and in *The Prayer-Book of Queen Elizabeth* (1559), we read: *"And there shall none be admitted to the holy communion; until suche tyme as he can saye the Catechisme and be confirmed."*[20]

In 1633, "Superliminare" was placed between "The Church-porch" and "The Church," rather than as the subtitle of the former, a change that tends to follow the Donnean figure; if, as in the Canticles, the Church is a walled garden, then baptism is the "Key in our hand to open the doore, that is, with the right and title, to the sacrament of Baptisme." By separating these liturgical synonyms, Herbert suggests a view of baptism similar to Donne's (5.127). Like Donne, Herbert sees baptism as an inception, or birth, in which affirmation of the Word is less important than later when, as an adult, the more prepared Christian participates fully in the sacramental life of the Church. Robert Hinman's representation of the speaker in "The Church-porch" as a con man may go too far,[21]

but it does recognize the distinction between the level of participation required by one whose innocence does and one whose does
not render the taking of Holy Communion supererogatory. Herbert's
revision points, then, to the way in which baptism only begins a
process of life in the Body of Christ. As with infancy in the natural
sense, responsibility for the most important functions of life necessarily remains with others—the spiritual parents, so to speak—
during the process of maturity.

Again, this process or movement is more temporal than spatial.
By associating the subtitle, "Perirrhanterium," with the sprinkling
of the worshipper upon entrance to the sanctuary, we risk construing
Herbert's figure as more Roman than Anglican. Thus, Calvin wrote:

But see, the Papistes would have a thousand baptismes. For what is the
holie water as they say? A thousand baptismes. Yea wis: as though God
had not beene wise inough to appoint that that he knewe to be necessarie
for us. His minde was that the faithfull should content them selves with
one Baptisme all their life long: in come men that marre it, and doe cleane
contrarie, and say it is not sufficient, unlesse there be a memoriall to renue
that baptisme that was once done. And so what are all their asperges of
holie water that the Papistes use?[22]

Full participation in the life of the Church—that is, in the Eucharist—came only after the baptized Christian had been taught
the meaning of the Sacrament and affirmed for himself undertakings
made at his christening by his sponsor and the congregation. Vendler
is mistaken to think of the didactic tone of "The Church-porch" as
indicative of the self addressing the self. Rather, the tone of "The
Church-porch" (pp. 6–24) reflects, as Stanley Fish rightly argues,[23]
the chastening tone appropriate to the relation between the catechizer and the youth being catechized:

> Thou, whose sweet youth and early hopes inhance
> Thy rate and price, and mark thee for a treasure;
> Hearken unto a Verser, who may chance
> Ryme thee to good, and make a bait of pleasure.
>   A verse may finde him, who a sermon flies,
>   And turn delight into a sacrifice.
>
>   (ll. 1–6)

As "Superliminare" later makes clear, "The Church-porch" implies
an earlier sprinkling and teaching: baptism followed by instruction.

The proverbial quality of these rhymed verses delineates the speaker's hortatory stance—preparation precedes transformation:

> Beware of lust: it doth pollute and foul
> Whom God in Baptisme washt with his own blood.
> It blots thy lesson written in thy soul;
> The holy lines cannot be understood.
> > How dare those eyes upon a Bible look,
> > Much lesse towards God, whose lust is all their book?
> >   (ll. 7–12)

Th aphoristic quality, simple syntax, and declarative tone fit not only the sense the speaker accords to the noncontroversial truths that he is charged to convey, but they also exhibit the difference in age and status between catechizer and catechumen.

Baptism was the sign of a hope, the public affirmation of which was made by the sponsor and the congregation for the infant. Now the responsibility to sustain the purity offered in baptism as a free gift falls on the youth himself. Thus, the movement from "Church-porch" to "Church" deals with a figure integral to the structure of *The Temple*. Man's entrance into the Body of Christ involves the only two Sacraments recognized by the Church of England (baptism and Holy Communion). So that just as "The Church-porch" ends with the passage of the soul from youth to maturity, likewise, "The Church" begins with the transformed soul entering into full participation in the life of the Church.

Further, the apposition in "The Church-porch" between the "sermon" and poetry's "bait of pleasure" is more than a rehash of the Horatian formula on poetry's power to teach and delight. Here the speaker recognizes the impropriety of sermonizing the unprepared. Thus it is also a criticism of clergymen who, as King James wrote, responded to Christ's injunction to "Pray without ceasing" by *"Preaching continually."*[24]

The Sanctuary of the Troubled Soul

As has already been suggested, most Herbert criticism focuses on the second part of *The Temple*, "The Church." Although a few poems do appear in manuscript that Herbert did not include in the copy sent to Ferrar, it is still the case that the poems in this section are those most often found in anthologies. These poems alone represent an extraordinary range of expression: sonnets, meditative reflections, hymns, prayers, verse paraphrases of Scripture, liturgical pieces, narrative, allegory, emblem poems, dialogues, pastorals, gnomic verses, anagrams, and so on. And though written in an often beguilingly simple style, they appear in many dozens of rhyme schemes and verse forms. Further, Herbert's lyrics form a sequence filled with lively contrasts, shifts, developments, and reversals, often within a single poem. Indeed, this latter feature may be the one that most effectively defines Herbert's poetic genius, and it certainly marks a sharp contrast between the poetic features of "The Church" and those of "The Church-porch."

The opening section of "The Church" is a series of poems organized around the most important event on the Christian calendar, Passion Week. As a result of the changes imposed on the sequence after composition of the Williams Manuscipt, the movement within this segment is never stiff or obvious. (Originally, the section was made up of "The Altar," "The Sacrifice," "The Thanksgiving," "The Second Thanksgiving," "The Passion," "Good Friday," "The Sinner," "Easter," "Easter Wings," "H. Baptism" [I and II], "Love" [I and II], and "The H. Communion.") The revised sequence amplifies, rather than the narrative of Holy Week, the worshiper's responses to it, and, as the imagery and allusiveness of "Sepulchre" shows, more tightly integrates the Passion Week poems with the opening of the series, and its central figure, "The Altar."

The narrative situation is this: the soul has entered "The Church" proper through baptism, catechism, and confirmation and is prepared as the guest at the Eucharist. But now—in the very first poem ("The Altar" [p. 26]—the dominant tension in *The Temple* emerges. Even though redeemed ("I acknowledge one baptisme for the remission of sinnes"),[25] the speaker cannot believe himself a worthy recipient of that free gift, does not feel himself the "new man," born of the spirit. And yet this sense of the unregenerate man within is implacably posed against ever-present signs of "Grace," first, in tears of contrition, second, in God's Word (evident even in the speaker's sense that he is nothing but hard and useless stone), and third, in "The Altar" itself:

> A broken Altar, Lord, thy servant reares,
> Made of a heart, and cemented with teares:
> Whose parts are as thy hand did frame;

No workmans tool hath touch'd the same.

(ll. 1–4)

Patrides's annotations to this poem suggest both how intricately the conflict—and its resolution—depend on an intertwining of Old and New Testament texts ("Collation of Scripture with Scripture" [p. 229]) and the way in which poems in *The Temple* exhibit a similar intertextuality. "The Altar," as Rosemond Tuve has eloquently demonstrated, "brings in associations with the Jordan River, introducing figures and motifs developed in such later texts as "The Bunch of Grapes" and the "Jordan" poems. Tuve reminds us of Moses' announcement in Deuteronomy:

And it shall be on the day when ye shall pass over Jordan unto the land which the Lord thy God giveth thee, that thou shalt set thee up great stones, and plaister them with plaister.

And thou shalt write upon them all the words of this law, when thou art passed over, that thou mayest go in unto the land which the Lord thy God giveth thee. . . .

Therefore it shall be when ye be gone over Jordan, that ye shall set up these stones. . . .

And there shalt thou build an altar unto the Lord thy God, an altar of stones: thou shalt not lift up any iron tool upon them. (27.2–6)

New Testament exegetes recognized in the Jordan a figure of the new covenant, which would be written, not in stone, but in man's heart. Accordingly, man entered the new Canaan of the Church through the Jordan of baptism.

The Jordan, baptism, the Passion—these are present to the speaker in the Eucharist, which, as Patrides points out, Lancelot Andrewes believed to be appropriately expressed by the metonymy of an "Altar" (p. 47). In the Eucharist, man's faults are measured, not by "Law," but by "Love." And this shift of judgment from justice to mercy provides an appropriate occasion for praise: "O let thy blessed Sacrifice be mine, / And sanctifie this Altar to be thine" (ll. 15–16). The last line of "The Altar" makes the title of the next poem, literally, an answer to prayer. "The Sacrifice" embodies that wonder of a "Name" ("Jesu" [p. 112]) which says to man *"I ease you."* Since man has been saved from the just condemnation of the Law, it is only just that, should he "hold [his] peace," the "stones" would cry out in "praise." The relevant New Testament text is from Luke.

Christ, having reached the end of his public ministry, enters Jerusalem, surrounded by an adoring multitude. Ever on the alert,
the Pharisees ask Jesus to rebuke his disciples: "And he answered
and said unto them, I tell you that, if these should hold their peace,
the stones would immediately cry out" (19.40). Herbert's readers
at Little Gidding would know, of course, that Christ's triumphal
entry into Jerusalem only shortly preceded the Lord's Supper.

Thus, Herbert closely links "The Altar" with "The Sacrifice" (pp.
26–34). Unlike most poems in "The Church" in length, "The
Sacrifice" differs also in that its speaker, being "The Sacrifice" (that
is, Christ), speaks directly to the audience as if from the Cross. This
address reverses the usual dramatic situation in "The Church," in
which the speaker remonstrates with Love (Divine Cupid, as he is
often represented in such works as Quarles's *Emblemes* [1635]). The
tone here is, then, markedly different:

> Oh all ye, who passe by, whose eyes and minde
> To worldly things are sharp, but to me blinde;
> To me, who took eyes that I might you finde:
> Was ever grief like mine?
>   (ll. 1–4)

And so that tone remains throughout the poem, ironic and harsh,
as Christ, borrowing the reproachful mode of Jeremiah, laments
man's treatment of his Creator. God gave the eyes, but they cannot
see him. God took on the humble perspective of those eyes, in order
to seek out man's redemption: "Was ever grief like mine?" Each
stanza develops a similar antithesis. In a monograph-length discussion of this poem Tuve presents a richly detailed study of relevant
material from illuminated manuscripts, stained glass windows, Books
of Hours, the *Biblia Pauperum,* medieval lyrics, and the liturgy.
Especially striking are the tonal similarities in Herbert's poem to
those utterances spoken by the priest in Christ's role during services
for Holy Week (Good Friday Complaints, for instance). Century
after century, congregations followed the liturgical calendar by en-
acting the last week of Christ's life, with the awfulness of the
proceedings represented in the severity of altar fixings and, especially
on Holy Thursday and Good Friday, in the caustic tone assumed
by the priest. Christ is sold, abandoned, betrayed, bound by those
whom he has freed. The story of the Passion unfolds indirectly, as

"The Sacrifice" protests the awful chasm between the gratitude that man owes and the ingratitude that he expresses—death for life:

> Heark how they crie aloud still, *Crucifie:*
> *It is not fit he live a day,* they crie,
> Who cannot live lesse then eternally:
>   Was ever grief, etc.
>   (ll. 97–100)

If man's ingratitude is the butt of Christ's scorn in "The Sacrifice," his feeble attempt to express its opposite occupies the following pair of poems, "The Thanksgiving" and "The Reprisall" (designated "The Thanksgiving" and "The Second Thanksgiving" in the Williams Manuscript). As in the opening two poems, here too Herbert makes his narrative intention known by linking the poems to earlier situations: "Was ever grief like mine"; "Never was grief like mine"; "Oh King of grief!" (pp. 34–35). In these two poems we encounter a situation typical in Herbert's lyrics. Walton figuratively described *The Temple* as *"a picture of the many spiritual Conflicts that . . . passed betwixt God and* [the speaker's] *Soul."* While he emphasizes the plurality of poetic conflicts, Herbert arranges these particular poems in such a way as to extend or recapitulate—in either case, to unify—two apparently discrete situations. "The Thanksgiving" (pp. 35–36) ends in a series of promises and, as critics have often observed, in a sense of exasperation and impotence. Throughout the poem the speaker, bent on his own notions of gratitude ("Surely I will revenge me on thy love" [1.17]), lays plans to repay "The King of grief." The poem is marked by a number of verbs in the future tense ("I will revenge," "I will restore," "I will tear thence") interrupted only by the occasional, intrusive doubt ("As for thy passion—But of that anon" [1.29]). But so earnest is the speaker's desire to act gratefully that he dismisses—or never really attends to—the meaning of his misgivings. So his doubt is swept away in fantasies of the future: "I'le contrive," "I'le build . . . mend . . . finde . . . prove." And yet here, as later in "The Crosse," the speaker's love of God, when expressed as determination to alter the world outside him—or within—does not set the stage for resolution of the poem's conflict:

> Nay, I will read thy book, and never move
> Till I have found therein thy love,

Thy art of love, which I'le turn back on thee:
O my deare Saviour, Victorie!
Then for thy passion—I will do for that—
Alas, my God, I know not what.
(ll. 45–50)

Because Passion Week elicits the most profound sense of man's inadequacy in relation to "The Sacrifice," the speaker strives to match that sense with plans for a new regime. He feels the moment as a challenge to shape his future. Hence, "The Reprisall" (pp. 36–37) begins where "The Thanksgiving" ends: "I have consider'd it, and finde / There is no dealing with thy mighty passion." It seems that the conflict is over. For this speaker, the past proceeds no further in his mind than the present, because, for the moment at least, he recognizes that it would make no difference if he *could* copy Christ's "art of love," since his "sinnes deserve the condemnation" (1.4) of death. It appears that the conflict stemming from the speaker's proposed "revenge" has been resolved, but in fact this fresh outlook provides no satisfaction. Instead, with it comes a new formula for discontent. If God would make him innocent, then his "attempts" might be acceptable. Thus, until the end of human time ("Death"), resolution of conflicts in the soul is always provisional. But when experienced, such moments of "rest" amid the turmoil of time provide the emotional content of the close of many of Herbert's most stunning poems. For example, "The Reprisall" ends when the speaker, vanquishing all notions of "revenge," surrenders completely: "in thee I will overcome / The man, who once against thee fought" (ll. 15–16).

The antithesis between the Sacrifice and man's feelings about it imparts a contrapuntal arrangement to the opening section of "The Church," which proceeds with events of Passion Week and expressions of the speaker's unworthiness: "The Agonie" and "The Sinner," "Good Friday" and "Redemption," "Sepulchre" and "Easter." As in "The Thanksgiving" and "The Reprisall," so in the following pairs we encounter a persistent recursiveness, as the coordinating figures (heart, stone, blood) are reconsidered, redefined, and, if only momentarily, understood in a new way. For example, in "The Sinner" (p. 38), prayer makes new sense following "The Agonie," which, as we observed in chapter 3, probably juxtaposed scenes from the life of Christ and Moses. As the sonnet unfolds, Herbert returns to imagery of "The Altar." "The Sinner" feels that his worthiness is like "quarries of pil'd vanities" (1.5) in contradistinction to mere "shreds of holinesse" (1.6). But this recurring sense of unworthiness is met by the promise of Scripture, introduced in "The Altar": "Yet Lord restore thine image, heare my call: / And though my hard heart scarce to thee can grone, / Remember that thou once didst write in stone" (ll. 12–14).

Herbert develops the same figure in a similar way in "Sepulchre" (pp. 40–41), which moves the narrative of Passion Week along, but provides a retrospective context for its consideration as well. Having recognized that his legal status has been changed by Christ's Sacrifice from tenant to freeholder ("Redemption" [p. 40]), the speaker relives the truth of Good Friday: "there I him espied, / Who straight, *Your suit is granted,* said, and died" (ll. 13–14). Again, this swift allegory seems to solve the speaker's problem. But after Good Friday comes Holy Saturday ("Sepulchre," pp. 40–41). As Christ's "Blessed bodie" lies in the tomb, the speaker addresses it, and the inevitable apprehension of his guilt and complicity recurs. Just as Christ was refused lodging at his Nativity, so in death he was denied all "lodging . . . but a cold hard stone" (1.2). The irony is, again, severe, as there are so many recipients of God's offered "Grace" on earth and so much room, as can be seen in man's capacity to store "transgressions by the score" (1.6). The speaker identifies himself with the Jews who prior to Christ's escape beyond the Jordan "took up stones again to stone him" (John 11.31) and with those who called out to Pontius Pilate: "Away with this man, and release unto us Barabbas" (Luke 23.18). As in "The Altar," so here, the Old and New Testaments mark the redemptive story, the truth that Christ died for man, not in spite of, but *because* of, man's faults:

> And as of old the Law by heav'nly art
> Was writ in stone; so thou, which also art
> The letter of the word, find'st no fit heart
>   To hold thee.
> Yet do we still persist as we began,
> And so should perish, but that nothing can,
> Though it be cold, hard, foul, from loving man
>   Withhold thee.
>   (ll. 17–24)

"Yet do we still persist as we began": this line could serve as a gloss on the temporal condition both of man and "The Church." The speaker struggles to find a way within himself to contradict the Word, and yet that Word is his only restorative: "For as much as ye are manifestly declared to be the epistle of Christ ministered by us, written not with ink, but with the Spirit of the living God; not in tables of stone, but in fleshy tables of the heart" (2 Cor. 3.3).

The opening sequence ends with a mighty affirmation. In response to the puzzling failure of the speaker's impulse in "The Thanksgiving" to write poetry as a means to repay God we read here: "My musick shall finde thee, and ev'ry string / Shall have his attribute to sing" (ll. 39–40). Paradoxically, he would write poetry, read Scripture, "and never move" until he finds the perfect means of imitating Christ. But, as Tuve argues in her splendid essay, "Herbert and 'Caritas,' "[26] his very distemper indicates that he has not understood the "dark instructions" of Scripture ("Divinitie," p. 135). In particular, he rejects the true meaning of the "dolefull storie" of "such a grief as cannot be." Christ intones this theme reiterated again and again in "The Church": *Follow my resigning* ("Dialogue," p. 115). Here in the Sacrifice itself is the "musick" to "prove one God, one harmonie," the very instrument for playing that heavenly song. Thus, in "Easter" (p. 40–41), we read:

> Awake, my lute, and struggle for thy part
> > With all thy art.
> The crosse taught all wood to resound his name,
> > Who bore the same.
> His stretched sinews taught all strings, what key
> Is best to celebrate this most high day.
>
> Consort both heart and lute, and twist a song
> > Pleasant and long:
> Or, since all musick is but three parts vied
> > And multiplied,
> O let thy blessed Spirit bear a part,
> And make up our defects with his sweet art.
> > (ll. 7–18)

Even the echo from "The Altar" ("O let thy blessed Sacrifice be mine, / And sanctify this Altar to be thine") emphasizes Herbert's recurrent motif: the Sacrifice is beginning, middle, and end of man's redemption. In Herbert, the Resurrection manifests a power similar to that of Christ's Nativity in Milton. With the rising of this "Sunne," time stops: "There is but one [day], and that one ever" (1.30). As the opening section draws to a close with Herbert's majestic "Easter" poem, numerous other poems interspersed throughout "The Church" come to mind: "Sunday," "Paradise," "Life," and "Time." Passion Week, which ends with commemoration of the Resurrection, conjoins life to death, and the Fall of Man to the new covenant of Grace ("Easter-wings"). As from the inception of man's struggle in "The Thanksgiving," we find man's will and unalterable unworthiness implacably posed against God's power and love, so from the beginning to the end of "The Church," time is interposed against the timeless.

Life and the Christian Year

We have already implied that in many of Herbert's most successful poems ("The Thanksgiving," "The Reprisall," "Redemption," the "Affliction" poems, "Divinitie," and "The Crosse" are a few) the dramatic tension emerges from man's stubborn attempt to impose his idea of the future—in service, especially—upon the Creator. It is a typical situation, known best perhaps in Herbert's often anthologized "The Collar," but seen also in the "Affliction" and "Employment" poems and in "The Flower" and other poems as well. This theme may be most powerfully expressed, however, in "The Crosse" (pp. 164–65), which, unlike "The Sacrifice," "Good Friday," and "The Agonie," is only secondarily concerned with the Passion. Here, the emphasis is on the Cross as a "designe," in the sense of an intention or desire. As in "The Thanksgiving," the speaker struggles "to serve," but life itself confounds the impulse to invoke his own "designes." As in the "Employment" and "Affliction" poems, it seems at first that the speaker resents the illnesses impeding his power to serve: "if once my grones / Could be allow'd for harmonie." But it is clear that the speaker's weakness is, as it has always been, in the very warp and woof of his being. Piety is no more effective than sin in palliating the horror of self-arrogation:

> Besides, things sort not to my will,
> Ev'n when my will doth studie thy renown:
> Thou turnest th' edge of all things on me still,

> Taking me up to throw me down:
> So that, ev'n when my hopes seem to be sped,
> I am to grief alive, to them as dead.
>
>   (ll. 19–24)

The speaker is like the archer, whose aim (crossing the bow by drawing the arrow) gives evidence of the underlying design. We are reminded of Donne's similar wordplay in his poem, also entitled "The Crosse":

> Who can deny mee power, and liberty
> To stretch mine armes, and mine owne Crosse to be?
> Swimme, and at every stroake, thou art thy Crosse,
> The Mast and yard make one, where seas do tosse.
> Looke downe, thou spiest out Crosses in small things;
> Looke up, thou seest birds rais'd on crossed wings;
> All the Globes frame, and spheares, is nothing else
> But the Meridians crossing Parallels.[27]

Herbert's poem, whose speaker perceives a similarly ubiquitous cruciform design in things, ends in prayerful address:

> Ah my deare Father, ease my smart!
> These contrarieties crush me: these crosse actions
> Doe winde a rope about, and cut my heart:
>   And yet since these thy contradictions
> Are properly a crosse felt by thy Sonne,
> With but foure words, my words, *Thy will be done.*
>
>   (ll. 31–36)

It is as if the speaker's frustrated willfulness has drawn him into a crucible. Contradictions bind, cut, crush, and crucify him. But, finally, the persistence of the image itself suggests the means of respite from this agony. By surrendering *his* "designes," in imitation of the "Sonne," the speaker takes refuge in the "Father's" "designe."

As so often in "The Church," here the speaker's meditation takes him from turmoil to peace, but that peace is evanescent in the extreme. Man's lot is, as in "The Pulley," more likely marked by a "repining restlesnesse" (p. 160). His state of mind ascends only as a necessary condition of its subsequent decline. In such dramatic surges and withdrawals of assurance lies one of the defining features of Herbert's poetic practice. If we look at the poem that follows "The Crosse," we find evidence of the way in which the contours of that dialectic provide the emotional link between poems and sections of "The Church." For "The Flower," which no less a critic than Arnold Stein considers "one of the greatest lyrics in the language,"[28] begins where "The Crosse" ends, with the peace of surrender:

> How fresh, O Lord, how sweet and clean
> Are thy returns! ev'n as the flowers in spring;
> To which, besides their own demean,
> The late-past frosts tributes of pleasure bring.
> Grief melts away
> Like snow in May,
> As if there were no such cold thing.
>
> (ll. 1–7)

But, as so often in "The Church," "rest" is no more than a moment between occasions of anxiety. As time passes, the same conflict recurs, and that repetition denies a necessary condition of Christian life. Change, though imperceptible at times, is inescapable, and yet it seems to contradict the eternal, unalterable love of God. In this respect, like time, these dramatic shifts imply the limitations of will.

As we have seen, "The Flower" (pp. 165–67) begins in a sense of exultant thanksgiving. The speaker is grateful at the moment for the tokens of spiritual rebirth. But underneath that gratitude lies the bitter memory of "late-past frosts." And since the past is the mirror of a possible future, it exercises a disturbing influence on the present. Just as winter passes, it returns. Thus, insofar as the sense of present "rest" includes recollection, it cannot exclude a measure of anxiety:

> But while I grow in a straight line,
> Still upwards bent, as if heav'n were mine own,
> Thy anger comes, and I decline:
> What frost to that? what pole is not the zone,
> Where all things burn,
> When thou dost turn,
> And the least frown of thine is shown?
>
> (ll. 29–35)

Swiftly the moment of assurance dissolves into its opposite: an awful sense of instability to which even earnest Christians are exposed. A winter tempest (the Creator's imagined frown) represents the ultimate danger of the Christian life for this speaker no less than for Spenser's Redcrosse Knight in *The Fairie Queene,* namely, spiritual despair. Even in the moment of security lies an occasion of doubt (as one season logically entails passage to another). Likewise, illness must be a sign of God's displeasure and impending wrath. For the meditant of "The Flower," the pendulum swing in human consciousness between assurance and despair becomes the overriding reality of Christian life: "These are thy wonders, Lord of power, / Killing and quickning, bringing down to hell / And up to heaven in an houre" (ll. 15–17).

As in the spiritual autobiographies of Saint Teresa and Saint John of the Cross, so here the flower image is a hieroglyphic of man's life: "And now in age I bud again, / After so many deaths I live and write" (ll. 36–37). The winter-death of despair recurs because, at any given moment, man's life is neither understood nor fully seen. Anxiously absorbed in the present and frightened of what his memory insists the future might hold, man fails to discern God's emerging "designe." Still, God's secrets are revealed to proper readers in his Book of Creatures. The flower shadows forth the mystery of Christian life:

> Who would have thought my shrivel'd heart
> Could have recover'd greennesse? It was gone
> Quite under ground; as flowers depart
> To see their mother-root, when they have blown;
> Where they together
> All the hard weather,
> Dead to the world, keep house unknown.
>
> (ll. 8–14)

Indeed, here is the mystery *behind* the mystery of the Christian's life. Even in the midst of death the restorative of the Incarnation sustains the life of man. The flower recedes, yet lives on, unaware both of its own life and of the source of that life. Although despair seems to overwhelm the spirit, the house of the Elect is sustained by God's love. "Repining restlesnesse" is a quality imposed on man as a condition of his existence in time. He cannot see what time will unfold; at one moment it seems that the flower is dead, at another, not. But from the heavenly point of view, nothing changes: "Jesus Christ the same yesterday, and today, and forever" (Heb. 12.8).

The reason for this paradox is simple. For Herbert, time is an illusion. He did not think of time in the physical, but in the Augustinian, sense, as a mysterious element of human existence.[29] In *The Flight of Time* (1634), Roger Matthew expresses an attitude typical of the seventeenth century:

What saith *David* to our daies? They are saith he, *as a shadow, and thers no abiding.* And what is *Hezekiahs* opinion? As a shepheards tent, of no long stay. A weavers shuttle is of no long race: a pilgrims tabernacle soone flitted. . . . So is life in the middest of its fortresse.

How durable is the state of grasse? *We fade away suddenly like the grasse.* Whats a tales grace? Shortnesse, *Our yeeres passe away as a tale that is told.* . . . Yea, as if these comparisons were yet defective, the Prophet addeth a sleighter manner of similitude, resembling mans life to a dreame, and that when its past, . . . it was but a thing (or rather a just nothing) of meere imagination.[30]

If in the spiritual sense, time is an illusion, then in the same sense, death must also be illusory. Such a view may seem to contradict the sense of "The Flower," but that contradiction is also only apparent.

It is true that in some cases the flower is a figure of death. It is used in this way, for instance, in Herbert's "Life" (p. 94). But even here the title gives the irony away; by reminding the speaker of death, the "posie" summons him to renewed spiritual vigor. Time may beckon to the flowers, but Time's intended audience is man, whom he wishes to guide to a proper understanding of the present experience. That experience, in turn, is the whole of life in miniature, for it is a confrontation with Time incarnate:

> My hand was next to them, and then my heart:
> I took, without more thinking, in good part
>   Times gentle admonition:
> Who did so sweetly deaths sad taste convey,
> Making my minde to smell my fatall day;
>   Yet sugring the suspicion.
>
>   (ll. 7–12)

Time's imperative concerns the value of what time in life remains, and yet duration itself is of little consequence. The inference is that

man must respond appropriately to Time's admonition. Herbert
uses the same figure in much the same way in "The Flower":

> These are thy wonders, Lord of love,
> To make us see we are but flowers that glide:
> Which when we once can finde and prove,
> Thou hast a garden for us, where to bide.
>
> (ll. 43–46)

Just as in "Life" Time renders man aware of the imminence of death,
so in "The Flower" the Almighty "makes" him recognize life's
impermanence.

Paradoxically, within the limits of that solemn recognition lies
a *hortus conclusus* of reassurance. In light of this recognition, experiences that once seemed like rehearsals of death are recognized as
the source of eternal life. Only man's limited point of view restrains
him from seeing that the "Lord of power" and "Lord of love" are
one and the same. Moreover, the swing between assurance and
despair may make life seem like an endless hurtling between heaven
and hell, but it is only the means by which God teaches man the
lesson of mortality. When man learns that lesson, he finds himself
at "rest" in "Paradise." Placed in time to make a simple choice,
man either accepts the limits imposed on all flesh or aims beyond
them. On the consequences of the latter choice Scripture was clear:
"Who would be more, / Swelling through store, / Forfeit their
Paradise by their pride" (ll. 47–49).

As the last stanza of "The Flower" suggests, just as time and
death are illusory, so is change apparent rather than real. The speaker's prayer ("O that I once past changing were, / Fast in thy Paradise,
where no flower can wither!" [ll. 22–23]) has been answered eons
before it was made. Indeed, in another context, the pilgrim seems
to know this. In "Paradise," he gives thanks for his inclusion in
that *hortus conclusus.* As I have elsewhere pointed out, Herbert knew
and used a rich medieval tradition, perpetuated in the literature
and iconography of the seventeenth century, which identified the
"Paradise" (pp. 132–33) of the Church with the text from the Song
of Songs: "A garden inclosed is my sister, my spouse; a spring shut
up, a fountain sealed."[31] In the literature and art of the Middle
Ages and the Renaissance, the garden wall alluded to the protection
of Christ's Spouse throughout all time, including the dispensation

of Grace. Probably Herbert had this tradition in mind in "Paradise": "What open force, or hidden CHARM / Can blast my fruit, or bring me HARM, / While the inclosure is thine ARM?" (ll. 4–6). By representing the division between nature and Grace, the wall indicates the distinction between the time-bound and the timeless. The mystery of Christian experience lies in this paradox: though living within time's strict limits, man exists also *outside* of them, for he is born of the spirit as well as of the flesh.

The structural implications of the dramatic feature we have been discussing are familiar to admirers of Herbert. These implications concern the drastic shifts in given stanzas and the shape and rhyme scheme of the poems as well. The movement from something like free verse to a colloquy in rhyme in "The Collar" (pp. 153–54) is perhaps the best-known example. Until that moment in the poem, the speaker engages in wild, rebellious fantasies of freedom and self-indulgence, with the disordered line endings being only one of many expressions of the speaker's undisciplined will. Further, that disorder seems, by contrast, all the more rude and impertinent:

> But as I rav'd and grew more fierce and wilde
> At every word,
> Me thoughts I heard one calling, *Child!*
> And I reply'd, *My Lord.*
>
> (ll. 33–36)

To this famous example we might add numerous instances of the Herbertian "turn" that marks the endings of so many poems in "The Church." Rebellion and anxiety are, after all, preconditions of surrender, with its concomitant "rest." We think of the close of many Herbert sonnets ("The Sinner," "Redemption," "Love" [I and II], "The H. Scriptures" [I and II]), of the "Jordan" poems, and of such poems as "Divinitie," "The Crosse," and, of course, "Love" (III).

With its stunningly dramatic close, "Love" (III) is indicative of another noteworthy structural aspect of "The Church." Most of the poems that come to mind as examples of the typically swift, dramatic, turnabout ending appear in the first half of "The Church," and they are often a result of Herbert's final revisions of *The Temple*.[32] The tendency—and I mean to imply only *that,* not a division of the sequence into two distinct and mutually exclusive halves—is toward more and more peaceful resolutions of anxieties of ever decreasing lengths and intensities. The early poems in "The Church" treat of the Christian's childhood in the Body of Christ. The imagery and tone of these lyrics often suggest birth, baptism, and Passion Week, with its association of spring and renewal. So the narrative movement begins in the springtime of the Christian year. We need register no surprise, then, that the close of the same sequence concerns the antithesis of birth and youth: age, sickness ("The Forerunners"), preparation for the Marriage of the Lamb ("The Invitation," "The Banquet"), death and the hereafter ("Death," "Dooms-day," "Judgement," "Heaven," and the Marriage of the Lamb ["Love" (III)]).

The overarching structural design results from a fusion of two temporal figures, the life span and the seasons. From "The Church-porch" through "The Church," the soul moves in stages—baptism, confirmation, communion, struggle—and that progress assumes the shape of a single year. As A. J. Festugière and others have pointed out,[33] "The Church" is arranged in accordance with familiar dates on the Christian calendar. Festugiere writes: "Les fêtes ou temps liturgiques commémorés dans *The Temple* sont: *Christmas, Lent, Good Friday* (à quoi se joignent naturellement *The Agonie, Redemption, Sepulchre), Easter* et *Easter-wings* (à quoi il faut ajouter *The Dawning), Whitsunday, Trinitie Sunday"* (p. 130). To these he adds, as indications of Herbert's nostalgia for the ten feasts honoring the Blessed Virgin, "Anagram" and "To all Angels and Saints"; and he ends his list by observing that the latter poem and "Marie Magdalene" also commemorate the saints.

Although the importance of the liturgical calendar to our understanding of the structure of *The Temple* has been generally recognized, Festugière's remarks need only be slightly extended to see how the close of "The Church" balances the opening suite of poems on the theme of Easter and rebirth. As a creature of time, the body must die. And as the sequence of Christian holidays in "The Church" suggests, man's year on earth passes swiftly. Yet while it passes man is able, with God's help, to recapitulate the wonder of Christ's death and transfiguration. To the Christian, Time is no enemy, but rather, as comparison between Herbert's "Time" and a poem like Aurelian Townshend's "A Dialogue Betwixt Time and a Pilgrime" shows, Time is the dresser of God's timeless garden. Herbert's sacramental understanding of the Incarnation places man's every experience within a timeless order. That is why in Herbert's "Time" (pp. 122–23) the figure of Time is reduced from the aggressive deliverer of homilies and poser of riddles of such poems as Towns-hend's "Dialogue" to a conciliatory figure—from an "executioner at best" to (like Christ) a "gard'ner." For, as we read in "Paradise," each moment is the beginning, as well as the end, of time. With respect to Christian truth, the prolongation of life becomes the scourge of the soul ("Time").

It seems to me that from this perspective the richness of Martz's remarks on the closing sequence in "The Church" may be more fully appreciated. The soul has entered time, passed through "this school" of the Church, and learned of its own sordid origins and humble destiny: "Comparing dust with dust, and earth with earth" ("Church-monuments" [pp. 64–65]). Having properly applied the meaning of his encounter with time, man knows that the body is like an hourglass, measuring out the sands of itself:

> Deare flesh, while I do pray, learn here thy stemme
> And true descent; that when thou shalt grow fat,
>
> And wanton in thy cravings, thou mayst know,
> That flesh is but the glasse, which holds the dust
> That measures all our time; which also shall
> Be crumbled into dust. Mark here below
> How tame these ashes are, how free from lust,
> That thou mayst fit thy self against thy fall.
>
> (ll. 17–24)

Beginning with "The Forerunners," we may trace the approach of "Death." "The Rose" reminds the reader that true pleasures wait upon the final union that is now but moments off. Except for reiteration of that theme in "Discipline," the sequence ("The In-vitation" and "The Banquet") heralds the end of time. "The Posie," with its delicate emphasis on God's mercy, is juxtaposed against the final recurrence of doubt ("A Parodie") before "Death."

In four poems on "the last things," we follow the soul's progress beyond death: "Dooms-day," "Judgement," "Heaven," "Love" (III). The last poem in "The Church," "Love" (III), completes the pattern begun in "The Church-porch." Having passed through time, the soul at last succumbs to the overpowering love of God and is seated at the banquet table in the Heavenly City. In this context, even the *"FINIS"* that follows fits this poetic design; the odyssey of the soul has ended, and with it the passage of the Church through time, seen from the individual's point of view.

"Providence" and "The Church Militant"

Since the speaker's life ends with the close of the second part of *The Temple,* we would expect the third section to employ a different point of view, and so it does. The effectiveness of the shift in perspective, and of "The Church Militant" as a poem, has often been questioned. Even Martz considers the poem only weakly integrated into the sequence: "Certainly the first two parts are much more closely related than the last two. And certainly the 'Church Militant,' in many respects, may seem to represent a rather desperate effort to salvage, if only by way of appendix, a very early poem" (p. 289). Signs of Herbert's own doubts about its inclusion are not hard to find. As Stanley Fish writes, "In both the Bodleian and the Williams manuscripts, 'The Church Militant' stands apart from the previous poems, separated in one by a blank page and in the other by five blank pages" (p. 142). Fish recalls F. E. Hutchinson's indictment of the poem as an early effort not suited to Herbert's primarily lyric gifts and notes Annabel [Endicott] Patterson's suggestion that "The Church Militant" "has no place in 'the structure of *The Temple'* " (p. 156)[34] As we have already seen, Vendler goes even farther, eliminating the work completely from her discussion of the Herbert canon. In answer to J. Max Patrick's charge that the evidence points to the authority of the first edition of 1633, Fish writes: "Of course, even if it were proved that Herbert intended to integrate 'The Church Militant' into *The Temple,* we would still be free to decide that he had failed" (p. 143). Fish exercises that freedom by arguing that the poem "does not seem to be a fit conclusion to the poems that precede it."

We have argued that the first two sections of *The Temple* include an ethical preludium and a lyric sequence, the latter of which subtly orchestrates two narrative strands. One suggests the order of the Christian calendar; the other follows the progress of the speaker's spiritual life through death to the heavenly banquet, in which the soul is joined in the promised union with her Spouse. In tandem, these narrative strands converge to represent the speaker's inner struggle seen within the comforting larger contours of the liturgical

calendar, whose repetitions bear the ultimate consolation of Christ's
life, death, and resurrection. By providing the preparation for entrance into the life of the Church, "The Church-porch" bears an
obvious temporal relation to the second part of *The Temple*. But
since the second portion of the work extends the narrative through
death to the promised union of the soul with God, we should not
expect part three of the work to exhibit the same temporal relation
to "The Church." From one point of view, man's story is over; the
soul's struggle has ended. The liturgical calendar has no further
relevance because there is no longer any passage of individual time.
The speaker sees now from a perspective in which events in "The
Church" can be reconsidered.

"The Church Militant" reflects a more detached perspective on
the soul's struggle and on all others like it. Thus, as with "The
Church-porch," the placement of the poem is a hieroglyphic of a
temporal relation. The relative lack of intensity and the difference
in form from most of the poems in "The Church," though a problem
for Fish and others, are neither as pronounced nor as important as
they have inferred. Fish claims to be persuaded by Lee Ann Johnson's
apprehensions about the length, form, and tone of "The Church
Militant." But in fact Herbert has prepared his reader for just this
kind of poem by including in "The Church" another long poem—
also in iambic pentameter couplets—on the same theme as that of
"The Church Militant," which is, I take it, "Providence." Herbert's
poem by that name is more than half as long as "The Church
Militant" and is, like the latter poem, closely linked to the Psalms.

We shall return to this point later. For now it is enough to
observe that, at least with respect to its theme, length, and metrical
form, "The Church Militant" exhibits some ligatures to "The
Church." But the poem is a conclusion, not a continuance only, of
The Temple, and we must consider its proprieties in that context,
too. The voice in "The Church Militant" does not sound with the
wonderfully intense tones of a soul in agony, but then we would
not expect the viewer, who now sees all of time, to be torturously
absorbed within a single segment of it. Here, that distance both
defines the speaker's point of view and explains his detached tone.
In "The Church," time was the defining feature of a world experienced through change and anxiety. The speaker in "The Church
Militant" sees the world with the vision of one in a state far removed
from the *"Conflicts . . . betwixt God and* [the] *Soul."* "The Church

Militant" is an apocalyptic poem. Its tone is austere because its speaker sees the past, present, and future with equal clarity.

"The Church Militant" is set off from "The Church" in such a way as to suggest a deliberate distancing of the sections. The reason for this is not obscure. The present transition differs from the earlier one in kind. Most obviously, the spatial analogy seen in the movement from the porch beneath "Superliminare" into "The Church" has no counterpart in the separation between "The Church" and "Church Militant," because this latter separation bears its own *kind* of finality (*"FINIS. | Glory be to* God *on high | And on earth peace | Good will towards men"* [p. 189]). This is no movement from one time and place to another, but rather from time to the timeless. The way has been laid for the recognition of an entirely new dimension in *The Temple.* "The Church Militant" is a poem concerned, not with the struggle of the soul in time, but with the progress of the Church throughout all time.

Don Cameron Allen, Frank Manley, and Louis Martz have noted the similarity in structure and content between "The Church Militant" and Donne's *First Anniversarie.*[35] Herbert's use of imagery from the Song of Songs is important here, given the manner in which the Bride invited to the Wedding Feast in "Love" (III) is also described in "The Church Militant." Likewise, Mary, a type of the Church, embodied the mystery of the timeless placed in time. Fish is wrong to emphasize the relevance of the hexameral tradition to "The Church Militant" (p. 148). The refrain from the Psalms divides "The Church Militant" into five parts, not six. And Herbert's quinquepartite division of the poem probably alludes to the practice of meditations on the mysteries of the Virgin in sequences of five, not to the six days that God took to create the world. "The Church Militant" (pp. 190–98) is a narrative sequence in five parts dedicated to the Bride of Christ, the Church:

> Early didst thou arise to plant this vine,
> Which might the more indeare it to be thine.
> Spices come from the East; so did thy Spouse,
> Trimme as the light, sweet as the laden boughs
> Of *Noahs* shadie vine, chaste as the dove;
> Prepar'd and fitted to receive thy love.
>
> (ll. 11–16)

Like Donne's *First Anniversarie,* "The Church Militant" deals
with history. Like the earlier poem, it is divided into parts by a
refrain. And like Donne's paean to Elizabeth Drury, Herbert's quinquepartite sequence bears at least a distant resemblance (for Jonson,
Donne's resemblances were not distant enough) to traditions surrounding the Virgin Mary.

Similarly, *The First Anniversarie* depicts the progressive alienation of man from nature, beginning with the Fall. During Donne's
"antiprogress," reflecting man's apostasy, the universe itself loses
its center ("The Sun is lost") and suffers irreversible decline to a
cadaverous state. In "The Church Militant," on the other hand, the
speaker interprets history through the use of three allegorical figures:
the Church, Religion, and Sin. Time is measured in the movements
of the sun, which are traced by the Church. In "The Church," life's
round was represented in the passage of one year; in "The Church
Militant," all of time is seen as the passing of one day: "one day is
with the Lord as a thousand years, and a thousand years as one day"
(2 Pet. 3.8).

This long day of history is divided into epochs by a refrain: *"How
deare to me, O God, thy counsels are! / Who may with thee compare?"*
Given the pessimistic bias of Fish's reading of this poem, it may
be well to observe that this quotation from the Psalms concerned
the sustaining value of God's Word, with its promises. To one
commentator this particular Psalm was: *"A meditation of the om-
nipresence of God, and a prayer that we may alwaies walk as in his
sight."*[36] Actually, Herbert's refrain is a pastiche of lines from verses
in Psalms 89 and 139, respectively:

> For who in the heaven can be compared unto the Lord?
> who among the sons of the mighty can be liked unto the Lord? (6)
> How precious also are thy thoughts unto me, O God:
> how great is the sum of them! (17)

Herbert's fusion of these verses into a refrain for his poem may help
to explain his purpose in making "The Church Militant" part of
The Temple and, having decided that, in placing the poem last,
rather than first or second, in the sequence. The issue hangs partly,
I think, on why he linked the two verses at all. Herbert did not
leave us a commentary on Scripture, much less one on the Psalms.
But as a clergyman and poet who loved and paraphrased the Psalms,

he was likely familiar with many of the popular expositions of the time. He may have believed, with one of his contemporaries, that the Eighty-ninth Psalm expressed the Prophet's gratitude for "the goodnes of God . . . For his testament and covenant, that he had made betwene him and his elect by Jesus Christ the sonne of David."[37] In the context of such a belief, much of Herbert's poem appears to be about "the great ruine and desolation of the kingdome of David, so that to the outward appearance the promes was broken." The corruption of the Church gave even the faithful reason to wonder at—and even doubt—the wisdom and benevolence of God's design. What, after all, was the meaning of a world in which the Church was overrun by Sin and in which darkness was always but one step behind the light? This is the drift of Fish's pessimistic view that the poem offers "less and less support for the speaker's periodic affirmations" (p. 151).

On the contrary, we must not underestimate the power of these "periodic affirmations." According to Calvin's exposition, Psalm 89 provides an eloquent answer to all doubts about God's governance of the world, for here King David addresses precisely those doubts encouraged by historical indications of Sin's hegemony, indications which Fish believes overwhelm the sense of Herbert's psalmic refrain. We need not quarrel with Fish's account of the power of Herbert's poem to elicit recognition of the havoc of Sin's progress in the world. The poem deals seriously with reasons for doubt. But then Michael's vision of the future, though intended to console Milton's Adam in *Paradise Lost* could be construed as support for Eve's defense of racial suicide: "Truth shall retire / Bestuck with sland'rous darts, and works of Faith / Rarely be found: so shall the World go on, / To good malignant, to bad men benign."[38] Until the third day, the fallen angels met Michael's legions "in even scale" (6.245). And on earth the balance between good and evil gives the faithless reason for despair. Why bear children if one son will kill the other? In *Paradise Lost,* Milton's theodicy requires the fullness of time to "justify the ways of God to men." Michael discharges his obligation to leave Adam "not disconsolate," but the hope that he gives man is not founded on the unreliable evidence of a given generation. Michael consoles Adam with the hope inherent in the total unfolding of the story of God's covenant with man. Hence, victory over the Adversary, and justification of man's existence as revealed in history, will be fully manifest only at the end of time.

It is just so with Herbert. As in *Paradise Lost,* so in "The Church Militant," passing generations appear "To good malignant, to bad men benign." And yet, for Herbert no less than for Milton, the promise of God's Word remains inviolate. Fish's lack of confidence in the numinous quality of the Psalmist's "counsel" as the antidote to historical evidences of Sin's triumph in time reflects no seventeenth-century theological opinion of which I am aware, and surely no attitude toward the Psalms amenable to Herbert's temperament. Indeed, Herbert resolves the relevant issue of such serious doubt as early in *The Temple* as "The Agonie." But earlier texts aside, Fish is wrong to describe "the speaker's periodic affirmations" in "The Church Militant" as weak and unconvincing, either in their use in organizing the whole into parts, or in their function as the basis of closure to the historical sequence. As the two sonnets on "The H. Scriptures" indicate, Herbert thought of God's Word as an all-sufficient affirmation, and so a valid basis for a powerful and convincing consolation. If, as Fish argues, "The Church Militant" suggests a "pessimistic, inconclusive, and anticlimactic" perspective (p. 144), it does so only to engage and absorb that point of view within a broader, more confident assurance. Fish's pessimistic misreading founders on a judiciously placed conjunction in the very passage that he takes to be the final evidence that Herbert's "chronicle does not end, but stops, offering less and less support for the speaker's periodic affirmations" (p. 151):

> Yet as the Church shall thither westward flie,
> So Sinne shall trace and dog her instantly:
> They have their period also and set times
> Both for their vertuous actions and their crimes.
> And where of old the Empire and the Arts
> Usher'd the Gospel ever in mens hearts,
> *Spain* hath done one; when Arts perform the other,
> The Church shall come, and Sinne the Church shall smother:
> That when they have accomplished their round,
> And met in th' east their first and ancient sound,
> Judgement may meet them both and search them round.
> Thus do both lights, as well in Church as Sunne,
> Light one anther, and together runne.
> Thus also Sinne and Darknesse follow still
> The Church and Sunne with all their power and skill.
> But as the Sunne goes both west and east;

So also did the Church by going west
Still eastward go; because it drew more neare
To time and place, where judgement shall appeare.
How deare to me, O God, thy counsels are!
  Who may with thee compare?

(ll. 259–79)

In the context of Herbert's Little Gidding audience, and of the poet's views on poetry, the Psalms, and Scripture in general, we cannot legitimately separate these lines from the wider poetic and religious context of the sequence. As in "The Flower" and elsewhere, so in "The Church Militant" it only *seems* that "The Church and Sunne" go more or less "entangled" on their way to a hopeless judgment. In the context of the Psalmist's "counsels," and of Herbert's syntax, the impasse implied by Fish's critical diction does not exist, because ("But as") as time passes toward the end that God's Word has promised, the Church comes closer and closer to the Marriage of the Lamb. Herbert's reader would have understood the way in which "The Church" and "The Church Militant" both end, though in different ways, with variations on an apocalyptic theme.

For believers, that is, Herbert's audience assembled at Little Gidding, God's "word is all." The "if" enters only with the limited understanding of the reader ("if we could spell"). To think of "The Church Militant" as pessimistic and / or unfinished is to advance a biblical perspective nowhere evident in Nicholas Ferrar's *Acta Apostolorum,* which proffers a more probable context for interpreting the close of *The Temple* than the hexameral tradition that Fish wants us to consider. "The Church Militant" does deal with history, which may seem to all but confirmed Pollyannas a profoundly unpromising narrative. But the poem's structure suggests the underlying figure of the Church as Christ's Spouse. However flawed the history of the Church is in time, she will meet her Spouse transfigured and in splendor. No serious estimate of "The Church Militant" can leave out of its account the underlying motif in *The Temple.* In its vast complexity, the Bible embodies man's total story. If "The Church" reconciles the life of some single "Christians destinie," "The Church Militant" records for the faithful reader the story of Christ's Spouse throughout history, from Old Testament times through the New Dispensation to the very end. And—for believers—that end is, as God's Word revealed, already complete and understood.

As Calvin wrote, then, Psalm 89 advanced an eloquent answer to precisely the questions posed by pessimism, "for here King David (or *whosoever he was that was the author of this Psalme*) . . . *commendeth in generall the power of GOD, whiche is seene in the whole governaunce of the world.*"[39] The verse paraphrased by Herbert (and rendered by Calvin, "For who shall be equall to the Lorde in the Cloudes, *or* bee like too the Lorde among the sonnes of the Gods" [fol. 49]) meant that "god reigneth alonly soveraien" in the heavens, and thus "that god doth actually dispose whatsoever is done in heaven and earth. For it were against reason, that the heavens beeyng created by God, should now be rolled by fortune: and that things should be mingled upon earth, either at the pleasure of men, or by chaunce and casualty" (fol. 49v). This passage from the Psalms was construed as a rejoinder to doubts raised by any particular in nature. All movements in space and time were perfectly guided, their ends known and ordained by an omniscient, omnipotent Creator. As we read in Ainsworth's *Annotations,* in Psalm 139 *"David praiseth God for his all seeing-providence."*[40]

Clearly, Herbert associated the Psalms with the idea of Providence. As F. E. Hutchinson points out, in Herbert's long poem entitled "Providence," "There are many echoes of Psalm civ which is headed in A. V. 'A meditation upon the mighty power and wonderfull providence of God' " (p. 518). Written in iambic pentameter, "Providence" (pp. 116–21) expresses the unique place of the poet in the divine scheme of things:

> Of all the creatures both in sea and land
> Onely to Man thou hast made known thy wayes,
> And put the penne alone into his hand,
> And made him Secretarie of thy praise.
>
> (ll. 5–8)

As "the worlds high Priest" (l. 13), man commits "a world of sinne" (l. 20) by refraining from praise of that "most sacred Spirit" (l. 25), which is "exact, transcendent, and divine" (l. 30). Here is a paradox that has proved difficult to more modern sensibilities. The poet can only express what he knows, and the only means of acquiring such knowledge is through gratitude for them:

> But who hath praise enough? nay, who hath any?
> None can express thy works, but he that knows them:

> And none can know thy works, which are so many,
> And so complete, but onely he that owes them.
>
> All things that are, though they have sev'rall wayes,
> Yet in their being joyn with one advise
> To honour thee: and so I give thee praise
> In all my other hymnes, but in this twice.
>
> (ll. 141–48)

The main theme of "Providence" concerns the harmonious plenitude of all created things. The speaker exults in the various orders of being, many of which are sensate creatures, whose eyes can see the evidences of God's power, but who never "know" their cause. Man is unique in his capacity to feel in debt. Gratitude is the means by which man knows the order that lies beneath the apparent diversity of things. Imitating the Psalmist, the poet sings a hymn of praise, imparting the evidence of his gratitude for and understanding of God's wonderful workmanship in making the world.

Likewise, in "The Church Militant," Providence guides history. As the progress of the Church unfolds, the speaker reminds himself at intervals of the orderliness of God's plan in creation. The lines treat of God's infinite "wisdom in the creation of man."[41] Thus, the refrain does more than invoke a meditative tone. Assuming that the special language employed enjoys (if I may coin a phrase) a privileged status, the refrain places the struggles depicted in "The Church" in a wider and final perspective. Affliction, doubt, despair—the painful experiences of life—are simply evidences of human limitation. Aspirations rooted in human powers share the insubstantial rewards of history. Only the real—that is, all that accords with God's will—endures. This was Herbert's theme in "The Church," and it is his theme in "Church Militant" as well:

> Almighty Lord, who from thy glorious throne
> Seest and rulest all things ev'n as one:
> The smallest ant or atome knows thy power,
> Known also to each minute of an houre:
> Much more do Common-weals acknowledge thee,
> And wrap their policies in thy decree,
> Complying with thy counsels, doing nought
> Which doth not meet with an eternall thought.
>
> (ll. 1–8)

Herbert's equation of God's "counsels" with this "eternall thought," and the identity of both with His "decree," though all-important to the shape of the poem, are not given sufficient weight in Fish's pessimistic account. Here in the opening lines of "Church Militant" Herbert states his providential theme. Throughout the poem, the progress of the minutes, hours, years, and ages that make up history unfolds, and in its entirety proves what is "Known also to each minute of an houre." At every moment—throughout all time— the world is governed by God's love.

Here and throughout "Church Militant" the emphasis is on God's Providence as seen in his creation. While it is true, as Fish observes, that Sin pursues the Church from the beginning of time "Much about one and the same time and place, / Both where and when the Church began her race, / Sinne did set out of Eastern *Babylon*, / And travell'd westward also"[ll. 101–104]), in the final analysis, Sin lacks substance. As the speaker exclaims in "Sinne" (II), "Sinne is flat opposite to th'Almighty, seeing / It wants the good of *vertue*, and of *being*" (p. 63). Like the darkness that will overtake the world before the dawn of eternal day, Sin and Death are creatures only of the illusory world of time. In God's mind, every instant and the sum of all instants aim at a single moment: "Nay, it [the Church] shall ev'ry yeare decrease and fade; / Till such a darknesse do the world invade / At Christs last coming, as his first did finde" (ll. 229–31). All of time past aimed at time present, all of time present aims at time future, and the sun moves steadily westward toward the nightfall of creation. The perfection of the providential design in history is nowhere better revealed than in this paradox of time. As the sun runs west, it comes east. As time fulfills its cyclic, self-destructive pattern, the Church moves unerringly toward the dawn of that wedding day envisioned by Saint John at Patmos:

> Thus also Sinne and Darknesse follow still
> The Church and Sunne with all their power and skill.
> But as the Sunne still goes both west and east;
> So also did the Church by going west
> Still eastward go; because it drew more neare
> To time and place, where judgement shall appeare.
>
> (ll. 272–77)

It is a mistake to omit emphasis where Herbert has resolutely imposed it: on the Second Coming. Pessimism appears only to critics who lend no credence to the Scriptures, which provide more to Herbert's text than a refrain: *"How deare to me, O God, thy counsels are! / Who may with thee compare?"*. One need not believe with Coleridge that only certain kinds of Christians are equipped to understand Herbert's poetry to concede that an appreciation of his notions of the Word might be helpful. From a purely human point of view, it may look as if the human race, with all its institutions (including the Church), has failed. But, for Herbert, as Sin and Darkness close around God's people—at just the moment when it seems the Adversary has prevailed—then will God's love be splendidly and finally manifest in Christ's return. Without that belief, the triumph of evil will seem as real, at the cosmic level of "The Church Militant," as the triumph of death seemed at times to the unenlightened pilgrim of "The Church."

The speaker of "The Church Militant" clearly sees what the speaker of "The Church" cannot see from the limited perspective of a single life, when time appears as a linear progression or decline (depending on the momentary placement of the soul in its inevitable swing between assurance and despair). As long as life exists, there will be physical motion and spiritual unrest. "The Pulley" is the relevant text, with its lovely balance between God's statement of the suffering imposed on man by his mere existence and his explanation of the eternal end of man's anxiety:

> Yet let him keep the rest,
> But keep them with repining restlesnesse:
> Let him be rich and wearie, that at least,
> If goodnesse leade him not, yet wearinesse
> May tosse him to my breast
> (p. 160, ll. 16–20)

But whether perceived from an individual or collective point of view, time tells only the one story of God's unchanging will. Just as in "The Church" the pain of human life was part of a larger design, so the trials and tribulations of the Church must also be seen in perspective of the timeless, only a part of which is available to man in time. Scripture, with the reader's hope based on its *"counsels,"* fills in the rest. It is true that "The Church Militant" seems like an appendix, but I suggest that it seems like an appendix to "The Church," and as such it is an appropriate denouement to the larger poetic structure of *The Temple*. The speaker of "The Church Militant," viewing creation in the fullness of time, emulates the soul's pilgrimage in "The Church" at a cosmic level. Here, the fits and starts involve whole civilizations. And the apparent basis for despair has found perceptive audiences in the twentieth century. But, for Herbert, the end, too, is known. Christ will be joined with his Spouse. The wedding celebration, known in time only through signs and hope, is nonetheless known through the poet's praise: "neare / To time and place, where judgement shall appeare." Then, the "bands of love" will be experienced as complete and uninterrupted joy: "So I did sit and eat."

Chapter Five

The School of
George Herbert

In 1961 A. Alvarez persuasively argued that a group of poets, notably Donne and Edward, Lord Herbert of Cherbury, wrote poetry to amuse each other. The coterie elements of their work tells something about the intellectual, social, and poetic tastes of a rather elite group. Its members were well educated—even a touch snobbish—and they were knowledgeable about the ways of London and the court. We have it on Ben Jonson's authority, Alvarez wrote, that when all England wept at the shocking news of Prince Henry's death, Donne took pains to compose "that Epitaph on Prince Henry . . . to match Sir Edward Herbert in obscurenesse."[1]

Modern critics, perhaps in rebellion against romanticism's emotional excesses, brought about a revival of interest in Donne, his associates, and his followers. The wit of their poetry, which Dryden ambiguously indicted as "metaphysical," suited the appetite of critics who wished to distance themselves from tastes and feelings of "the great unwashed." Donne's insouciant tone, even his tongue-in-cheek misogyny, met with favor as the banners of realism and pessimism were raised to signal a new sophistication in the intellectual centers of the Western world. With the revival of the metaphysicals came an appreciation of Donne's influence on poets beyond his immediate coterie of intellectuals in the first two decades of the seventeenth century. Echoes of Donne were heard and admired in Marvell, Lovelace, Cowley, Cleveland, and others. Some critics reduced the metaphysical revival to a renewal of interest in Donne and in those poets who sought to imitate him. A colleague of mine once said that the term *metaphysical poetry*, as normally used, refers only to certain aspects of certain parts of certain poems written by Donne. More pointedly, he argued that discussions of those poetic features described as metaphysical usually focus upon images found in the last three stanzas of "A Valediction: forbidding Mourning."

This argument may have been intended only to provoke discussion, but it is nevertheless a suggestive one. Donne's characteristic use of far-fetched comparisons, especially if they involve abstruse vocabulary from arcane disciplines, has much to do with what F. R. Leavis aptly called the "line of wit."[2] Edward, Lord Herbert of Cherbury, Marvell, Cowley, Crashaw, Cleveland—and even Milton (in "On the Death of a Fair Infant")—imitated the master's flair for the bizarre metaphor. In this chapter, we will examine the relationship of George Herbert to such typical features of Donne's poetry, and then consider the justice of including him in "The School of Donne." Finally, we will look at the impact of Herbert's own poetic practice on religious verse of the seventeenth and early eighteenth centuries, especially on those poets who sought to imitate Herbert, that is, to align themselves with the school of George Herbert.

Herbert and The School of Donne

It is probable, of course, that George Herbert knew Donne's poetry well. Alvarez writes:

The main channel of his [Donne's] influence was the Herbert family. The two sons of Donne's friend Magdalen Herbert were both deeply in debt to his poetry and both were friends of other writers supported in the same way. Edward, Lord Herbert of Cherbury, knew Donne well. . . . George Herbert, Edward's brother, was at Westminster with Henry King, who had been Prebendary of St. Paul's shortly before Donne became its Dean. Both he and Herbert received copies of the seal which Donne, according to Walton, sent to 'his dearest friends.' (pp. 46–47)

Significantly, Alvarez follows these biographical remarks with this statement: "It was, nominally, by following Herbert's example that Vaughan and Crashaw were gathered into the Metaphysical fold."

The validity of this genetic interpretation aside, we should observe the important differences between Donne and Herbert. If Herbert's was the example that others followed, in what way was that example different from Donne's? As Alvarez indicates, the personal connection between Donne and the Herbert family was strong. But the most important figures in that relationship, at least for Donne, were Edward and Magdalen Herbert, with whose names many of his poems are rightly linked. Herbert was twenty-one years younger than Donne and was only three years old when Donne took part in the Cadiz expedition. Herbert, of course, was a student of Trinity College, Cambridge. But, like Donne, he contributed to a volume commemorating the untimely death of Prince Henry. It should be noted, however, that the differences between Donne's poem and Herbert's two Latin poems on the subject are more interesting than the similarities. First, and most obviously, Herbert did not seek to compete with his brother, Lord Herbert—or with Donne—in writing sophisticated, torturous, obscure English verse.

Donne's "Elegie upon the untimely Death of the imcomparable Prince Henry" and Lord Herbert's "Elegy for the Prince," published in *Lachrymae Lachrymarum,* employ the macabre notion that the world, rather than Prince Henry, has died. Their mutual emphasis is on verbal pyrotechnics. Lord Herbert pursues a familiar theme in metaphysical poetry:

> For what are souls but love? Since they do know
> Only for it, and can no further go.
> Sense is the Soul of Beasts, because none can
> Proceed so far as t'understand like Man:
> And if souls be more where they love, then where
> They animate . . .
> Do we then dye in him, only as we
> May in worlds harmonique body see
> An universally diffused soul
> Move in the parts which moves not in the whole?[3]

Donne's poem, likewise, is concerned with such matters as "Gods essence, place, and providence,"[4] and the disposition of souls. Prince Henry was a stunning presence ("a torpedo" [l. 30]) in a world-sea of passive angler-princes. In taking Prince Henry to himself, the Deity has "spent his store" (l. 45). Since the prince was the essence of "Reason" in the world, it follows that the world's present unreason proves the past existence of the opposite state:

> But, now, for us, with busie proofs to come,
> That w'have no Reason, whould prove we had some:
> So would just lamentations. Therfore wee
> May safelier say, that wee are dead, then hee.
>
> (ll. 77–80)

The argumentative speaker pursues his disjunctive logic with admirable single-mindedness: the world and mankind are the opposite of what they might have been had the prince not departed. Though dead, the speaker summons the strength to wish that he "were an angel, singing" in the presence of Prince Henry. The apotheosis of the dead may be a traditional consolation of funeral elegies, but Donne's poem develops a line of thought and pursues it so relentlessly that the new god has only a world of cadavers left to worship him. Both poems draw outrageously on the apparatus of academic disputation. And both move away from the vocabulary and tone of consolation toward a diction that, with the best will in the world, must be described as strained, artificial, and speciously intellectual.

In contrast to both poems, Herbert's *"In Obitum Henrici Principis Walliae"* is marked by verbal restraint. For instance, its speaker strikes a self-effacing pose by rejecting the far-removed demands of Parnassus and Helicon:

> Muse, and also Phoebus, goodbye: let sorrow
> Tell me what to sing. Thus will I begin:
> O straying eyes of intellect, slowly
> Accumulate a timid strength, live
> While I portray a death.[5]

This pose presents us with a striking contrast: for this speaker, the prince *has* died. He was no "torpedo," nor does he, by some linguistic legerdemain, live on, while the corpses of those usually thought to be alive on earth stink in corruption. For Herbert's speaker, the pain of being alive has something to do with the arbitrariness of "the Fates," who could have taken Prince Henry in the Gunpowder Plot, but chose instead this inexplicable moment, as if to punish England: "Would not have famine or the plague's bleak / Visitation been a lesser punishment / Than the Prince's painful fate?" (p. 159). Just as the poem began, so it ends with a disclaimer regarding the power of poetry:

> Why then do I attempt to spill from me in words
> Dolorous concerns, as though for all our misery
> This were the medicine? In soundless fire
> Immoderate lamentation eats the heart,
> Just as when a river flows, the shallows
> Cry, and the depths are still.
>
>   (p. 161)

Noticeable here is Herbert's obeisance to the traditional aim of the funeral elegy to console, hardly the purpose of Donne and Lord Herbert. And yet we recognize in their posturing and ingenuity precisely what we often admire in metaphysical poetry. Its speakers wrack their brains with novel premises, relentless arguments, and unexpected comparisons. Herbert's self-effacing poem presents the reader with a less obstreperously arrogant speaker.

And in this self-effacing quality the poem is typical of Herbert. Notwithstanding the fact that Herbert wrote much poetry besides *The Temple,* comparisons between his verse and that of Donne are difficult, largely because Herbert did not write about secular love, a favorite topic of Donne and Lord Herbert. On this point, F. E. Hutchinson writes: "Apart from some complimentary verses to Bacon and other public personages, he wrote on religious themes only, whether in Latin or English, and Gosse has no warrant for asserting that Herbert destroyed his 'amatory verse' when at last he entered the ministry."[6] With respect to aspects of Donne's poetry admired by Cowley and Cleveland, we must hold, with Hutchinson, that at no time did Herbert write poetry in the mold of Donne's "The Extasie" or "A Valediction" or of Lord Herbert's "The Thought" or "Platonick Love" (I), (II), and (III). And if we consider such examples as "Communitie" and "The Flea," the disparity is only increased.

Although, on the one hand, the relationship between Donne and Herbert has always appealed to critics, on the other, when subjected to close analysis, it proves to be a problematic one. True, both men were priests. They were friends, if not close friends. And at times their poetry seems to be strikingly similar. Both poets draw on a wide range of human activities: law, real estate, commerce, horticulture, the Bible, history, astronomy, music, and so on. And yet, if Herbert belongs to "The School of Donne," he must be marked for limited matriculation. For the most part, though not exclusively, Herbert must be a student of Donne's relatively slim canon of religious poetry. The proviso is not merely precautionary, for as we have seen in chapter 4, Donne's *First Anniversarie,* a poem that Ben Jonson faulted because it was *not* one of Donne's *Divine Poems,* is similar in certain ways to Herbert's "Church Militant." But it could easily be pointed out that neither poem is typical of its author's poetic practice. Indeed, the examples that we find most often cited as indicative of metaphysical poetry are precisely those that make a strict yoking of Herbert and Donne more than a little awkward.[7]

Consider Dryden's remark that, rather than making love to his mistress, Donne's poet "affects the metaphysicks."[8] Four Herbert poems come immediately to mind: the two sonnets that he sent to his mother (but did not include in *The Temple*) and the "Jordan" poems. In the sonnets written, according to Walton, in the same year as Donne's *First Annivarsarie* (1610), the speaker complains about the state of poetry, which does not exhibit the passion of the *"Martyrs"*:

> Why are not *Sonnets* made of thee? and layes
> Upon thine Altar burnt? Cannot thy love
> Heighten a spirit to sound out thy praise
> As well as any she? Cannot thy *Dove*
> Out-strip their *Cupid* easily in flight?
>
> (p. 206)

More than faintly reminiscent of Sidney's "Leave me, ô Love," this sonnet presents the audience with a choice between mutable or transcendent love objects. Since divine love is not subject to despoliation ("which one day Worms may chance refuse"), the speaker chooses the spiritual alternative. As we read in the second of Herbert's sonnets sent to his mother, beauty passes, and therefore womankind is not a proper subject of poetry. So Herbert replaces Cupid with Divine Cupid.

The speaker in "Jordan" (I) even more trenchantly questions the propriety of romantic love as a poetic concern:

> Who sayes that fictions onely and false hair
> Become a verse? Is there in truth no beautie?
> Is all good structure in a winding stair?
> May no lines passe, except they do their dutie
> Not to a true, but painted chair?
>
> (p. 56)

The conflict here is between the speaker and the authority behind prevailing taste. Rhetorical questions delineate the adversary's argument, which values falsity above truth, and they insinuate, too, the appropriate answers. In effect, the very thing must take priority over a disguised (or "painted") version of it. The apposition here is similar to that in the companion sonnet; earthly love is tame in contrast to its pure, heavenly, authentic counterpart.

Again, these rhetorical questions leave no room for doubt about their expected responses:

> Is it no verse, except enchanted groves
> And sudden arbours shadow course-spunne lines?
> Must purling streams refresh a lovers loves?
> Must all be vail'd, while he that reades, divines,
>   Catching the sense at two removes?
>   (ll. 6–10)

Artifice and art diverge at all levels and in all areas of expression. Not only do painters and architects disguise the utility of their work, and in so doing draw attention to their craft, but poets transform these deceptions into fiction. And the same is true in poetry's treatment of love. Too often poets imitate the coyness and obtuseness of trite lovers by hiding their affections in poetic riddles. They are witty, finding out abstruse affinities in things seemingly unlike. They are, by all accounts, of "The School of Donne." But in so distinguishing their ideas from common sense, these poets separate themselves from the model of poetry with which the speaker resolutely aligns himself:

> Shepherds are honest people; let them sing:
> Riddle who list, for me, and pull for Prime:
> I envie no mans nightingale or spring;
> Nor let them punish me with losse of rime,
>   Who plainly say, *My God, My King*.
>   (p. 57, ll. 11–15)

Witty, artificial, secular poetry—the butt of the speaker's scorn— is nothing more than a game of chance. Its creators merely bet on the next figure of speech, the next quiddity of thought, the next startling image.

Clearly, Herbert's poem registers misgivings about those very features of poetry held in high esteem among Donne's coterie. Obscurity and plainness, like "Loves *oblique* . . . can never meet."

Herbert reminds his reader that Christ was the "good Shepherd," and that the Psalmist was a shepherd, too. He not only recalls that the good news of Christ's birth was first announced to humble shepherds, but he alludes also to the fact that God Incarnate humbled himself to be baptised in the Jordan River. The self-importance of the poet who labors to display his craft is inevitably at loggerheads with this model, which is one not only of virtue, but of art.

Although "Jordan" (II) similarly treats the subject of poetic pretense, it is a more personal poem, written in a more confessional mode. The poem is closely related to the first sonnet of Sidney's *Astrophil and Stella,* likewise a poem about poetic "invention" (Herbert's original choice for the title of this poem). Addressed to the self, Sidney's poem urges honest expression as the best means of writing to Stella: " 'Foole,' said my Muse to me, 'looke in thy heart and write.' "[9] Herbert's poem, addressed to a third party (one presumably interested in a narrative concerning the origins of poetry), deals with the lure of excellence in one's chosen craft:

> When first my lines of heav'nly joyes made mention,
> Such was their lustre, they did so excell,
> That I sought out quaint words, and trim invention;
> My thoughts began to burnish, sprout, and swell,
> Curling with metaphors a plain intention,
> Decking the sense, as if it were to sell.
>
> (p. 102, ll. 1–6)

Spurning fictions contrived with trite settings and phony sentiments, this poet takes for his theme a subject without reproach. Likewise, his intention is admirably plain. Thus, the one difficulty considered in "Jordan" (I), that of preoccupation with earthly subjects, does not appear. In "Jordan" (II), the speaker relates, in the past tense, his "plain intention" to describe his "heav'nly joyes." Unfortunately, during the process of composition, something happened to that "plain intention." Indeed, it seems that the poet became preoccupied with technical skills typical of the Donne coterie. Diction became an issue, with the implicit understanding that ordinary expression must be avoided. So the poet's thoughts changed, almost as if involuntarily, in luster, quality, and size (they just "began to burnish, sprout, and swell"), as during the process of composition, the poet changed places with the vendor.

Herbert's narrative delineates a laborious process, involving many possibilities considered and many revisions undertaken, during which the poet's focus shifts from "plain intention" to art. For how can ordinary language suffice to "deck" the august "sense" he has in mind ("Nothing could seem too rich to clothe the sunne" [l. 11])? Considering the "Jordan" poems as companion pieces, we see that "Jordan" (II) reverses the situation in the earlier poem. In "Jordan" (I), the poet criticizes conventional love-poets for their inordinate emphasis on secular love, with its attendant artifice. In "Jordan" (II), he confesses his own preoccupation with poetic technique. He has chosen the worthiest subject, but like the speaker of "The Thanksgiving," he has sought to respond to it with his own exertions and by his own gifts. And as in that response to "The Sacrifice," so here those gifts and those exertions being inadequate and pretentious, are (as self-conscious witticisms in poetry often prove to be) obtuse:

> As flames do work and winde, when they ascend,
> So did I weave my self into the sense.
> But while I bustled, I might heare a friend
> Whisper, *How wide is all this long pretence!*
> *There is in love a sweetnesse readie penn'd:*
> *Copie out onely that, and save expense.*
>
> (ll. 13–18)

In Sidney's *Astrophil and Stella,* the rhetorical problem is quite different: the poet, unable to decide what to say to his mistress, wonders how to avoid ridicule. He is anxious to conform his expression to the social situation, which is subject to perils of competition in love and in art as well:

> I sought fit words to paint the blackest face of woe,
> Studying inventions fine, her wits to entertaine:
> Oft turning others' leaves, to see if thence would flow
> Some fresh and fruitfull showers upon my sunne-burn'd braine.
>
> (ll. 5–8)

Although the stakes in "Jordan" (II) are different, sincerity is still the answer to writer's block: "Loving in truth, and faine in verse my love to show" (l. 1). Similarly, Herbert's speaker must express a "sweetnesse" that has already been "penn'd." Similarly aware of prior efforts to express the same feelings, the poets resolve their problems in different, even contrary, ways. Sincerity will liberate Sidney's poet from the bondage of "others' leaves" (that is, from conventional modes of expression), allowing him to express his own feelings. In Herbert, the poet finds that the business of writing has too much preoccupied him. He has thought too much, planned too much, written too much, and now recognizes that it is this baggage of himself as thoughtful, careful poet that impedes him from writing a truthful poem. A universe of linguistic possibilities exists and will remain forever. Aware of this, the poet becomes too taken with his status as a poet—thinking, choosing, revising without end. Rather than focus on his subject, the poet concerns himself *with* himself. The image behind "Jordan" (II) and "The Thanksgiving" is, of course, the Passion, and that image renders the poet's suffering ridiculous and phony as well. Until the middle of the final stanza, "Jordan" (II) is the poetic counterpart of "The Thanksgiving." In conclusion, the poem echoes Sidney's sonnet in such a way as to provide a poetic analogue to "The Reprisall."

As Rosemond Tuve has pointed out, in Herbert, remembrance of the Sacrifice has, as we see in "Divinitie" (pp. 134–35), poetic, as well as theological, meaning. [10] Men may use their wit as a weapon against the Almighty, but just as in the "Jordan" poems poetry often masks the truth, so in the highest matters, man's pretensions obscure what was originally "cleare as heav'n, from whence it came" (l. 14):

> But he doth bid us take his bloud for wine.
> Bid what he please; yet I am sure,
> To take and taste what he doth there designe,
> Is all that saves, and not obscure.
>   (ll. 21–24)

Likewise, in "Dialogue" (pp. 114–15), the conflict between guest and host is resolved by simple, direct instruction. The "honest" poet imitates the Passion by subduing the self (*"Follow my resigning"* [l. 28]).

Sidney's poet resolves to ignore external models: "Biting my trewand pen, beating my selfe for spite, / 'Foole,' said my Muse to me, 'looke in thy heart and write' " (ll. 13–14). This affirmation

of "the spontaneous overflow of powerful feelings" might have pleased
Wordsworth, but it is not the method of composition affirmed in
"Jordan" (II). Herbert's poet dispells the creative impasse by surrendering completely to a text already "penn'd," by *"resigning"* the
poetic self to the model of resignation. Sidney's poet-lover dissociates
creative expression from the reading of "others' leaves"; in contrast,
Herbert's poet commits himself to a species of divine plagiarism.

We see, then, that whereas Donne's spectacular linguistic gifts
are often marshalled without apology in the service of Eros, human
no less than divine, Herbert not only avoids the former, but even
in the service of the latter exhibits, if only in a rhetorical ruse,
ambivalent feelings toward the self-consciously poetic. It has not
escaped critics that even in the "Jordan" poems Herbert employs
the very tricks of language against which his speaker purports to
protest. He compares the formation of poetic figures with a game
of "Primero," but in so doing he also subordinates the writing of
poetry to the higher imperative *("Follow my resigning")* that is his
major theme in *The Temple: "the many spiritual Conflicts that have past
betwixt God and* [his] *Soul."*

The School of George Herbert

If seems clear, then, that George Herbert adjusted "the [Donnean]
line of wit" to suit his own purposes and that, if he belongs to the
school of Donne, he belongs to it in a different sense than does his
brother, Lord Herbert, whose poetry so often resembles that of
"Jack" Donne. Herbert's almost polemical efforts to distinguish his
aims and methods from those of contemporary love-poets express,
in fact, a sentiment at the farthest pole from Donne's typical employment of religious figures—sainthood, relics, martyrology—in
the service of profane love ("The Canonization," "Loves Deitie,"
"The Relique," "The Funeral"). It is true that Cleveland, Cowley,
Marvell, and others imitate Donne in his sometimes rakish, sometimes philosophical poses. On the other hand, younger poets also
emulated Herbert's stance of the isolated poet, dedicated to divine
poetry in a world slavishly committed to lyrics inspired by Venus.
Indeed, the evidence is strong that, during the same period that
saw the establishment of a "School of Donne," something like a
"School of Herbert" also arose. Poets who aligned themselves with
Herbert not only imitated or paraphrased his verse, but sought to

identify themselves with the attitudes so prominently exhibited in the "Jordan" poems. Indeed, they sought to identify themselves, not just with Herbert's poetic aims and practices, but with George Herbert himself.

First and most obvious, poets demanded that their works be recognized in relation to Herbert's *The Temple*. Volumes of verse issued from the pens of Herbert's successors with titles intended to declare Herbert's literary heritage. The most famous of these may be Richard Crashaw's *Steps to the Temple* (1648), but we think also of Christopher Harvey's *The Synagogue, Or, The Shadow of The Temple: Sacred Poems and Private Ejaculations: In imitation of Mr. George Herbert* (1640), Ralph Knevet's *A Gallery to the Temple*, Henry Vaughan's *Silex Scintillans* (1650), and the poetry of such other contemporaries and near-contemporaries as Thomas Washbourne, Mildmay Fane, Henry Colman, Samuel Speed, and Thomas Traherne. Of these, Harvey's work most closely follows the structural metaphors of *The Temple*, if with admittedly very different results. But all of these poets in their different ways harken back to Herbert's rhetorical pose reflecting a felt antagonism between the poets of divine and those of secular love.

Harvey's poetry may not be the most successful work composed by the school of Herbert, but it may be the most assertive of its Herbertian loyalties. A quotation from Pliny on the title page claims that *"Not to imitate the best example is the greatest folly."*[11] It does not take Harvey long to distance himself from such foolishness. Herbert's "The Dedication" begins, *"Lord, my first fruits present themselves to thee"* (p. 5); Harvey's "The Dedication" begins, "Lord, my first fruits should have been sent to thee' (sig. A3). *The Temple* moves from "The Church-porch" to "Superliminare" to "The Church." The opening sequence in *The Synagogue* (1640) goes: *"Subterliminare.* A stepping-stone to the threshold of Mr. *Herberts* Church-porch," "The Church-yard," "The Church-stile," "The Church-gate," "The Church-wals," "The Church," and "The Church-porch." Harvey associates himself with Herbert by virtually expropriating what he sees as the structural design of *The Temple*.

In *A Gallery to the Temple* [1641–1652?], Ralph Knevet's method is more discursive and yet more to the point. In his address "To the Reader," while allowing that he cannot "come neare [Herbert] in the excellencye of his high Enthusiasmes,"[12] Knevet takes comfort in his belief that he follows Herbert "in his Devotions" (p. 281).

It should be noted that Knevet considers Herbert one of the greatest poets who ever lived. Like Harvey, then, Knevet models himself after the best of poets. Knevet sees in Herbert the only modern evidence of the fact that "the Harpe, hath bene more glorious, and antique among Gods People, then famous with the Infidells" (p. 279). Indeed, he looks, not to the Greeks, but to the Hebrews of old for the source of true poetry: "For though it bee reported, that Orpheus by an harmonious touche of this instrument, did appease the strife of his mutinous Argonautes; yet wee are assured, that Hee who was the best of Kings, and of Men, by the like meanes expelled Satan the Prince of discorde" (p. 279). Just as King David surpassed his contemporaries in government and in poetry, so have divinely inspired authors in other ages accomplished feats loftier than those attributed to the noblest pagan authors:

And . . . yet it really appeares, that Moses, David, and Salomon have so farre surmounted, even bothe those Quires of the Greeke and Latine Lyrickes, in all those excellencyes, and ends, which hav[e] relation to this kind of poesye, that from a most divine Angelicall transcendencye, they seeme to looke downe on those laborious Antes of Helicon, and Parnassus. (pp. 279–80)

Moses occupies a special place in Knevet's pantheon. The most ancient of poets, Moses was also the best poet in two modes, "Epinician Song," a type employed upon the overthrow of the pharaoh, and "Panegiricke," a form used in Deuteronomy, chapter 32. But despite his great literary achievement, Moses would have been forgotten had it not been for Herbert, who, because of the *kind* of poetry in which he excelled, distinguished himself above all English poets. For the same reasons, Herbert also surpassed the greatest Italian poets, and so, implicitly, became the premier poet of the civilized world:

But I wonder not so much at the perfection of this entheated Heroe, as at the inadvertencye of our moderne wittes, who in this maturity of sciences, have appeared so barren concerning the production, of this most divine sorte of Poesye, that the species thereof might have bene number'd amongst lost Antiquities if our Pious Herbert (a name which I dare confidently affirme most aptly aggrees with the past and present condition of the person whom it denoted) had not by a religious cultivation, added new life to the wither'd branches, of this celestiall Balme Tree.—whereby

Hee hath not onely surpassed those of his owne Nation, but even the haughty Italians, who chalenge a priority in art, as well as devotions. (p. 280)

We cannot miss the cultural serendipity of this remark. Just as the Roman Catholic Church arrogates to itself "a priority in" religion, so its poetic counterparts arrogate to themselves "a priority in art." Thus, Knevet's regard for Herbert's poetry accords with his loyalty to the Church of England:

It is true, that their glorious Temples abounde with musicke, both vocall, and instrumentall, But all their Academicall Societyes of wittes cannot showe a Paralell to Herberts Temple. Their Inflammati of Padua, their Elevati of Ferrara, their Affidati of Pavia, their Intronati of Sienna etc: were so taken up with court-Corinna's, or countrey Laura's, that they quite forgott those lawes of duety, and gratitude, wherein they stood obliged to Heaven, for their endowments. (p. 280)

So, while conceding that Dante, Petrarch, Ariosto, Marino, and Tasso have written some creditable poetry, even (in Marino's case) poetry with admirably moral perspectves, Knevet finds the lot culpable in that they alike ignore "the principall end of Poesye," namely, composition of "that divine Poesye, which immediately aymes at the glory of the Almighty."

Knevet's main objection to the state of Continental poetry is that it reflects what today might be called secular humanism, but what would in more traditional nomenclature be designated that species of humanism associated with the Renaissance: Florentine syncretism, the frescoes of Michelangelo, and the like. Knevet's attitude makes him something of a seventeenth-century curmudgeon:

Yet concerning that divine Poesye, which immediately aymes at the glory of the Almighty (which at first was, and ever ought to bee the principall end of Poesye) They are all as mute as Seriphian Frogs: And in their bookes they render more expressions that tend to the flatterye of Man, then to the praises of the liveing God: And though they pretend to deliver incentives to vertue, yet they intend nothing more, then the interest of their owne vaineglory. (pp. 280–81)

Knevet does allow that one Italian has held to the high, original aims of true poetry, but that one exception, Dame Vittoria Colonna, only provides him with the rhetorical means of turning attention to her English contemporaries, on whom her lofty example is lost: "But it hath bene the ordinary taske of the moderne, and sublimated wittes of our Nation, to idolize some silly scornfull woman into a fooles Paradise of self admiration, and with store of such stuffe our late Rapsodyes abound; but in respect of these ingenious Brutes, I may say of Herbert: Sanctius his animal, mentisq capacius altae Deerat adhuc—For it was Hee who rightly knew to touch Davids Harpe" (p. 281). Amy M. Charles points out (p. 398) that Knevet may have admired Dame Vittoria Colonna's association with an elite group, including "Marguerite of Navarre, Cardinal Pole, Galeazzo da Tarsia, and Michelangelo (the two latter of whom addressed poems to her)," dedicated to reform of the Roman Catholic Church. But he may have valued her sonnets, too, because they daringly broke with Renaissance tradition by celebrating the nonadulterous love between her and her husband (p. 398n). Again, religious and poetic aims fuse in Knevet's mind as the single underlying criterion for judging poetry. This leaves only one poet in English history for him to admire. In the quotation from Ovid's *Metamorphoses* (1. 76–77), Knevet not only praises Herbert's mind, but more to the point, he sees him as holier than his fellow poets. In this holiness lay the secret of his—and Dame Vittoria Colonna's—poetic success.

Richard Crashaw's *Steps to The Temple* (1646) is probably the best-known work modeled on Herbert's *Temple*. But Crashaw's success as a poet, which is only now coming to be justly recognized, cannot be attributed to his fidelity to Herbert's poetic practices. As has often been observed, Crashaw is an English poet, sui generis. The manner in which he identified himself with the Roman communion makes his poetry seem, in comparison to that of other metaphysicals, outrageously sensual. And yet many of the linguistic pyrotechnics typical of Donne and Herbert are also those of Crashaw. Why, then, associate him with Herbert rather than with Donne? For two reasons: First, although he wrote, as Herbert did not, secular verse (including one of the more sensual of the many seventeenth-century paraphrases of Catullus's Carmen V), he is nonetheless remembered, as Donne is not, almost solely for his religious poetry. Second, like Harvey and Knevet, Crashaw sought to associate himself and his poetry with Herbert and *The Temple* rather than with Donne and *The Songs and Sonnets.*

The year after Herbert died, Crashaw made the acquaintance of

Herbert's friend Nicholas Ferrar, and in 1635 he visited Little Gidding. In the first edition of *Steps to the Temple* (1646), Crashaw included a poem entitled *"On Mr. G. Herberts booke intituled the Temple of Sacred Poems, sent to a Gentlewoman."* Had any reader missed the import of the volume's title, this poem would have brought Crashaw's admiration for Herbert to mind. As in Knevet, so in Crashaw, the speaker emphasizes the nature of Herbert's poetic interest: "Know you faire, on what you looke? / Divinest love lyes in this booke."[13] The figure of "Divinest love" is, in this context, complex, referring not only to the inspiration behind Herbert's poetry (the Holy Spirit), but also to Herbert himself: "Expecting fire from your eyes, / To kindle this his sacrifice." When the words of the poet meet the fire from this loving reader's eyes, the effect is the lighting of "his [Herbert's] sacrifice." George Williams suggests that Crashaw is punning on the title of Herbert's long poem, "The Sacrifice" (p. 68n). If so, we see how effectively the figure of "Divinest love" controls the movement of the speaker's thought. Inspired by God, the poet's lines come to life through the igniting power of a receptive reader, who not only understands Herbert's poem, but the Passion that is its true subject and the source of the poet's inspiration.

Indeed, Crashaw praises Herbert more enthusiastically and less critically than either Harvey or Knevet in that he does not view him as a mere poet who has wisely turned from secular to religious subjects. Crashaw presents Herbert (in much the same manner as he does Saint Teresa) as a being who has transcended human limits:

> When your hands unty these strings,
> Thinke you have an Angell by th' wings.
> One that gladly will bee nigh,
> To wait upon each morning sigh.
> To flutter in the balmy aire,
> Of your well perfumed prayer.
> These white plumes of his heele lend you,
> Which every day to heaven will send you.
> (ll. 5–12)

Just as he has subtly alluded to "The Sacrifice," Crashaw alludes also to "Easter-wings." Herbert is "an Angell," waiting on the "Gentlewoman," ready to lend his wings ("white plumes"), which are, as Williams notes, both the leaves of the book (especially the

leaf on which the two wings of Herbert's shaped Easter poem appear)
and the wings of Herbert's angelic spirit.

As is often the case when one poet aligns himself with the virtues
of another, Crashaw draws attention to his own accomplishments
and virtues. Herbert may be "an Angell," but as the giver of a
particular copy of *The Temple*—such is the legal nature of possessions
and gifts—the speaker insinuates himself into the very place rhe-
torically accorded to Herbert:

> And though *Herberts* name doe owe
> These devotions, fairest; know
> That while I lay them on the shrine
> Of your white hand, they are mine.
>   (ll. 15–18)

Again, the controlling figure of "Divinest love" permits the speaker
to identify completely with Herbert, both as the owner of the
"devotions" in *The Temple* and as the agent capable of transporting
the owner of that receiving "white hand" to heaven. "Divinest love"
transforms the reading of a poem ("The Sacrifice") into appreciation
of "Divinest love" behind the Sacrifice itself, just as God's love
transformed Herbert into "an Angell" waiting to transport the reader
"every day to heaven." And, at last, the same God whose loving
spirit had inspired *The Temple*, by the same means, prompts the
speaker to give this perfect gift, and in so doing transforms the
admirer into the owner of those "devotions" elsewhere attached to
"*Herberts* name."

Still, Crashaw's invocation of the Roman Muse distinguishes his
religious sensibility from Herbert's Anglo-Catholicism. If he sought
to emulate Herbert, and if he believed that he succeeded in that,
he nevertheless bent Herbert's texts to his own needs. "The Weeper"
lacks Herbert's typical restraint, and even at his best, as in "The
Flaming Heart," Crashaw's use of anaphora and of the periodic
sentence reflects an interest in altered states of mind that does not
sort well with Herbert's concern for the integrity of the individual
stanza or with his less mystical turn of mind. But Crashaw did write
poems that would not be out of place in *The Temple*. "Charitas
Nimia" (pp. 48–50), for instance, begins with a psalmic echo not
unlike the opening of many of Herbert's lyrics: "Lord, what is man?
why should he coste thee / So dear?" The intense, personal tone of

the soliloquy is typical of Herbert and his "School." And, as in poems like "The Thanksgiving," "The Reprisall," and " The Collar," the sequence of rhetorical questions, followed by a serene reply, is also a staple of the conflict between the soul and God in "The Church":

> What if my faithlesse soul and I
>   Would needs fall in
>   With guilt and sin?
> What did the Lamb, that he should dy?
> What did the lamb, that he should need,
> When the wolf sins, himself to bleed?
>
>   (ll. 49–54)

Perhaps Crashaw's poem emphasizes color somewhat more than do the relevant analogues in Herbert: "Why should the white / Lamb's bosom write / The purple name / Of my sin's shame?" (ll. 57–60), but the tone of remonstrance and self-doubt are familiar enough.

And the enormous disproportion between God's love and man's unworthiness is also their common theme. But Crashaw is closest to his master when he resolves his speaker's doubts in the closing quatrain of the poem:

> O my Saviour, make me see
> How dearly thou hast payd for me;
>   That lost again my Life may prove
> As then in Death, so now in love.
>
>   (ll. 63–66)

Not only Crashaw, but other imitators of Herbert were not monolithic in their aims and attitudes. In some ways, Joseph Beaumont resembles Crashaw more than he does Herbert, this in spite of the fact that twenty-one of the verses in his *Poems* bear titles in common with poems in *The Temple,* putting the literary relationship between the two works beyond question. And yet Beaumont's sensuality is reminiscent of Crashaw, as is his obvious fascination with Roman Catholicism. We may recall that Beaumont's friend Bishop Wren spent eighteen years in the Tower for such offenses as reading prayers in a surplice and that Beaumont himself was suspected of similar offenses. But suspicion aside, Beaumont wrote poems on such topics as the Virgin Mary in language that invites comparison with Crashaw:

> Haile, *Queen of Love,*
> Whose Sweets can move
> The *Spouse of Hearts* to lodge with Thee,
> And hither come
> From his bright Home
> To shrowd in thy Virginitie.
>
> Inlarge thy Breast
> To make a Nest
> For the *Eternall Dove . . .*
>   *("Annuncio B.V.")*[14]

And yet, like Ralph Knevet, Beaumont looked to Herbert as the savior of English poetry. In his long Spenserian poem, *Psyche* (1648), he praises *The Temple* as *"Devotion in Verse,"*[15] comparing Herbert favorably with Pindar. Again, "Loves Monarchie" sounds very much like "Love" (I) and (II), poems which, in turn, are related in form, theme, and tone to Herbert's two sonnets to his mother on the state of poetry. They begin: "Immortall Love, author of this great frame," and "Immortall Heat, O let they greater flame / Attract the lesser to it" (p. 54). Beaumont's poem begins "O MIGHTY LOVE" and, like Herbert's sonnets, employs typical Petrarchan conventions, while arguing that the true flame of love is known only by the divine poet. As in Herbert, so here, the poet's allegiance must be to the world's creator—authentic Love—Divine Cupid:

> Let other Muses
> Goe court the Wanton Mysterie
> Of lewd abuses
> Into a young Spruce Deitie:
> Mine does no homage owe, but unto Thee,
> Who, whilst the other's blind, do'st all Things see.
>   (p. 94)

But it is in the specific strategy of certain poems that Beaumont betrays his greatest indebtedness. He borrowed, if not as abundantly as from *The Temple,* titles and topics from poets other than Herbert: Donne, Crashaw, Vaughan. But we cannot miss the influence of Herbert's dramatic technique in such Beaumont poems as "The Little One's Greatness," "Love's Adventure," "The Sluggard," "The Combat," and "The Complaint." Again and again, he develops the Herbertian conflict as a speaker struggles in a situation in which his only hope lies in being overwhelmed: "MIGHTY *Love,* oh how dost Thou / By not fighting, overthrow" ("The Complaint," p. 310). But it is in those moments of direct address to Divine Cupid, as in "The Complaint," that Beaumont's allegiance to the school of Herbert shows most clearly:

> Gentle Love, oh neerer still,
> Neerer yet, that I may feel
> What thou art, by feeling Thee;
> Not by Contrarietie.
> (pp. 310–11)

Beaumont may lack the intensity and restraint of Herbert, but he does often grasp a thematic constant of "The Church." He recognizes and tries to emulate the tension often developed within Herbert's speaker between his own "restless importunitie" and the "*DE-SIGNE*" intended by the "Great *Lord of Love.*" In "Submission" (pp. 337–39), one of his most interesting attempts to imitate this aspect of Herbert's poetic technique, the speaker recognizes a recurrence of familiar distress: "Storms of Disquiet," "Tyrranous Delight," "pleasing Restlesness":

> A thousand times my Thoughts I chode,
> And then as oft those Chideings did recant:
> Against my Self I boldly stood,
> And when I firmly ment
> This Side should Victor be, the other
> Soon trampled down his dareing Brother.
> (p. 338)

Beaumont's expression of "design" reminds us of Herbert's similar use in "The Crosse," and it seems directed toward a similar apposition between the speaker's will and God's. The poem may close less succinctly or surprisingly than does "The Crosse," but the dramatic resolution is nonetheless reminiscent of that poem, and of " The Reprisall" and "The Flower" as well:

> O mighty LORD of GOODNES, my
> Most aenigmatik Greif appeals to Thee:

Use, Use thine own Authority
Both upon it, and Me.
No more will I own this DESIGNE
Unless it may comply with Thine.

(p. 339)

I realize that we find elements of the same conflict in Donne,
too, in "Batter my heart" and "Good Friday, 1613. Riding Westward." But in Herbert it is a defining feature of his best poems,
and I doubt that we can say this of Donne, whose striking versatility
can be a bane (as in "La Corona") as well as a blessing. This is the
aspect of Herbert's poetry that poets sought to emulate—not the
scintillating verbal skill, but the intimate rapprochement of a de-
spairing soul with the source of "Rest." Again, this is what we see
in Henry Colman's poetry. Karen E. Steanson, to whom we owe
gratitude for making Colman's work available to scholars, thinks
of Herbert as "a spiritual pattern and a literary master—the ground
from which Colman's own achievement would spring,"[16] and almost
the same could be said of others who wrote during the period of
the Civil War and shortly after: Thomas Washbourne, Mildmay
Fane, Samuel Speed, Henry Vaughan, and Thomas Traherne. Steanson points out how Colman's *Divine Meditations* (1640) imitates not
just the context but the form of *The Temple*. Thus, we find poems
shaped like altars and wings, acrostics on the name of Jesus, companion poems on the Eucharist modeled on Herbert's "The Invitation" and "The Banquet" ("The Invitation" and "On the Lords
Supper"). Moreover, the entire sequence is divided into "sections
of the Eucharistic ritual" (p. 40); the sequence begins with a shaped
poem entitled "The Altar" and ends with one shaped like a Cross
("Sinnes Sacrifice"). But, as Steanson cogently argues, Colman or-
ganizes the parts concerning the Eucharist into one whole, in which
the speaker struggles to make sense out of the vicissitudes of Christian life: "the poet's search for his true identity" (p. 34).

Again, with this feature we can discriminate the Donneans from
the Herbertians. Colman disclaims wit and eloquence as devices.
He writes only as a remedy to affliction. If, as in Beaumont, the
liturgy provides a structural framework for Colman's *Divine Meditations,* affliction remains the speaker's primary theme and focus. It
is this thematic interest that links Colman more securely to Herbert
than to Donne. Donne cannot take affliction seriously. Even when

his speaker is on his deathbed, with doctors peering down at him, he grasps for the fortuitous linguistic coup. The doctors are cartographers, and he's their map. Primero! The witty poet wins.

Colman's "On Affliction" aims in another direction. And yet, if that is toward Herbert's thematic interest, it must be said that the emotional content of the poem is very different indeed. Colman's meditant repudiates almost from the start the source of anxiety of many Herbert lyrics, as he declares that "Affliction is a sure and certaine signe / Of Gods exceedinge love" (p. 143). Where Herbert's speaker often opens with a serious case of conscience, sensing his affliction as a sign of God's displeasure, Colman's speaker begins with certainty rather than doubt. And the meditant's state of mind is apt only to improve on that sense of assurance. Indeed, unlike Beaumont's sufferer, Colman's meditant prays for "Grace" just in case the situation of distress should ever arise (which, we know from the author's own statement, it has in the past). He remembers pain, but never cries out from the depths of its despair. He may not even recall those depths. Instead, he sees affliction as a sign of "guilt," and so he prays that should that occasion ever arise, he will be made grateful for it:

> But this the least, for thou in mercy hast
> Still scourg'd me from
> My ill, and by affliction made me tast
> My guilt, I pray thee let it be
> Happie for me, thou hast afflicted me.
>
> (p. 144)

Thus the poem moves from certainty to gratitude. Suffering is in the remote past, and although the poem deals with affliction, it does so only indirectly.

Poets of the school of George Herbert exhibited a range of skills and aptitudes. Thomas Washbourne is truer to Herbertian *practice* in handling the typically Herbertian theme of affliction. When at his best Washbourne was very effective in achieving the dramatic, deftly turned ending that we associate with Herbert. I am thinking now of such poems as "Math. 26.39," "1 Cor. 6.19," "2 Cor. 12.10," "Upon Divine Love," "Upon his walking one day abroad," and "Upon his late Ague, or the new Feaver, as it was call'd." In "Upon his late Ague," the speaker cries out (in language reminiscent

of "The Crosse"), "What a strange thing's this Ague?"[17] Unlike
Colman's speaker, he does not merely remember suffering. He suf-
fers. He sweats. He reviles his physicians, concluding that even
Faustus, by casting a spell, could do a better job of healing him.
By his fevered train of thought the speaker is prepared for the
resolution of doubts articulated in the poem:

> I wil turne Conjurer, but an holy one,
> And with my prayers to heaven exorcise
> This evil spirit thus; Let God arise
> With healing in his wings, and first begin
> To heal my souls disease and sicknesse, sin,
> Then let this great Physician apply
> A salve to cure my bodies malady;
> Thou that didst legion with a word expel,
> But speak the word, thy servant shal be wel.
>
> (pp. 134–35)

The closing couplet surprises and satisfies, not only because of the
neat way in which the figure of Faustus conjuring is developed in
apposition to Christ's ministering to the man possessed: "For he
said unto him, Come out of the man, thou unclean spirit" (Mark
5.7). The fevered recollection of the Faustus narrative has a demented
relationship in the speaker's mind to his own condition, which is
desperate. He is suffering with a fever that his doctors cannot cure,
just as Faustus suffered with a hunger for power that worldly success
could not satisfy. But the difference is that, in his dreamlike, fevered
state, Washbourne's speaker only intimates his doctors' impotence
by his fantasied alternative of employing black magic for a cure. By
trafficking with the devil, Faustus separated himself from God.
Christ expelled the demons from the man possessed, who, drawn
to him, wished to be his servant. It is the way in which just the
right biblical text is "collated" in just the right way at the right
time—here, to heal the mind by a fortuitous analogy between one
rendered hopelessly demented (Faustus) and another mercifully redeemed ("My name is Legion")—that exhibits Washbourne's pre-
cocious study of Herbert.

Mildmay Fane, it seems to me, is like Washbourne in that he
often successfully imitates Herbert at his best. He does so not only
in his dramatic technique, but also in his experimental attitudes
toward stanzaic patterns and rhyme schemes. In *Otia Sacra* (1648),

echoes from Herbert are common, and we find here, too, the Herbertian play on words, acrostics, and emblems. From the outset,
the poet in the work proclaims his sole interest to be those subjects
"consonant with holy things."[18] By now we recognize this as nothing
less than a leitmotiv of the school of Herbert. Perhaps "My Reformation" is Fane's most graceful imitation. In stanzas of fifteen
lines, the speaker meditates on the disproportion in man's life between what God has given and what man returns in virtuous action.
The uneven line lengths and bewildering rhyme scheme (the first
stanza scans, if I am not mistaken, *a b a c b a d e a f d f g f e*) remind
us of "The Collar," and it seems clear that Fane intends the un-
evenness here to reflect the "Crackt estate" of man's soul (p. 52).
Like Herbert, Fane explores this mental condition through various
figures, one of which—that of the captive—provides the basis for
resolution of what the earlier stanzas established as an irreconcilable
conflict between God and man. The speaker associates the figure of
capture with that of hostage, which suggests, in turn, the possibility
of liberation in a third, apposite, association of "Ransome." Accordingly, the poem closes with a sense of ease and renewed perspective, reminiscent of Herbert, derived from that sequence of
thought:

> Not what I will
>   To speak,
>   Or doe My fill,
>   As Appetite,
> Not Reasons Fescue shall direct;
>   But with that Skill,
> Thy Gracious Mercies shall infuse
> To make me truly sensible of those;
>   Whilst I the Fetters break,
>   And so detect
>   That which did me abuse,
>   My Young years,
>   Which were light,
>   Too void of fears,
> That so I might the rest for Thee compose.

> (p. 53)

It is to such lines as this that Donald M. Friedman refers when he
writes that throughout the volume Mildmay Fane echoes Herbert

"most often."[19] Fane's poem effectively sets up this last pentameter line, and we enjoy it partly because we remember another closing line (from *The Temple*): "That thou mayst fit thy self against thy fall" (p. 65).

The more one reads in the period, the more convinced one will become that the school of Herbert had a large and enthusiastic student body. Consider the joyful spirit with which Samuel Speed openly avows his poetic affiliation with Herbert in *Meditations Divine and Moral* (1677):

I know it is a general humour in this Age, to think no Verse good but what is scurrilous and profane; nor do I promise Elegancy in my stile, that being more proper for dramatick than divine Poesie. Nay, such is the looseness of this Age, that many are of opinion, that Divinity in verse is unpleasant to the ear and to the heart: let such be convinced by the Psalms of *David*, or the Song of his Son *Solomon*. Divine Verse hath these two operations: it is pleasant, and makes an impression in the memory of the Reader; so true is that of the excellent Geo. *Herbert*, University-Orator of *Cambridge:*

> *A verse may take him who a Sermon flies,*
> *And turn delight into a Sacrifice.*[20]

Obviously, Speed had read "The Church-porch" often enough to believe that he had memorized this couplet. More important than his mistaken belief is the fact that many of the poems in *Prison-Pietie* are modeled on specific texts from *The Temple*. For instance, "The Petition" is Speed's experiment with three stanzas of triplets, with trimmed rhymes, in imitation of Herbert's "Paradise" ("brought . . . rought . . . ought"). We have poems with Herbertian titles ("The Thanksgiving," "Antiphon,") and a sequence on "the last things": "On Death," "On Judgment," "On Heaven," ["On Hell"]. We find the virtual lifting of lines and figures from *The Temple,* as in "On Sin" ("Sin is such an uncouth thing, / I cannot well define it" [p. 147]) and in "The Wish" ("Oh, that I once were in that City" [p. 112]). Speed shamelessly expropriates figures of land tenancy, landlords, rent, and the like, in such a way as to render his borrowings impossible to miss. Like Henry Colman, he writes a shaped poem entitled "The Altar," replete with paraphrases from his Herbertian model (p. 72). But, in an important sense, Speed's address to the "Christian Reader" is more revealing than all of the echoes, imitations, and paraphrases of Herbert. He thinks of Herbert's poetry on the same level as Scripture, equating *The Temple* with the Psalms and the Song of Songs. Father and son built one temple of wood and stone, and in their divinely inspired poetry they provided the models for the construction of Herbert's *Temple*. Speed understood this providential connection to be the outcome of a literal and spiritual genealogy, leading from the House of David through Christ to Herbert, and thence to such followers—Vaughan called them *"Converts"*—as Speed, Traherne, and Vaughan.

Traherne and Vaughan

We turn now to the two most talented followers of Herbert, Thomas Traherne and Henry Vaughan. Like Herbert, both poets are remembered for their religious verse, but their work reflects rather different literary and religious sensibilities. And, of course, Vaughan wrote poetry dedicated to those very profane subjects that the school of George Herbert seems consistently to disparage. Furthermore, unlike Herbert, both Vaughan and Traherne exhibit imagery and themes closer to the mystical Neoplatonism popular at Cambridge than to the prevailing thought of such Anglican apologists as Richard Hooker. Neither poet was especially attracted to the Passion as the central focus of his poetry; as we have seen, in Herbert, that event is the emotional center of the speaker's doubts and anxieties and, as such, the major thematic interest in "The Church."

If the validity of this assertion can be conceded, we have a significant basis for comparison between Herbert and these two latter-day followers. One can point, for instance, to the fact that Vaughan's "The Passion" is seldom anthologized and seems atypical of his poetic sensibility. Likewise, even though the Crucifixion provides an emphatic structural focus in the "First Century" ("And our Saviors Cross like the Centre of Eternity is in Him" [1.54, p. 188]), for Traherne that event with its associated images suggests a means of union between the self and "all" that is Divine: "He that is in all, and with all, can never be Desolat. All the Joys and all the Treasures, all the Counsels and all the Perfections, all the Angels and all the Saints of GOD . . . All the Kingdoms . . . All . . . all."[21] As is often the case with Traherne, repetition is a syntactic key to his use of what I have elsewhere called a "rhetoric of erosion."[22] The more the speaker emphasizes the composite totality of "all," the less significant becomes the isolated, eccentric particular. In Traherne, the Crucifixion is an event which transforms all time and all goodness into one amalgamated act of love:

The Cross of Christ is the Jacobs ladder by which we Ascend into the Highest Heavens. There we see Joyfull Patriarchs, Expecting Saints . . . Apostles . . . Doctors . . . All Nations . . . Angels Praising. That Cross is a Tree set on fire with invisible flame, that Illuminateth all the World. The Flame is Lov. (1.60, p. 191)

The emphasis here and often elsewhere in Traherne is on dissolving boundary lines between people and things, or between images and their commonly believed opposites. He does this by loading his lines and sentences with thoughts, images, considerations, statements, tergiversations, reservations, additions, subtractions—any apposite mental concern that might shift the mind from the definite and finite, and therefore limited and misleading, conception of the subject. Even the soul's colloquy with Christ as he hangs upon the Cross (1.64) must slide into its opposite (blood, tears, adoration, "GLORY," riches) and into the inevitable return to Traherne's major theme of gratitude: "Had I been alive in Adams steed, how should I hav Admired the Glory of the world!" (1.65, p. 194).

Likewise, Vaughan is more at ease with figures and developments of them suggesting the tenuousness of spatial and temporal distinctions than he is with those associated with the Eucharist and the liturgy. This can be so even when his subject involves figures prominent in the Passion story. For instance, in "Cock-crowing," one of Vaughan's greatest poems, the crowing of a cock does not remind the speaker of the Sacrifice ("a Sunne, by rising set"), but of the coming of the light, which the speaker—like Peter, who denied Christ three times before the cock crowed twice—is somehow not yet the proper vessel to receive. But in Vaughan the emphasis is always on the tenuousness of the barrier separating the soul from God. In "Cock-crowing," it is like the veil torn asunder at the Crucifixion:

> Onely this Veyle which thou hast broke,
> And must be broken yet in me,
> This veyle, I say, is all the cloke

> And cloud which shadows thee from me.
> This veyle thy full-ey'd love denies,
> And onely gleams and fractions spies.[23]

As in "The Retreate," here Vaughan suggests the ephemeral nature of man's apprehension of God. Only in isolated moments of rapt attention does the soul catch the longed-for "glimpse" of those "shadows of eternity" (p. 419). Indeed, what is interesting in both of these typically Vaughanian poems is the conviction, similar to that often found in Traherne, that one sense is too narrow to perceive or convey the nature of this transcendent experience. Thus, the visual sense is suddenly abandoned for the tactile: "But felt through all this fleshly dresse / Bright *shootes* of everlastingnesse" (ll. 19–20). And yet while the shift from the visual *seems* appropriate to the speaker's insight, it is presented only to be itself abandoned. The speaker feels the quality of brightness once apprehended in "a white, Celestiall thought."

Similarly, toward the end of "Cock-crowing," the speaker senses the tenuousness of the light that remains through the darkest night, like a seed, inside the cock, and inside of man:

> O thou immortall light and heat!
> Whose hand so shines through all this frame,
> That by the beauty of the seat,
> We plainly see, who made the same.
> Seeing thy seed abides in me,
> Dwell thou in it, and I in thee.
>
> (ll. 19–24)

Here, the clear echo from Herbert's "Love" (I) and (II) ("Immortall Love," "Immortall Heat" [p. 54]) only points up an interesting difference between the two poets. In Herbert, even the sonnet form, with the tightly closed voltas, delivers the typically Herbertian sense of reassured and calm resolution of the material within the poem: "All knees shall bow to thee; all wits shall rise, / And praise him who did make and mend our eies" ("Love [II], ll. 13–14). This is not the usual development in Vaughan, and it is not the development in "Cock-crowing." Comparison between the fourth stanza and the seventh (quoted earlier) suggests that the speaker's prayer is only partially answered. The speaker prays for an indwelling of the light, only to observe that a hindrance stands between that "immortall

light and heat" and his soul. As in "The Retreate"—and also in
"Regeneration"—Vaughan elicits a sense of the imminent, but elusive, rush of the Spirit, which will overwhelm the tenuous impe-
diment between the soul and God.

Vaughan's typical emphasis is on the yearning for a union that
eludes man as he strays further and further from the source of light.
In a manner typical of such mystics as Saint Teresa and Saint John
of the Cross, he represents the quality of that union as tenuous and
elusive: sudden, brief, often only remembered from childhood ("The
Retreate"). For the most part, humankind is estranged from the
light, though as in the cock, a tiny seed of radiance remains, yearning
for absorption in an ocean of dawn's light. In the "dark night of
the soul" (man's "second race" through time), clouds and shadows
temporarily and tenuously bar man from immediate union with
God. Thus, both "Regeneration" and "Cock-crowing" end in echoes
from the Canticles, long a favorite of mystical writers, who inter-
preted its erotic figures as expressions of that desired union:

> O take it off! make no delay,
> But brush me with thy light, that I
> May shine unto a perfect day,
> And warme me at thy glorious Eye!
>   O take it off! or till it flee,
>   Though with no Lilie, stay with me!
>   (ll. 43–48)

The speaker of Herbert's "Church" "sighs and "grones" for reassurance, which comes in a fortuitous recognition of the way in which
the present problem has already been resolved in Scripture, especially
in the life of Christ. Vaughan turns to Scripture, too, but, as here,
his speaker is more inclined to texts associated with what the mystics
thought of as its "unitive" or "experimental" meaning.[24] Herbert's
meditant looks for "rest," Vaughan's for union with God as experienced through an altered state of mind. Thus, since Traherne's
interests are closer to Vaughan's than to Herbert's, we might expect
their poetry to exhibit structures, thought, imagery, and tensions
reflecting religious aims and interests quite different from those of
Herbert.

And yet, despite these apparent contrasts in religious and poetic sensibilities, both Traherne and Vaughan *are* of the school of George Herbert. With respect to the latter, as Jonathan F. S. Post points out in *Henry Vaughan: The Unfolding Vision* (1982), there are virtually no limits to the number of specific "verbal parallels" one can find between *The Temple* and *Silex Scintillans* (1650).[25] And although, as has been said, Vaughan did write secular poetry, he follows Knevet, Crashaw, Washbourne, and others in repudiating the dominant poetic interest of the Donneans. Thus, as Post correctly observes, Vaughan declares himself a *"Convert"* to Herbert's "holy *life* and *verse*" (p. 391). Further, in Vaughan, we find many instances of the poet's declaration of allegiance to the poetics of George Herbert. Like Harvey and Knevet, he associates his first volume of religious verse with *The Temple* by sharing the subtitle of Herbert's work: *Silex Scintillans: or Sacred Poems and Private Ejaculations.* And in his "Preface To the following Hymns," published with part 2 of the work five years later, Vaughan questions the state of English poetry, especially as evidenced in "those ingenious persons, which in the late notion are termed *Wits*" (p. 388). The impact of their self-indulgence has been the proliferation of *"impure thoughts* and *scurrilous conceits"* (p. 389), which defile both author and audience. Unhappily, Vaughan recognizes his own culpability in this matter: "And here, because I would prevent a just *censure* by my free *confession,* I must remember, that I my self have for many years together, languished of this very *sickness"* (p. 390). Sensuality has joined with impiety, and even with the dashing of Scriptures and of holy things, in the writings of the most honored authors of the nation. In a line of thought that would not be out of place in *Areopagitica,* Vaughan admits that "the suppression of this pleasing and prevailing *evil,* lies not altogether in the power of the *Magistrate"* (p. 391). If the presses are silenced, then these vile entertainments will be promulgated in manuscript form.

Just as he has admitted how thoroughly his poetic impiety was a fault which only he could remedy, Vaughan extends the same notion to the state of English poetry. Poets themselves require a change of attitude: "The true remedy lies wholly in their bosoms, who are the gifted persons, by a wise exchange of *vain* and *vitious subjects,* for *divine Themes* and *Celestial praise."* One ought not to be surprised that at this point Vaughan declares himself to be an imitator of and a *"Convert"* to the poetic practices of Herbert:

The first, that with any effectual success attempted a *diversion* of this foul
and overflowing *stream*, was the blessed man, Mr. *George Herbert*, whose
holy *life* and *verse* gained many pious *Converts*, (of whom I am the least)
and gave the first check to a most flourishing and admired *wit* of his time.
After him followed diverse,—*Sed non passibus aequis.* (p. 391)

Vaughan pays homage here to Herbert, not only as a poet, who has
already turned to divine themes and therefore shown him the way
to alter his vain course, but as a "blessed man, . . . whose holy
life," implicitly, takes precedence over his *"verse."* The reason that
Herbert surpasses him is that he wrote from "a true, practick piety."
Those who practice only his poetic techniques cannot hope to be
convincing. Hence, Vaughan presents himself as a novice following
in the footsteps of a saint: "but he that desires to excel in this kinde
of *Hagiography*, or holy writing, must strive (by all means) for
perfection and true *holyness*, that a *door may be opened to him in heaven*,
Rev. 4. 1. and then he will be able to write (with *Hierotheus* and
holy *Herbert*) A *true Hymn*" (p. 392). Post points out how completely
this view required Vaughan to repudiate his earlier secular verse:
"One of Vaughan's first duties was to erase from his verse the
memory of his past masters. Under Herbert's schooling, nearly all
books of poetry other than *The Temple* become, at best, 'broken
letters scarce remembred.' " ("Vanity of Spirit" [p. 77]).

Conversely, Traherne had no reason to renounce his earlier work,
but he did nevertheless make a clear statement of his poetic association with Herbert. In *"The Author to the Critical Peruser"* (pp. 3–
4), purportedly speaking in his own voice, he states his aim of
writing so as to expose with his "Simple Light" and "transparent
Words . . . the highest Mysteries" (l. 3–5). Like the speaker of
the "Jordan" poems, and that of *Astrophil and Stella* before him,
"The Author" juxtaposes the "Simple," "lowly" poet and the more
leaden minds able to perceive only what is obvious to the senses.
Indeed, in this declaration of his poetic views, Traherne clearly has
the "Jordan" poems in mind:

> No curling Metaphors that gild the Sence,
> Nor Pictures here, nor painted Eloquence;
> No florid Streams of Superficial Gems,
> But real Crowns and Thrones and Diadems!

> That Gold on Gold should hiding shining ly
> May well be reckon'd baser Heraldry.
>
> (ll. 11–16)

Like the "Jordan" poet, the speaker distinguishes the "easy Stile" from the problematic language of those "blazing Prodigies" who speak in a mysterious language only to "amaze" the reader. As in Herbert and Sidney, so here the sharpest distinction is also the simple one between the real and the phony ("A clearer Stream than that which Poets feign" [l. 18]). Some poets only play linguistic games:

> Ransack all Nature's Rooms, and add the things
> Which *Persian* Courts enrich; to make Us Kings:
> To make us Kings indeed! Not verbal Ones,
> But reall Kings, exalted unto Thrones;
> And more than Golden Thrones! 'Tis this I do,
> Letting Poëtick Strains and Shadows go.
>
> (ll. 31–36)

Clothing, jewelry, riches—the problem is that poets too often value such trivial artifacts above the highest art, which is best seen in the wonderful workmanship of the body itself. The lines in praise of man's eyes and bones and joints are typical of Traherne. By failing to appreciate the smallest details of the body, poets of limitation limit the soul as well as the body, and in so doing separate themselves from God:

> Nor yet the *Soul,* in whose concealed Face,
> Which comprehendeth all unbounded Space,
> GOD may be seen; tho she can understand
> The Length of Ages and the Tracts of Land
> That from the *Zodiac* do extended ly
> Unto the *Poles,* and view *Eternity.*
>
> (ll. 55–60)

This statement of the poet's credo is only one of many indications of Traherne's link with the school of Herbert. As we see in the *Thanksgivings,* Traherne like Herbert looked to David as his model, not only as a poet, but as a proper man. The Psalms were to be emulated (as was Herbert, who emulated them) because David was

the one who perfectly "Enjoyed Himself." As I have elsewhere
pointed out (*Expanded Voice,* p. 141), David was, for Traherne as
for Herbert, the poet who embodied the comprehensive soul:

> A Shepherd, Soldier, and Divine,
> A Judge, a Courtier, and a King,
> Priest, Angel, Prophet, Oracle did shine
> At once; when He did sing.
>
> (p. 300)

Like Herbert, Traherne drew heavily on Scripture, often paraphras-
ing it; and like Herbert he wrote a wide variety of types of poems:
meditative poetry, verse paraphrases, apothegms, epigrams, hymns,
long poems in heroic couplets, and the like. But probably it is in
the meditative poetic sequence that Traherne reveals his strongest
alliance with the Herbertians. He wrote two of them, and both
begin with poems about birth. The Dobell *Poems* begins with "The
Salutation," the other with "An Infant-Ey."[26] And although neither
sequence gives evidence of the kind of structure found in *The Temple*—
Traherne's method of association moves in an entirely different manner—the Dobell *Poems* ends with an apocalyptic vision ("Good-
nesse") following a suite of poems in which Traherne suggests a
prolonged mental state of ecstatic contemplation: "Thoughts. I,"
"Blisse," "Thoughts. II," "Ye hidden Nectars," "Thoughts. III,"
"Desire," and "Thoughts. IV."

If I had to pick one poem that places Traherne *thematically* in the
school of George Herbert, it would be "The Circulation." The poem
has a tone reminiscent of Herbert's "Man," and its theme is similar
too. In this poem, Traherne treats the idea of circulation by developing a comparison between the eye that sees God's works and a
mirror. Thus giving and receiving, circulating and expanding, the
"Celestial Eys" of this Trahernean soul encompass both the source
of light and its reflection:

> All Things to Circulations owe
> Themselvs; by which alone
> They do exist: They cannot shew
> A Sigh, a Word, a Groan,
> A Colour, or a Glimps of Light,
> The Sparcle of a Precious Stone,
> A virtue, or a Smell; a lovly Sight,

> A Fruit, a Beam, an Influence, a Tear;
> But they anothers Livery must Wear:
> And borrow Matter first,
> Before they can communicat.
>
> (p. 46)

Wherever he looks, the speaker finds evidence of this divine principle of emanation: Love first infuses life, and then sustains it. If this sense of order and generosity in the universe is like that of Herbert's "Man," it is so because of the psalmic features that the poems share, as their respective authors internalize the same poetic model. And yet it must be said that Traherne's rumination aims at a sense of boundlessness atypical of Herbert:

> He is the Primitive Eternal Spring
> The Endless Ocean of each Glorious Thing.
> The Soul a Vessel is
> A Spacious Bosom to Contain
> All the fair Treasures of his Bliss
> Which run like Rivers from, into the Main,
> And all it doth receiv returns again.
>
> (p. 47)

In Traherne, the rush to add a noun or adjective, a consideration or thought—or *anything*—is meant to suggest the inexplicable nature of the topic. Infinity cannot be expressed, but the idea of addition can be suggested, as can that of multiplication, and so on. Structurally, the impact of such a rhetorical aim is considerable. Traherne seldom conveys a sense of the tautly framed and integral stanza. "The Circulation" is thematically similar to Herbert's "Man," but it is not structurally so. We sense the same adulation, the same innocence of spirit, the same assertion of the ultimate artistry manifest in God's wonderful workmanship in making the world. Here the comparison ends, as Traherne's rhetoric of infinity takes over.

This is not so with Vaughan. And despite all the differences discussed earlier, I think this fact makes him the truest "Son of George." We see this if we compare the two poems entitled "Man." Herbert's poem (pp. 90–92) is addressed to God ("My God, I heard this day"), Vaughan's (p. 477) to an audience that is not clearly specified. We get the sense, not of someone praying, but of one reflecting upon a subject:[27]

Weighing the stedfastness and state
Of some mean things which here below reside,
Where birds like watchful Clocks the noiseless date
And Intercourse of times divide,
Where Bees at night get home and hive, and flowrs
Early, aswel as late,
Rise with the Sun, and set in the same bowrs.

(ll. 1–7)

The subject is time, which is measured in an orderly way by God's creatures ("some mean things"), who function "like watchful Clocks," measuring out the days in their precise movements. Even the poet's stanza marks a tightly finished point, as the rhyme scheme matches the progress of a full day, interlocking the final rhyme with the first line (a b a b c a c).

George Ryley, one of Herbert's early editors and critics, considers Herbert's "Man" to be about the microcosm, identifying the poem as a companion piece to "The World," about which he has this to say:

One may Apply Every Article in this poem to the aeconomy of the world we live in; tho, I think Scarcely, without Straining Some of the Terms. But I think it most Naturally Runs into the State of Man; who is called the *Microcosme,* or little world. so that the Subject of this poem, and that Entitled Man, are the Same; which I am convinced the more of from the parity of their beginnings. (*Love built* etc. to the End.) Here the Contemplation on Man is carryed on under the Notion of a house. so is he Called *Heb: 3.6* and *1 Pet. 2.5*[28]

Ryley's comment that the "stately house" that "Love built" ("The World," p. 84) is the same "stately habitation" that the speaker in "Man" imagines God building points to a difference as well as a similarity between Herbert and Vaughan. Post rightly stresses their shared poetic emphasis on the integrity of the stanza. Thus, the stanzaic form of the two poems is quite similar:

Man is all symmetrie,
Full of proportions, one limbe to another,
And all to all the world besides:
Each part may call the furthest, brother:
For head with foot hath private amitie,
And both with moons and tides.

> Nothing hath got so farre,
> But Man hath caught and kept it, as his prey.
> His eyes dismount the highest starre:
> He is in little all the sphere.
> Herbs gladly cure our flesh; because that they
> Finde their acquaintance there.
>
> (ll. 13–24)

Vaughan also links the figure of the house with man's place in the world, but the difference is that he is outside the house, just as he feels himself to be outside the orderly, time-measuring functions of the "meaner" creatures on the earth. Indeed, man has a "home" in Vaughan's poem only so he can express his bewilderment about it:

> Man hath stil either toyes, or Care,
> He hath no root, nor to one place is ty'd,
> But ever restless and Irregular
> About this Earth doth run and ride,
> He knows he hath a home, but scarce knows where,
> He sayes it is so far
> That he hath quite forgot how to go there.
>
> He knocks at all doors, strays and roams,
> Nay hath not so much wit as some stones have
> Which in the darkest nights point to their homes,
> By some hid sense their Maker gave;
> Man is the shuttle, to whose winding quest
> And passage through these looms
> God order'd motion, but ordain'd no rest.
>
> (ll. 15–28)

Again, the echoes from Herbert's "The Pulley" are not as significant as the means to which the two poets put the same figure. In Herbert, man's "repining restlessnesse" is the means by which God draws man to his "breast." The poem is a clever, but warm, expression of a pun, in which God himself speaks in reassuring tones about man's anxiety. In this way, it relates very nicely to the close of Herbert's "Man," which presents the speaker in impassioned colloquy with God:

> Since then, my God, thou hast
> So brave a Palace built; O dwell in it,

That it may dwell with thee at last!
Till then, afford us so much wit;
That, as the world serves us, we may serve thee,
And both thy servants be.

(ll. 49–54)

Herbert's poem emulates the Psalmist in expressing gratitude for God's gifts to man. The figure of domestic service is the key: "Oh mightie love! Man is one world and hath / Another to attend him" (ll. 47–48). We recall, of course, that "The Church" ends beautifully as the speaker, an unworthy guest, is coaxed to "sit and eat," while "Love" himself waits on him. Herbert's "Man" emphasizes the orderliness of God's creation, as does Vaughan's, but it ends in a prayer of petition and resolve, as Vaughan's does not. In Herbert, the reader is left with a sense that "Man is all symmetrie" insofar as, with the Psalmist, he is thankful. Vaughan's poem ends in the same mode of detached reflection as it began. In man's alienation from his "home," his very quest, which *seems* absurd ("He knocks at all doors"), is part of the divine order. Birds know what time it is; bees find their way to the hive. Even lodestones always point in the same direction "to their homes." And yet for all his seeming awkward nonparticipation in the scheme of things, man does exhibit his place in the cosmic order—in his very sense of alienation from it. Unlike Herbert's title figure of "The Pulley," Vaughan's striking visual image of the shuttle and the loom comes abruptly, at the close of the poem. In constant motion, the shuttle races this way and that, never at rest, but also imparting to the fabric the pattern of its maker's design. It is this suddenness that makes the poem typically Vaughanian. If we look to compare Vaughan's "Man" with his "World," we will see (as we did with Herbert) an apposite sense of the mind's sudden glimpse of the divine order: "I saw Eternity the other night / Like a great *Ring* of pure and endless light" (p. 466). In Vaughan, man is an exile, longing for home. In Herbert, he is an unworthy servant, rescued from his diffidence and his sense of unworthiness, which is its true cause, and restored to his rightful place at the heavenly banquet.

Conclusion

In this chapter I have argued that, rather than being a conduit for the export of poetic practices typical of the school of Donne,

George Herbert directly influenced a generation of poets himself, and might justifiably be called the master of a school of his own. In recognizing the shaping influence of Herbert on such poets as Crashaw, Harvey, Colman, Washbourne, Speed, Vaughan, and Traherne, we seek not to diminish the importance of Donne, but only to acknowledge that we appreciate him and the Donneans (Lord Herbert, Cleveland, Cowley, Sherburne, Marvell, and in certain moods, Lovelace) precisely because they practiced so well the very poetic techniques from which Herbert and his followers earnestly sought to separate themselves. It must be said that our appetite to enjoy the rough insouciance of love poetry fashioned in the Donne workshops cannot be satisfied by Herbert and his *"Converts,"* as Vaughan referred to himself and his fellow Herbertians. Nor do I mean to question our frequent use of the term *metaphysical.* The schools of Donne and Herbert, though distinguishable, nevertheless share many poetic traits, and if the term is useful in describing those traits, no good purpose would be served by questioning its validity. It is only that the remark by Dryden from which the term is derived is so directly aimed at Donne's love poetry that we must pay attention to the ways in which Herbert and his followers avoided the basis of Dryden's scorn. Plainly, if one abstains from profane love, it makes no sense to fault one's techniques of lovemaking.

Then, too, by looking carefully at the way in which poets modeled themselves after Herbert we have another means by which to measure his achievement—and *theirs.* (Washbourne, for instance, deserves more serious attention than he has yet received.) We can see, however, that though his followers often thought they were imitating Herbert, they were also reading him in a certain way, reflecting their own interests, and responding to a swiftly changing world— a world of revolution, as it happened, in the area of religion most important to our understanding of Herbert's poetics. Change is inevitable. Indeed, it is evidence of the contrary—stasis in society— that would challenge our credulity. Poets may try to imitate an admired literary forebear, and they may succeed, up to a point. As they do, they create schools of laudatory likenesses. But while they imitate, establishing schools, they also impose their different personalities, in response to different social contexts. These, in turn, point the way to dissolution of the very school the imitators have established. For, after all, imitation is a form of interpretation, and as times change so do the values that inform this sine qua non of critical and poetic practice. Just as hymnologists of the eighteenth century re-created Herbert in a form amenable to their congregational needs (see chapter 1), so did later generations of poets look for new sources of inspiration, turning from the Mount of Olives and the Jordan to other mountains and other streams for more relevant alternatives to Mount Parnassus and the Helicon. In so doing, they turned also from the poetic stance that had shaped the credo and practices of the school of George Herbert.

Notes and References

In all quotations I have regularlized the use of i/j and u/v, expanded contractions and ignored meaningless capitals and small capitals. Unless otherwise noted, all books published before 1700 bear a London imprint.

Chapter One

1. The following account owes much to Amy M. Charles, *A Life of George Herbert* (Ithaca: Cornell Univ. Press, 1977); Joseph H. Summers, *George Herbert: His Religion and Art* (London: Chatto and Windus, 1954); and F. E. Hutchinson, ed., introduction to *The Works of George Herbert* (Oxford: Clarendon Press, 1953). Unless otherwise noted, all citations from Herbert in my text will be from this edition and cited as *Works*.

2. Charles, *Life*, 112–13.

3. *Herbert's Remains, Or, Sundry Pieces Of that sweet Singer of the Temple, Mr. George Herbert* (1652), sig. a1, hereafter cited in the text.

4. Except for quotations from Herbert's "Sonnets" written to his mother, available in Hutchinson, all references to Walton's *The Life of Mr. George Herbert* (cited in the text as *Life*) will be to the first edition of *The Lives of Dr. John Donne, Sir Henry Wotton, Mr. Richard Hooker, Mr. George Herbert* (1670). I am aware that *The Life of Mr. George Herbert* (Wing W669) was published separately the same year.

5. *Select Hymns, Taken out of Mr. Herbert's Temple, And Turn'd into the Common Metre (1697)*, edited with an introduction by William E. Stephenson (Los Angeles: Augustan Reprint Society, 1962), title page; hereafter, cited in my text as *Select Hymns*.

6. All quotations from John and Charles Wesley in my text will be from the first edition of *Hymns and Sacred Poems* (1739), hereafter cited in text as *Hymns* (1739).

7. C. A. Patrides, ed., *The English Poems of George Herbert* (London: J. M. Dent & Sons, 1974), 103.

8. *The Works of George Herbert* (W. Pickering edition), 2 vols. (London, 1853), 2:6; hereafter cited in text.

9 Richard Baxter, "The Epistle to the Reader," *Poetical Fragments* (1681), sig. A7; hereafter cited in text.

10. George Gilfillan, ed., *The Poetical Works of George Herbert* (Edinburgh, 1853), v; hereafter cited in text.

11. Charles, *Life*, 209.

Chapter Two

1. John Carey, *John Donne: Life, Mind and Art* (New York: Oxford Univ. Press, 1980), Chap. 1 ("Apostasy"), esp. 15.

2. Charles, *Life,* 121–31, 151.

3. J. E. B. Mayor, *Nicholas Ferrar* (Cambridge, 1855), xxi. A copy of Edward Lenton's original letter to Sir Thomas Hetley, on which *The Arminian Nunnery* is loosely based, is reprinted, xxvi–xxxvi. Lenton dissociated himself from the pamphlet; see T. T. Carter, ed., for Jane Frances Mary Carter, *Nicholas Ferrar: His Household and His Friends* (London, 1892), 291. For an early discussion of the relation between Edward Lenton's correspondence and *The Arminian Nunnery,* see P. Peckard, *Memoirs of the Life of Mr. Nicholas Ferrar* (Cambridge, 1790), 236, 278, 281, 283, and Appendix; hereafter cited in text.

4. *The Latin Poetry of George Herbert,* trans. Mark McCloskey and Paul R. Murphy (Athens, Ohio: Ohio Univ. Press, 1965), 37; hereafter, unless otherwise noted, all quotations from Herbert's Latin poems will be from this fine translation, cited in the text as *LP.*

5. The translation from Andrew Melville is by Alexander B. Grosart, in *The Complete Works in Verse and Prose of George Herbert,* ed. Alexander B. Grosart, 3 vols. (London, 1874), 2:98; hereafter, all citations from Melville in my text will be from this edition, cited in text as Grosart ed.

6. Izaak Walton, *The Life of Mr. George Herbert,* in *The Lives of Dr. John Donne, Sir Henry Wotton, Mr. Richard Hooker, Mr. George Herbert* (1670), 24.

7. For a witty discussion of the slipperiness of the term, see Patrick Collinson, "Concerning the Name Puritan," in *English Puritanism,* General Series, no. 106 (London: The Historical Association, 1983), 7–11; Collinson's remarks on the Admonition (pp. 15–20) are most helpful in suggesting how divisions developed in the Elizabethan Church. See also chapter 2, " 'But Halfly Reformed,' " in Collinson's *The Elizabethan Puritan Movement* (Berkeley: Univ. of California Press, 1967), 29–44.

8. C. A. Patrides, "A Crown of Praise: The Poetry of Herbert," in *The English Poems of George Herbert* (London: J. M. Dent, 1974), 211–23.

9. Richard Hooker, *Of The Lawes of Ecclesiasticall Politie* (1597), bk. 5, 56.

10. John Greenwood, *An Aunswer to George Giffords Pretended Defence of Read Prayers and Devised Leitourgies* ([Dort], 1590), sig. A2v; Greenwood refers to the Portuary, or Roman Breviary *(OED).*

11. George Fox, *A Journal or Historical Account of the Life, Travels, Sufferings, Christian Experiences and Labour of Love in the Work of the Ministry, of that . . . Servant of Jesus Christ, George Fox* (1694), 1:134–35.

12. Anonymous letter to John Ayrey, in *The Journal of George Fox,*

edited by Norman Penney, with an introd. by T. Edmund Harvey (Cambridge: Cambridge Univ. Press, 1911), 2:370.

13. *Elizabethan Nonconformist Texts: The Writings of John Greenwood,* (1587–90) ed. Leland H. Carlson (London: George Allen and Unwin, 1962), 4:23.

14. James I, *A Meditation Upon the Lords Prayer* (1619), 11.

15. Ibid., 9.

16. Ibid., 11.

17. Ibid., 9.

18. Ibid., 6.

19. Ibid., 5–6.

20. Ibid., 18.

21. Ibid., 23.

22. John Greenwood, *An Aunswer,* sig. A2v.

23. *The Works of Joseph Hall* (1624–25), 557.

24. John Greenwood, *An Aunswer,* sig. A3.

25. Richard Bernard, *Christian Advertisements and Counsels of Peace* (1608), 176.

26. George Gifford, *A Short Treatise Against the Donatists of England* (1590), 25.

27. Henry Barrow, *A True Description Out of the Worde of God, Of the Visible Church* (1589), sig. A2v.

28. John Donne, *Devotions upon Emergent Occasions* (Ann Arbor: Univ. of Michigan Press, 1959), 86.

29. Chauncey Wood, "A Reading of Herbert's 'Collos. 3.3,' " *George Herbert Journal 2,* no. 2 (1979):15–24.

30. Judy Z. Kronenfeld, "Probing the Relation between Poetry and Ideology: Herbert's 'The Windows,' " *John Donne Journal* 2, no. 2 (1983):55–80.

31. Jeanne Clayton Hunter, " 'With Winges of Faith': Herbert's Communion Poems," *Journal of Religion* 62 (1982):57–71.

32. For a statement of her assumptions, see Rosemond Tuve, *A Reading of George Herbert* (London: Faber and Faber, 1952), 84–111, but the entire book is essential to the study of Herbert.

33. See my "Time and *The Temple,*" *Studies in English Literature 6,* no. 1 (1966):97–110, esp. 104–05, and chap. 4, below; for the commentary on "Love" (III) from which Hunter dissents, see C. A. Patrides, *English Poems,* 20–21, 192.

34. Joseph H. Summers, *George Herbert: His Religion and Art* (London: Chatto and Windus, 1954), 54.

35. Ira Clark, *Christ Revealed: The History of the Neotypological Lyric in the English Renaissance,* Univ. of Florida Monographs, Humanities no. 51 (Gainesville: Univ. of Florida Press, 1982), chap. 1 et passim.

Chapter Three

1. Heather A. R. Asals, *Equivocal Predication: George Herbert's Way to God* (Toronto: Univ. of Toronto Press, 1981), 5–6; Asals sees Sister Maria Thekla and Richard Hughes, Malcolm Ross and Rosemond Tuve as instances of this critical polarization.

2. Barbara Lewalski, *Protestant Poetics and the Seventeenth-Century Religious Lyric* (Cambridge: Harvard Univ. Press, 1979), 283.

3. For a discussion of "the theological and attitudinal connections between Herbert and the radicals of the Reformation and English Revolutions" (p. xx), see Richard Strier, *Love Known: Theology and Experience in George Herbert's Poetry* (Chicago: Univ. of Chicago Press, 1983), passim, but esp. chaps. 6–7; and see n. 37, below. My differences with Strier can be briefly indicated by the fact that the index of this 277-page book includes many dozens of entries for Stanley Fish and Helen Vendler, but reflects no mention at all of the most important member of Herbert's intended audience, Nicholas Ferrar.

4. J. Max Patrick, "Critical Problems in Editing George Herbert's *The Temple*," in *The Editor as Critic and the Critic as Editor* (Los Angeles: William Andrews Clark Memorial Library, 1973), 13. Amy M. Charles writes: "A comment of Ferrar's to Woodnoth . . . makes clear that Ferrar had been entrusted with at least some of Herbert's remaining manuscripts and that he regarded himself as Herbert's literary executor," in *A Life of George Herbert* (Ithaca: Cornell Univ. Press, 1977), 179.

5. Joseph H. Summers, *George Herbert: His Religion and Art* (London: Chatto and Windus, 1954), chap. 3, esp. 49–50.

6. *The Book of Common Prayer* (1630), sigs. B3 and C2v (STC 16381).

7. A. L. Maycock, *Nicholas Ferrar of Little Gidding* (London: Society for Promoting Christian Knowledge, 1938), 48–49; Maycock writes that the "Harmonies" were "famous throughout England and . . . count amongst the most remarkable feats of book production ever carried out in" England (pp. 148–59).

8. Copies of this work were regularly produced at Little Gidding during the period from 1630 to 1637. Several are extant. I was able to examine the two volumes of *The Actions and Doctrine and other Passages Touching Our Lord and Saviour Jesus Christ* at the British Library (C.23.e.2; C.23.e.4) and the related *Acta Apostolorum* (C.23.e.3). Unless otherwise noted, all citations from *The Actions and Doctrine Touching Our Lord* will be from the copy once in the possession of Charles I (C.23.e.4). For a bibliographic account of the remaining "Harmonies," see J. E. Acland, *Little Gidding and its Inmates in the Time of King Charles I, with an Account of the Harmonies Design and Constructed by Nicholas Ferrar* (London: Society for Promoting Christian Knowledge, 1903), 34–60. For a valuable discussion of these volumes from the viewpoint of Bible illustration, see George Henderson, "Bible Illustrations in the Age of Laud," *Transactions*

of the Cambridge Bibliographical Society 8 (1982):173–216; hereafter, cited in text.

9. *The Ferrar Papers,* ed. B. Blackstone (Cambridge: Cambridge Univ. Press, 1938:42–46, 86; hereafter, unless such citation would be misleading or vague, cited in the text.

10. T. T. Carter, ed., for Jane Frances Mary Carter, *Nicholas Ferrar: His Household and his Friends* (London, 1892), 182–83; hereafter, cited in the text.

11. Judy Z. Kronenfeld, "Probing the Relation between Poetry and Ideology: Herbert's 'The Windows,' " *John Donne Journal* 2 (1983):55–80.

12. *The Works of George Herbert,* ed. F. E. Hutchinson (Oxford: Clarendon Press, 1953), 228; hereafter, cited in the text.

13. *The Arminian Nunnery* (1641), an anonymous pamphlet addressed to Parliament several years after Ferrar's death, is based on a letter written by Edward Lenton to Sir Thomas Hetley, and is an interesting example of a Puritan response to the life of Little Gidding. The engraved title page of the work depicts a woman dressed as a nun, holding a book (presumably a prayer book) and a rosary (Maycock, facing p. 136).

14. *Ferrar Papers,* 42.

15. The fact may be inferred from Arthur Woodnōth's letter, written during a visit to Herbert's household on 13 October 1631 (*Ferrar Papers,* 268).

16. *The Works of Aurelius Augustine, Bishop of Hippo,* trans. and ed. Rev. Marcus Dodds, D. D., 15 vols. (Edinburgh, 1871–83), 8:136; Augustine makes his remarks in lectures 12 and 17 of his *Tractates on the Gospel According to St. John,* 11:472, 503.

17. Thomas Middleton, *Mariage of the Old and New Testament* (1620), 41; hereafter, cited in the text.

18. John Lightfoot, *The Harmony of the Foure Evangelists: Among themselves, and with the Old Testament* (1644), sig. A4. In *The Storie of Stories, Or The Life of Christ, According to the foure holy Evangelists: With a Harmonie of Them* (1632), John Huid insists that the four sources establish a "continual coherence of time and order" (sig. A8).

19. For a fuller discussion of this point, see my *The Enclosed Garden: The Tradition and the Image in Seventeenth-Century Poetry* (Madison: Univ. of Wisconsin Press, 1966), chap. 1, esp. 17–19. For a compatible approach to the same texts, see Chana Bloch, "Spelling the Word: Herbert's Reading of the Bible," in *"Too Rich to Clothe the Sunne": Essays on George Herbert,* ed. Claude J. Summers and Ted-Larry Pebworth (Pittsburgh: Univ. of Pittsburgh Press, 1980), 15–31; see n. 3, above.

20. Helen Vendler, *The Poetry of George Herbert* (Cambridge: Harvard Univ. Press, 1975), 198.

21. Column 217–18 (top) and middle panel (below); for the sake of

convenience (the folios are unnumbered), further references to *The Actions and Doctrine Touching Our Lord* will be to the column numbers.

22. Rosemond Tuve, *A Reading of George Herbert* (London: Faber and Faber, 1952), 112–17.

23. See pls. 6, 7, 8a. The major differences between representation of the bunch of grapes in pl. 6 (from the *Biblia Pauperum*) and the Little Gidding engraving of the same subject lie in the detail of the latter (the earlier illustration being printed from a relatively unsophisticated woodblock) and Ferrar's curious interpretation of the forked hat worn by one of the carriers.

24. Louis L. Martz, *The Poetry of Meditation: A Study in English Religious Literature of the Seventeenth Century* (New Haven: Yale Univ. Press, 1954), 107–112; hereafter, cited in the text.

25. A. L. Maycock, *Nicholas Ferrar*, 281; Maycock adds that, likewise, "Charles' enthusiasm knew no bounds."

26. A. L. Maycock, *Nicholas Ferrar*, p. 149; Maycock writes that "the Concordance Room" was hung with many "texts from the Scriptures . . . aphorisms or exhortations" (pp. 148–49). He adds: "The most striking of these inscriptions . . . had been shown in draft to George Herbert, who had been much struck by it and had urged that it should be engraved on brass and put up where everyone coming to the house should see it" (p. 149). The inscription was headed by Little Gidding's ubiquitous insignia, *IHS*. The importance of this Jesuit monogram will be discussed below. For a discussion of the role of the senses in Ferrar's decoration of the church at Little Gidding, and an interior, see C. Leslie Craig, *Nicholas Ferrar Junior: A Linguist of Little Gidding* (London: Epworth Press, 1950), fac. p. 45.

27. In *A Priest to the Temple*, Herbert describes *"The Parson in his house"*: "Even the wals are not idle, but something is written, or painted there, which may excite the reader to a thought of piety." (p. 240). Again, the Parson makes sure the church is decorated in accordance with "the middle way," which meant that, at times, it be "perfumed with incense" (p. 246). I take it that Herbert's attitudes toward stained glass windows are exhibited in "The Windows" and "Love-joy."

28. John Greenwood, *An Aunswer to George Giffords Pretended Defence of Read Prayers and Devised Leitourgies* ([Dort], 1590), sig. A2v.

29. Richard Hooker, *Of the Lawes of Ecclesiasticall Politie* (1597), bk. 5, 56.

30. James I, *A Meditation upon the Lords Prayer* (1619), 18–19.

31. John Greenwood, *An Aunswer*, sig. A2v.

32. Anonymous letter to John Ayrey, in *The Journal of George Fox*, ed. Norman Penney, with an introduction by T. Edmund Harvey, 2 Vols. (Cambridge: Cambridge Univ. Press, 1911), 2:370.

33. Amy M. Charles, *Life*, pp. 122–27, esp. 123; see also 151.

34. See, for instance, the representations of *Maria dolorosa* (cols. 27–28, 35–36), of Saint Catherine and Saint Peter (cols. 117–18), and of Saint Nicholas (cols. 125–26). For an extensive discussion of the supposed Roman Catholicism at Little Gidding, see Patrick Grant, *The Transformation of Sin: Studies in Donne, Herbert, Vaughan, and Traherne* (Amherst: Univ. of Massachusetts Press, 1974), 118–23.

35. Thomas Rogers, *The Catholic Doctrine of The Church of England, An Exposition of the Thirty-Nine Articles* [1586], ed. Rev. J. J. S. Perowne (Cambridge, 1854), 222–23, 226–27; Rogers is only one example among many possible Protestants who registered the most vigorous opposition to representations of the saints and the Virgin Mary with halos, representation of the body of Christ on the Cross, and representations of many of the saints found in the engravings of the Little Gidding "Harmonies."

36. J. A. W. Bennett, *Poetry of the Passion: Studies in Twelve Centuries of English Verse* (Oxford: Clarendon Press, 1982), 153–58, esp. his discussion of Friar William Herbert's "version of *Populae meus*" (p. 154).

37. I am grateful to Chana Bloch for permitting me to read relevant portions of the manuscript of her book-length study *Spelling the Word: George Herbert and the Bible* (Berkeley: Univ. of California Press, 1985). Especially relevant are the first two chapters, which deal with Herbert's ideas of scriptural collation. As I understand her views, Professor Bloch's approach is compatible with, and supports, my own argument for the similarities between Herbert's poetic practice and the conceptions underlying the making and use of the "Harmonies" of Little Gidding.

38. See Amy M. Charles's introduction to *The Williams Manuscript of George Herbert's Poems* (Delmar, N. Y.: Scholars' Facsimiles and Reprints, 1977), vii–xxxi.

39. C. A. Patrides, ed., *The English Poems of George Herbert* (London: J. M. Dent, 1974), 94.

40. For a recent expression of the view that in this poem "one can see at work . . . some of the most historically characteristic and significant features of the Puritan mind" (p. 132), see Richard Strier, " 'To all Angels and Saints': Herbert's Puritan Poem," *Modern Philology* 77 (November 1979):132–45; see also his *Love Known*, 104, 211.

41. T. S. Eliot, *George Herbert*, Writers and Their Work, no 152, gen. ed. Bonamy Dobrée (London: Longmans, Green & Co., 1962), 10. Eliot's opinion finds support in Ira Clark's valuable study, *Christ Revealed: The History of the Neotypological Lyric in the English Renaissance* (Gainesville: Univ. of Florida Press, 1982), esp. chaps. 1 and 4; I agree with Clark's argument that Herbert and others like him are more accurately designated "Reformed" than "Protestant."

Chapter Four

1. Izaak Walton, *The Life of Mr. George Herbert* (1670), 74; see chap. 1, n. 4.

2. David Novarr, *The Making of Walton's "Lives"* (Ithaca: Cornell Univ. Press, 1958), esp. 494–96; and Amy M. Charles, *A Life of George Herbert* (Ithaca: Cornell Univ. Press, 1977), esp. 147–48, 167–68, 201–3.

3. Helen Vendler, *The Poetry of George Herbert* (Cambridge: Harvard Univ. Press, 1975), 137.

4. A most recent example: Diana Benet thinks that "the length of 'The Church-porch' vitiates its impact" (*Secretary of Praise: The Poetic Vocation of George Herbert* [Columbia: Univ. of Missouri Press, 1984], p. 35); the following pages are more in sympathy with the views of Sheridan D. Blau (originally published in *Genre*) in "The Poet as Casuist: Herbert's 'Church-porch,' " in *Essential Articles for the Study of George Herbert's Poetry*, ed. John R. Roberts (Hamden, Conn.: Archon Books, 1979), 408–15.

5. Louis L. Martz, *The Poetry of Meditation* (New Haven: Yale Univ. Press, 1954), 290; hereafter cited in text.

6. Michael C. Schoenfeldt, "Submission and Assertion: The 'Double Motion' of Herbert's 'Dedication,' " *John Donne Journal 2*, no. 2 (1983):39–49.

7. *The Works of George Herbert*, ed. F. E. Hutchinson (Oxford: Clarendon Press, 1953), 25; unless otherwise noted, all citations from Herbert in this chapter will be from this edition.

8. C. A. Patrides, ed., *The English Poems of George Herbert* (London: J. M. Dent, 1974), 33; see also Hutchinson, *Works*, 476–77.

9. See Alexander B. Grosart, *The Complete Works in Verse and Prose of George Herbert*, 3 vols. (London, 1874), 1:234; and George Herbert Palmer, *The English Works of George Herbert*, 3 vols. (Boston: Houghton Mifflin, 1905), 2:5; both editors follow the commentary of G. Ryley.

10. John S. Bumpus, *A Dictionary of Ecclesiastical Terms* (London: T. Werner Laurie, n. d.), 23–25.

11. Adrian Fortescue, *The Ceremonies of the Roman Rite Described*, rev. by J. B. O'Connell (London: Burns Oates and Washbourne, 1934), 92–95; hereafter referred to as Fortescue and O'Connell.

12. John S. Bumpus, *Dictionary*, 23.

13. Fortescue and O'Connell, *Ceremonies of the Roman Rite*, 366, 373, 439.

14. Jeremy Collier, *An Ecclesiastical History of Great Britain, Chiefly of England*, 9 vols. (London, 1845–46), 4:337–41, but esp. item 49, p. 340; and Convocation of 1542, 5:86.

15. John Fox, *Actes and Monuments*, 8 vols. (London, 1849), 6:380.

16. See H. B. Walters, *London Churches at the Reformation, With an Account of Their Contents* (London: Society for Promoting Christian Knowledge, 1939), 393, 472, 643.

17. Thomas Jackson, *A Treatise Containing the Original of Unbelief, Misbeliefs, or Mispersuasions, The Works of Thomas Jackson,* 9 vols. (Oxford, 1844), 4:291; see also 9:531.

18. *The Sermons of John Donne,* ed. George R. Potter and Evelyn M. Simpson, 10 vols. (Berkeley and Los Angeles: Univ. of California Press, 1953–1962), 6:283; hereafter, all citations from Donne's *Sermons* in my text will be from this edition.

19. Patrick Collinson informs me (in conversation at the Henry E. Huntington Library and Art Gallery [Summer 1984]) that, in his opinion, especially when one passed much beyond the privileged sanctuaries around London, actual practice did not necessarily follow, and often completely contradicted, the liturgical order of confirmation; but see William Maskell, *Monumenta Ritualia Ecclesiae,* 3 vols. (Oxford, 1882), 1:38, and n. 20, below.

20. *The Prayer-Book of Queen Elizabeth* (1559), ed. Edward Benham (Edinburgh: John Grant, 1909), 121.

21. Robert B. Hinman, "The 'Verser' at *The Temple* Door: Herbert's 'The Church-porch,' " in *"Too Rich to Clothe the Sunne": Essays on George Herbert,* ed. Claude J. Summers and Ted-Larry Pebworth (Pittsburgh: Univ. of Pittsburgh Press, 1980), 55–75.

22. *Sermons of M. John Calvin on the Epistles of St. Paule to Timothie and Titus,* trans. L. T. (1579), 428 *(OED).*

23. Stanley Fish, *The Living Temple: George Herbert and Catechizing* (Berkeley: Univ. of California Press, 1978), esp. chap. 1; the reader will note my indebtedness to portions of Fish's argument in this book (hereafter cited in the text), but my differences with him should also be evident.

24. James I, *A Meditation Upon the Lords Prayer* (1619), 5–6; See chap 2, above.

25. *The Booke of Common Prayer,* (1604), sig. P6v (STC 16328).

26. Rosemond Tuve, "George Herbert and *'Caritas,' " Journal of the Warburg and Courtauld Institute 22,* (1959):303–31, repr. in her *Essays,* ed. T. P. Roche (Princeton: Princeton Univ. Press, 1970), 167–206.

27. John Donne, *The Divine Poems,* ed. Helen Gardner (Oxford: Clarendon Press, 1952), 26.

28. Arnold Stein, *George Herbert's Lyrics* (Baltimore: The Johns Hopkins Univ. Press, 1968), 196.

29. See *The Confessions of Saint Augustine,* trans. and ed. Rev. Marcus Dods (Edinburgh, 1876), bk. 11.

30. Roger Matthew, *The Flight of Time* (1634), 3; see also Samuel Chew's discussion of time in seventeenth-century literature in *The Pilgrimage of Life* (New Haven: Yale Univ. Press, 1962).

31. See my *The Enclosed Garden: The Tradition and the Image in Sev-

enteenth-Century Poetry (Madison: Univ. of Wisconsin Press, 1966), esp. chap. 1.

32. See Amy M. Charles, "The Williams Manuscript and *The Temple*" (originally published in *ELH*), in *Essential Articles,* ed. John R. Roberts, 416–32.

33. A. J. Festugière, O. P., *George Herbert: Poète Saint Anglican (1593–1633)* (Paris: Librairie Philosophique J. Vrin, 1971), 127–40.

34. Annabel M. Endicott-Patterson, "The Structure of George Herbert's *Temple:* A Reconsideration" (originally published in *University of Toronto Quarterly*), in *Essential Articles,* ed. John R. Roberts (pp. 351–62), 361.

35. See Frank Manley, Introduction to *John Donne: The Anniversaries* (Baltimore: The Johns Hopkins Univ. Press, 1963); Louis L. Martz, *Poetry of Meditation,* chap. 6; Don Cameron Allen, *Image and Meaning* (Baltimore: The Johns Hopkins Univ. Press, 1960), chap. 4.

36. *The Psalter of David . . . Whereunto is Added, Devotions* (1646), p. 285. For an account of the importance of the Psalms in the order of worship at Little Gidding, see chap. 3, above.

37. *The Boke of Psalmes . . . With Breife and Apt annotations in the margent* (Geneva, 1559), 228.

38. *John Milton: Complete Poems and Major Prose,* ed. Merritt Y. Hughes (New York: Odyssey, 1957), 466 (*PL,* 12: 535–38); all citations from Milton in this chapter are from this edition.

39. *The Psalmes of David and others, With M. John Calvins Commentaries* (1571), pt. 2, fol. 47v.

40. Henry Ainsworth, *Annotations Upon the Booke of Psalmes* (1626), 180.

41. *The Boke of Psalmes,* 357.

Chapter Five

1. A. Alvarez, *The School of Donne* (London: Chatto and Windus, 1961), 31; hereafter, all citations from Alvarez in my text will be from this edition.

2. See F. R. Leavis, "The Line of Wit," repr. from *Revaluation: Tradition and Development in English Poetry* (London: Chatto and Windus, 1936), in *Seventeenth-Century Poetry: Modern Essays in Criticism,* ed. William R. Keast (New York: Oxford Univ. Press, 1982), 31–49; see also George Williamson's discussion, *The Proper Wit of Poetry* (London: Faber and Faber, 1961), chap. 1, esp. 11–12.

3. Edward, Lord Herbert of Cherbury, *The Poems English and Latin of Edward, Lord Herbert of Cherbury,* ed. G. C. Moore Smith (Oxford

Clarendon Press, 1923), 22; hereafter, all citations from Lord Herbert of Cherbury in my text will be from this edition.

4. John Donne, *The Epithalamions Anniversaries and Epicedes*, ed. W. Milgate (Oxford: Clarendon Press, 1978), 63–66; hereafter, unless otherwise indicated, all citations from Donne in my text will be from this edition.

5. George Herbert, *The Latin Poetry of George Herbert*, trans. Mark McCloskey and Paul R. Murphy (Athens: Ohio Univ. Press, 1965), 157; hereafter, all citations from Herbert's Latin poems in my text will be from this bilingual edition.

6. Introduction to *The Works of George Herbert*, ed. F. E. Hutchinson (Oxford: Clarendon Press, 1953), xxv; hereafter, unless otherwise indicated (see n. 5, above), all citations from Herbert in my text will be from this edition.

7. Classical statements on the subject by H. J. C. Grierson and T. S. Eliot are reprinted in Keast (pp. 3–30), and the collection, now revised, provides a wide range of commentary on typical features of metaphysical poetry.

8. John Dryden, "Discourse on the Original and Progress of Satire" (1693), in *The Critical and Miscellaneous Prose Works of John Dryden*, ed. Edmond Malone, 3 vols. (London, 1800), 3:79.

9. Sir Philip Sidney, *The Poems of Sir Philip Sidney*, ed. William A. Ringler, Jr. (Oxford: Clarendon Press, 1962), 165; hereafter, all citations from Sidney in my text will be from this edition.

10. Rosemond Tuve, "George Herbert and 'Caritas,' " *Journal of the Warburg and Courtauld Institute 22* (1959):303–31, repr. in her *Essays*, ed. T. P. Roche (Princeton: Princeton Univ. Press, 1970), 167–206.

11. Christopher Harvey, *The Synagogue, or, The Shadow of The Temple. Sacred Poems, and Private Ejaculations. In imitation of Mr. George Herbert* (1640), title page; hereafter, all citations from this work in my text will be from this, the first, edition.

12. Ralph Knevet, *The Shorter Poems of Ralph Knevet*, ed. Amy M. Charles (Columbus: Ohio State Univ. Press, 1966), 281; hereafter, all citations from Knevet in my text will be from this edition. For Charles's remarks on the dating of *A Gallery to The Temple*, see 53.

13. Richard Crashaw, *The Complete Poetry of Richard Crashaw*, ed. George Walton Williams (Garden City: Doubleday, 1970), 68; hereafter, all citations from Crashaw in my text will be from this excellent edition.

14. Joseph Beaumont, *The Minor Poems of Joseph Beaumont, D. D.*, ed. Eloise Robinson (Boston: Houghton Mifflin, 1914), 169; hereafter, unless otherwise indicated, all citations from Beaumont in my text will be from this edition.

15. *The Complete Poems of Dr. Joseph Beaumont,* ed. Rev. Alexander B. Grosart, 2 vols. (Edinburgh, 1880), 1:68.

16. Henry Colman, *Divine Meditations* (1640), ed. Karen E. Steanson (New Haven: Yale Univ. Press, 1979), 21; hereafter, cited in the text.

17. Thomas Washbourne, *Divine Poems* (1654), 134; hereafter, cited in the text.

18. Mildmay Fane, *"Ad Libellum suum,"* in *Otia Sacra (1648),* 2; hereafter, all citations from this work will be from this, the first, edition.

19. Donald M. Friedman, Introduction to facsimile of *Otia Sacra (1648)* (New York: Scholars' Facsimiles and Reprints, 1975), viii.

20. Samuel Speed, *Prison-Pietie; or, Meditations Divine and Moral* (1677), sig. A5v (roman/italics reversed); hereafter, all citations from Speed in my text will be from this edition.

21. Thomas Traherne, *Poems, Centuries and Three Thanksgivings,* ed. Anne Ridler (London: Oxford Univ. Press, 1966), 188; hereafter, all citations from Traherne in my text will be from this edition.

22. Stanley Stewart, *The Expanded Voice: The Art of Thomas Traherne* (San Marino: The Huntington Library, 1970), chaps. 5 and 6, esp. 136–38.

23. Henry Vaughan, *The Works of Henry Vaughan,* ed. L. C. Martin (Oxford: Clarendon Press, 1957), 489; hereafter, all citations from Vaughan in my text will be from this edition.

24. The terms are synonymous with *anagogical;* see Stanley Stewart, *The Enclosed Garden: The Tradition and the Image in Seventeenth-Century Poetry* (Madison: Univ. of Wisconsin Press, 1966), 19–30, 95–96.

25. Jonathan F. S. Post, *Henry Vaughan: The Unfolding Vision* (Princeton: Princeton Univ. Press, 1982), 81; hereafter cited in the text.

26. See my discussion of the two poetic sequences, in *The Expanded Voice,* chaps. 6 and 7, esp. 155–58.

27. This and the following remarks owe much to Louis L. Martz, "Henry Vaughan: *The Caves of Memory,"* in *The Paradise Within: Studies in Vaughan, Traherne, and Milton* (New Haven: Yale Univ. Press, 1964), chap. 1.

28. *Mr. Herbert's Temple and Church Militant Explained and Improved By a Discourse Upon Each Poem Critical and Practical by George Ryley: A Critical Edition,* ed. John Martin Heissler (Ph.D. diss., Univ. of Illinois, 1960), 254; for Heissler's comparison between Ryley's commentary on Herbert's "Man" and Matthew Henry's approach to biblical commentary, see xxi–xv. Heissler dates the MS on which his edition is based "March the 24 1714 / 5" (lxxviii).

Selected Bibliography

Primary Sources

1. Works Published after 1800
Augustine, Saint, Bishop of Hippo. *The Works of Aurelius Augustine, Bishop of Hippo.* Edited by Rev. Marcus Dods, D. D. Translated by Rev. Marcus Dods, et al. 15 vols. Edinburgh, 1871–83.
Beaumont, Joseph. *The Complete Poems of Dr. Joseph Beaumont.* Edited by Rev. Alexander Grosart. 2 vols. Edinburgh, 1880.
———. *The Minor Poems of Joseph Beaumont, D. D.* Edited by Eloise Robinson. Boston: Houghton Mifflin, 1914.
The Calendar and the Collects, Epistles, and Gospels For the Lesser Feasts and Fasts. New York: The Church Pension Fund, 1963.
Colman, Henry. *Divine Meditations* (1640). Edited by Karen E. Steanson. New Haven: Yale University Press, 1979.
Crashaw, Richard. *The Complete Poetry of Richard Crashaw.* Edited by George Walton Williams. Garden City: Doubleday, 1970.
Donne, John. *John Donne: The Anniversaries.* Edited by Frank Manley. Baltimore: The Johns Hopkins University Press, 1963.
———. *Devotions upon Emergent Occasions.* Ann Arbor: University of Michigan Press, 1959.
———. *The Epithalamions Anniversaries and Epicedes.* Edited by W. Milgate. Oxford: Clarendon Press, 1978.
———. *The Sermons of John Donne.* Edited by George R. Potter and Evelyn M. Simpson. 10 vols. Berkeley: Univ. of California Press, 1953–62.
Dryden, John. *The Critical and Miscellaneous Prose Works of John Dryden.* Edited by Edmond Malone. 3 vols. London, 1800.
Elizabethan Noncomformist Texts: The Writings of John Greenwood (1587–90). Edited by Leland H. Carlson. 4 vols. London: George Allen and Unwin, 1962.
Herbert, Edward, Lord Herbert of Cherbury. *The Poems English and Latin of Edward, Lord Herbert of Cherbury.* Edited by G. C. Moore Smith. Oxford: Clarendon Press, 1923.
Herbert, George. *The Complete Works in Verse and Prose of George Herbert.* Edited by Rev. Alexander B. Grosart. 3 vols. London, 1874.
———. *The English Poems of George Herbert.* Edited by C. A. Patrides. London: J. M. Dent, 1974.

————. *The English Works of George Herbert.* Edited by George Herbert Palmer. 3 vols. Boston: Houghton Mifflin, 1905.

————. *The Latin Poetry of George Herbert.* Translated by Mark McCloskey and Paul R. Murphy. Athens: Ohio University Press, 1965.

————. *The Poetical Works of George Herbert.* Edited by Rev. George Gilfillan. Edinburgh, 1853.

————. *The Works of George Herbert* (W. Pickering edition). 2 vols. London, 1853.

————. *The Works of George Herbert,* Edited by F. E. Hutchinson. Oxford: Clarendon Press, 1953.

The Ferrar Papers, Containing a Life of Nicholas Ferrar; The Winding-Sheet, An Ascetic Dialogue; A Collection of Short Moral Histories; A Selection of Family Letters. Edited by B. Blackstone. Cambridge: Cambridge University Press, 1938.

Fox, John. *The Acts and Monuments of J. Foxe.* Introduction by Rev. George Townsend. 8 vols. London, 1843–49.

Fox, George. *The Journal of George Fox.* Edited by Norman Penney, with an introduction by T. Edmund Harvey. 2 vols. Cambridge: Cambridge University Press, 1911.

Knevet, Ralph. *The Shorter Poems of Ralph Knevet.* Edited by Amy M. Charles. Columbus: Ohio State University Press, 1966.

Mayor, J. E. B., ed. *Nicholas Ferrar.* Cambridge, 1855.

Milton, John. *Complete Poems and Major Prose.* Edited by Merritt Y. Hughes. New York: Odyssey, 1957.

The Prayer-Book of Queen Elizabeth (1559). Edited by Edward Benham. Edinburgh: John Grant, 1909.

Rogers, Thomas. *The Catholic Doctrine of The Church of England, An Exposition of the Thirty-Nine Articles {1586}.* Edited by Rev. J. J. S. Perowne. Cambridge, 1854.

Ryley, George. *Mr. Herbert's Temple and Church Militant Explained and Improved By a Discourse Upon Each Poem Critical and Practical By George Ryley: A Critical Edition.* Edited by John Martin Heissler. Ph. D. diss., University of Illinois, 1960.

Select Hymns, Taken out of Mr. Herbert's Temple, And Turn'd into the Common Metre (1697). Edited by William E. Stephenson. Los Angeles: Augustan Reprint Society, 1962.

Sidney, Sir Philip. *The Poems of Sir Philip Sidney.* Edited by William A. Ringler, Jr. Oxford: Clarendon Press, 1962.

Traherne, Thomas. *Poems, Centuries and Three Thanksgivings.* Edited by Anne Ridler. London: Oxford University Press, 1966.

Vaughan, Henry. *The Works of Henry Vaughan.* Edited by L. C. Martin. Oxford: Clarendon Press, 1957.

2. Works Published before 1800 (unless otherwise noted, published in London)

Acta Apostolorum. N.d. (British Library shelf no. C.23.e.3)

The Actions and Doctrine and other Passages Touching Our Lord and Saviour Jesus Christ. [Little Gidding, 1635.] (British Library shelf no. C.23.e.4)

The Actions Doctrine and other Passages Touching our Lorde and Saviour Jesus Christ [Little Gidding, 1636.] (British Library shelf no. C.23.e.2)

Ainsworth, Henry. *Annotations Upon the Booke of Psalmes.* 1626.

Barrow, Henry. *A True Description Out of the Worde of God, Of the Visible Church.* 1589.

Baxter, Richard. *Poetical Fragments.* 1681.

Bernard, Richard. *Christian Advertisements and Counsels of Peace.* 1608.

The Book of Common Prayer. 1630.

The Booke of Common Prayer. 1604.

The Boke of Psalmes . . . With Briefe and Apt annotations in the margent. Geneva, 1559.

Calvin, John. *A Harmonie upon the Three Evangelists, Matthew, Mark and Luke, with the Commentarie of M. John Calvine.* Translated by E. P. 1584.

————. *Sermons of M. John Calvin, on the Epistles of S. Paule to Timothie and Titus.* Translated by L. T. 1579.

Fane, Mildmay, earl of Westmoreland. *Otia Sacra.* 1648.

Fox, George. *A Journal or Historical Account of the Life, Travels, Sufferings, Christian Experiences and Labour of Love in the Work of the Ministry, of that . . . Servant of Jesus Christ, George Fox.* 2 vols. 1694–98.

Greenwood, John. *An Aunswer to George Giffords Pretended Defence of Read Prayers and Devised Leitourgies.* [Dort] 1590.

Hall, Joseph. *The Works of Joseph Hall.* 2 vols. 1624–25.

Harvey, Christopher. *The Synagogue, or, The Shadow of The Temple. Sacred Poems, and Private Ejaculations. In imitation of Mr. George Herbert.* 1640.

Herbert's Remains, Or, Sundry Pieces Of that Sweet Singer of the Temple, Mr. George Herbert. 1652.

Hooker, Richard. *Of The Lawes of Ecclesiasticall Politie.* 1597.

Huid, John. *The Storie of Stories, Or The Life of Christ, According to the foure holy Evangelists: With a Harmonie of Them.* 1632.

James I. *A Meditation Upon the Lords Prayer.* 1619.

Lightfoot, John. *The Harmony of the Foure Evangelists: Among Themselves, and with the Old Testament.* 1644.

Matthew, Roger. *The Flight of Time.* 1634.

Middleton, Thomas. *The Mariage of the Old and New Testament.* 1620.

Peckard, P. *Memoirs of the Life of Mr. Nicholas Ferrar.* Cambridge, 1790.

The Psalmes of David and others, With M. John Calvins Commentaries. 1571.

The Psalter of David . . . Whereunto is Added, Devotions. 1646.

Speed, Samuel. *Prison-Pietie: Or, Meditations Divine and Moral.* 1677.

Walton, Izaak. *The Lives of Dr. John Donne, Sir Henry Wotton, Mr. Richard Hooker, Mr. George Herbert.* 1670.

Washbourne, Thomas. *Divine Poems.* 1654.

Wesley, John, and Charles Wesley. *Hymns and Sacred Poems.* 1739.

Secondary sources

1. Historical, Biographical, and Critical Studies (Book length)

Acland, J. E. *Little Gidding and its Inmates in the Time of King Charles I, With an Account of the Harmonies Designed and Constructed by Nicholas Ferrar.* London: Society for Promoting Christian Knowledge, 1903. A valuable source of bibliographical information on the Little Gidding "Harmonies."

Alvarez, A. *The School of Donne.* London: Chatto and Windus, 1961. Argues cogently for the coterie aspects of poetry written by the metaphysicals.

Asals, Heather A. R. *Equivocal Predication: George Herbert's Way to God.* Toronto: University of Toronto Press, 1981. A learned study of Herbert's poetry in the context of Anglican commentary on Scripture and the liturgy.

Benet, Diana. *Secretary of Praise: The Poetic Vocation of George Herbert.* Columbia: University of Missouri Press, 1984. Approaches Herbert through the theme of vocation.

Bennett, J. A. W. *Poetry of the Passion: Studies in Twelve Centuries of English Verse.* Oxford: Clarendon Press, 1982. Impressive analysis of poetry of Passion Week from its earliest examples through the Renaissance.

Carey, John. *John Donne: Life, Mind and Art.* New York: Oxford University Press, 1980.

Carter [Jane Frances Mary]. *Nicholas Ferrar: His Household and His Friends.* Edited by T[homas] T[helluson] Carter. London, 1892.

Charles, Amy M. *A Life of George Herbert.* Ithaca: Cornell University Press, 1977. Based on all the known sources for the study of Herbert's life, this fine work has already become the standard biography of Herbert.

————. *The Williams Manuscript of George Herbert's Poems.* Delmar, N.Y.: Scholars' Facsimilies & Reprints, 1977. Valuable comparison between the sequence of poems in the Williams MS and that of the 1633 *Temple.*

Chew, Samuel. *The Pilgrimage of Life.* New Haven: Yale University Press, 1962.

Clark, Ira. *Christ Revealed: The History of the Neotypological Lyric in the English Renaissance.* University of Florida Monographs, Humanities no. 51, Gainesville: University of Florida Press, 1982. An insightful study of lyrics written in the seventeenth century, suggesting an idiom based on typological associations that were familiar in the emblem books and biblical exegesis.

Collinson, Patrick. *The Elizabethan Puritan Movement.* Berkeley: University of California Press, 1967. Learned inquiry into the origins of Puritanism in Tudor England.

―――. *English Puritanism.* General Series, no. 106. London: The Historical Association, 1983. Witty definition of English Puritanism.

Craig, C. Leslie. *Nicholas Ferrar Junior: A Linguist of Little Gidding.* London: Epworth Press, 1950. An account of the community at Little Gidding and of some extant artifacts, including the "Harmonies."

Eliot, T. S. *George Herbert.* Writers and Their Work, edited by Bonamy Dobree, no. 152. London: Longmans, Green & Co., 1962. Magisterial evaluation of Herbert.

Festugière, A. J. (O. P.) *George Herbert: Poète Saint Anglican (1593–1633).* Paris: Librairie Philosophique J. Vrin, 1971. Distinguishes Herbert's Anglicanism from Roman Catholicism, showing the poet's use of the liturgical calendar.

Fish, Stanley. *The Living Temple: George Herbert and Catechizing.* Berkeley: University of California Press, 1978. Lively discussion of *The Temple* in the context of Renaissance catechisms, ending with pessimistic misreading of "The Church Militant."

Fortescue, Adrian. *The Ceremonies of the Roman Rite Described.* Revised by J. B. O'Connell. London: Burns Oates and Washbourne, 1934. Learned, standard work.

Grant, Patrick. *The Transformation of Sin: Studies in Donne, Herbert, Vaughan, and Traherne.* Amherst: University of Massachusetts Press, 1974. Perceptive study of the major metaphysical poets.

Lewalski, Barbara. *Protestant Poetics and the Seventeenth-Century Religious Lyric.* Cambridge: Harvard University Press, 1979. Important statement of the influence on seventeenth-century literature in England of typical Protestant habits of thought.

Martz, Louis L. *The Poetry of Meditation: A Study in English Religious Literature of the Seventeenth Century.* New Haven: Yale University Press, 1954. Seminal study of the metaphysicals in the context of Renaissance techniques of devotion; one of the most important critical studies of the last three decades.

―――. *The Paradise Within: Studies in Vaughan, Traherne, and Milton.* New Haven: Yale University Press, 1964. Discussion of Augustinian influence on certain metaphysicals, and on Milton.

Maycock, A. L. *Nicholas Ferrar of Little Gidding.* London: Society for Promoting Christian Knowledge, 1938. The most thorough book on Nicholas Ferrar.

Novarr, David. *The Making of Walton's "Lives."* Ithaca: Cornell University Press, 1958. Important study of Walton's creative handling of his sources.

Post, Jonathan F. S. *Henry Vaughan: The Unfolding Vision.* Princeton: Princeton University Press, 1982. Impressive critical study, with emphasis on Vaughan's relation to Herbert.

Roberts, John R. *George Herbert: An Annotated Bibliography of Modern Criticism 1905–74.* Columbia: University of Missouri Press, 1978. Essential tool for Herbert scholars, very well annotated and indexed.

Stewart, Stanley. *The Enclosed Garden: The Tradition and the Image in Seventeenth-Century Poetry.* Madison: University of Wisconsin Press, 1966. Discusses the poetic uses of the Song of Songs by seventeenth-century poets, including Herbert.

———. *The Expanded Voice: The Art of Thomas Traherne.* San Marino: The Huntington Library, 1970. Discusses Traherne's relation to Herbert.

Stein, Arnold. *George Herbert's Lyrics.* Baltimore: The Johns Hopkins University Press, 1968. Powerful analysis of key lyrics in the Herbert canon.

Strier, Richard. *Love Known: Theology and Experience in George Herbert's Poetry.* Chicago: University of Chicago Press, 1983. Places Herbert's thought and art in the context of Protestant thought and practice.

Summers, Joseph H. *George Herbert: His Religion and Art.* London: Chatto and Windus, 1954. The most influential book on Herbert, treating the author's life and work.

Tuve, Rosemond. *A Reading of George Herbert.* London: Faber and Faber, 1952. An outstanding study of Herbert's poetry in the context of its liturgical and iconographic backgrounds.

Vendler, Helen. *The Poetry of George Herbert.* Cambridge: Harvard University Press, 1975. A close analysis of the poems in Herbert's "Church."

2. Historical, Biographical, and Critical Studies (Essay length)

Blau, Sheridan D. "The Poet as Casuist: Herbert's 'Church-porch.' " In *Essential Articles for the Study of George Herbert's Poetry,* edited by John R. Roberts, pp. 408–15. Hamden, Conn.: Archon Books, 1979. Reprinted from *Genre.* Considers "The Church-porch" in the rhetorical context of "practical divinity" ("cases of conscience"), which stressed conduct rather than belief.

Bloch, Chana. "Spelling the Word: Herbert's Reading of the Bible." In *"Too Rich to Clothe the Sunne": Essays on George Herbert,* edited by Claude J. Summers and Ted-Larry Pebworth, pp. 15–31. Pittsburgh: University of Pittsburgh Press, 1980. Argues relevance of Herbert's exegetical views to understanding of his poetic practice.

Endicott-Patterson, Annabel M. "The Structure of George Herbert's *Tem-*

ple: A Reconsideration." In *Essential Articles for the Study of George Herbert's Poetry,* edited by John R. Roberts, pp. 351–62. Hamden, Conn.: Archon, 1979. Reprinted from *University of Toronto Quarterly.* Rejects analogy between tripartite structure of Hebraic Temple and Herbert's *Temple,* arguing that the sequence more closely resembles Donne's division of the Temple into two, not three, parts (hence, "The Church-porch," "The Church").

Friedman, Donald M. Introduction to facsimile of *Otia Sacra (1648).* New York: Scholars' Facsimiles and Reprints, 1975. Sound commentary on Fane's relation to Herbert.

Henderson, George. "Bible Illustration in the Age of Laud." *Transactions of the Cambridge Bibliographical Society* 8 (1982):173–216. One of the very few twentieth-century discussions of the illustrations to the "Harmonies."

Hinman, Robert B. "The 'Verser' at *The Temple* Door: Herbert's 'The Church-porch.' " In *"Too Rich to Clothe the Sunne": Essays on George Herbert,* edited by Claude J. Summers and Ted-Larry Pebworth, pp. 55–75. Pittsburgh: University of Pittsburgh Press, 1980. Sophisticated approach to complex rhetorical aspect of the speaker in "The Church-porch," whom Hinman compares to the carnival pitchman as well as to the "Country parson."

Hunter, Jeanne Clayton. " 'With Winges of Faith': Herbert's Communion Poems." *Journal of Religion* 62 (1982):57–71. Important study of Herbert's views on the Eucharist, suggesting his settled position as a Calvinist.

Kronenfeld, Judy Z. "Probing the Relation between Poetry and Ideology: Herbert's 'The Windows.' " *John Donne Journal* 2, no. 2 (1983):55–80. Penetrating analysis of "The Windows" in the context of Herbert's ideas on preaching.

Leavis, F. R. "The Line of Wit." In *Seventeenth-Century Poetry: Modern Essays in Criticism,* edited by William R. Keast, pp. 31–49. New York: Oxford University Press, 1982. Influential early statement of poetic features peculiar to metaphysical poetry.

Patrick, J. Max. "Critical Problems in Editing George Herbert's *The Temple.*" In *The Editor as Critic and the Critic as Editor.* Los Angeles: William Andrews Clark Memorial Library, 1973. A provocative challenge to the customary view that, on his deathbed, Herbert sent a manuscript of *The Temple* to Nicholas Ferrar; suggests that the facts better fit his sending a manuscript of *A Priest to the Temple.*

Patrides, C. A. "A Crown of Praise." In *The English Poems of George Herbert,* pp. 6–25. London: J. M. Dent, 1974. A thoughtful, balanced commentary on Herbert's religious and poetic practices.

Schoenfeldt, Michael C. "Submission and Assertion: The 'Double Motion' of Herbert's 'Dedication.' " *John Donne Journal* 2, no. 2 (1983):39–49. Analysis of Herbert's courtly manner in "Dedication," suggesting broader application of the courtesy books to Herbert's poetics.

Stewart, Stanley. "Time and *The Temple.*" *Studies in English Literature* 6, no. 1 (1966):97–110. Discusses temporal figures in *The Temple.*

Strier, Richard. " 'To all Angels and Saints': Herbert's Puritan Poem." *Modern Philology* 77 (November 1979):132–45. Sets "To all Angels and Saints" in context of Puritan thought and practice.

Tuve, Rosemond. "George Herbert and *'Caritas.'* " *Journal of the Warburg and Courtauld Institute* 22 (1959):167–206. Argues that Christ's self-abnegating love is the central focus of the soul's struggle—and of its succor—in *The Temple.*

Wood, Chauncey. "A Reading of Herbert's 'Collos. 3.3.' " *George Herbert Journal* 2, no. 2 (1979):15–24. Analysis of Herbert's "Collos. 3.3," suggesting that the form of the poem presents a deliberately "hidden" expression of its biblical theme.

Index

Aaron, 63
Acta Apostolorum, 112
Adam, 110
Ainsworth, Henry, 34, 72, 113
Allen, Don Cameron, 108
altar, position of, 72
Alvarez, A., quoted, 118, 119
Anabaptists, 34
Andrewes, Lancelot, 1, 91
Apostle's Creed, 59
apparel, priest's, 42
Ark of the Covenant, 43
Arminian Nunnery, The, 26, 158n,
Asals, Heather A. R., *Equivocal Predication,*
    57
Ascension Day, 86
Ash Wednesday, 86
Asperges, 86, 87
aspergillum, 86, 87
astrologer, figure of, 67–68
Aubrey, John, 4
Augustine, Saint, 63, 64, 84, 101
Augustinianism, 57

Bacon, Francis, 2, 5
Baxter, Richard, 12, 20, 81
baptism, 88, 90–91, 104
Barrow, Henry, 30, 34, 39, 40, 72, 73, 80
Beaumont, Joseph, 135–38
Bemerton, 4, 5, 10, 74
Benet, Diana, 164n
Bennett, J. A. W., 75
Bentley, James, 64
Bernard, Richard, 35, 38
Bible and biblical commentary, 6, 7, 9–10,
    12, 14, 29, 32, 37, 38, 39, 40, 41, 43–
    46, 53, 56, 59, 60–62, 68, 75, 87, 91,
    95–96, 101, 109, 112, 116, 130, 139–
    40, 143, 146–50
Biblia Pauperum, 57, 58, 92
biretta, 30, 39
Blau, Sheridan D., 164n
Bloch, Chana, 75, 163n
Bolswert, Boethius, 74
Books of Hours, 57, 92
breviaries, 58

Broughton, Hugh, 64
Browne, Robert, 30, 34, 72
Brownists, 34, 35
Bunyan, John, 23

Calvin, John, 110, 113
Canaan, see Promised Land
Cambridge University, 1, 2, 3, 30; Censors
    at, 77; and Neoplatonism, 143
Canticles, 57, 102, 108, 143, 146
Carey, John, 25
Carter, Jane Frances Mary, 60, 62, 81, 82
catechisms, 57, 87, 90; importance to un-
    derstanding Herbert, 61
Catherine, Saint, 74
Catholic, as category, 59
Catholic Church, 72
Catullus, 132
Charles I, 26, 56, 71, 73, 81
Charles, Amy M., 3, 23, 73, 83, 132
Christ, 10, 11, 19, 21, 22, 23, 32, 37, 38–
    42, 63, 68, 79, 92, 94, 95, 103, 110,
    117, 125, 144, 146–47
Civil War, 33
Church of England, 33, 55, 72, 87, 131;
    government of, 30
Clark, Ira, 55, 163n
Cleveland, John, 118, 119, 128
Coleridge, Samuel Taylor, 20–22
Collection of Divine Hymns, 12
Collinson, Patrick, 29, 165n
Colman, Henry, 129, 138–39, 142
Colonna, Dame Vittora, 131–32
confirmation, 87, 90, 104
Convocation of 1536, 86
Cowley, Abraham, 20, 118, 119, 122, 128
Crashaw, Richard, 25, 26, 32, 119, 125,
    129, 136, 155; *Steps to the Temple,* 132–35
Creighton, Robert, 3
Crucifixion, 144

Dante, 131
Danvers, Jane, 3
Danvers, Sir John, 2, 3
Danvers, Henry, Earl of Danby, 3

821.3
#536

119 427